T0336534

The Hedge Fund Fraud Casebook

Founded in 1807, John Wiley & Sons is the oldest independent publishing company in the United States. With offices in North America, Europe, Australia, and Asia, Wiley is globally committed to developing and marketing print and electronic products and services for our customers' professional and personal knowledge and understanding.

The Wiley Finance series contains books written specifically for finance and investment professionals as well as sophisticated individual investors and their financial advisers. Book topics range from portfolio management to e-commerce, risk management, financial engineering, valuation and financial instrument analysis, as well as much more.

For a list of available titles, please visit our Web site at www.WileyFinance.com.

The Hedge Fund Fraud Casebook

BRUCE JOHNSON

WILEY

John Wiley & Sons, Inc.

Copyright © 2010 by Bruce Johnson. All rights reserved.

Published by John Wiley & Sons, Inc., Hoboken, New Jersey.
Published simultaneously in Canada.

No part of this publication may be reproduced, stored in a retrieval system, or transmitted in any form or by any means, electronic, mechanical, photocopying, recording, scanning, or otherwise, except as permitted under Section 107 or 108 of the 1976 United States Copyright Act, without either the prior written permission of the Publisher, or authorization through payment of the appropriate per-copy fee to the Copyright Clearance Center, Inc., 222 Rosewood Drive, Danvers, MA 01923, (978) 750–8400, fax (978) 646–8600, or on the Web at www.copyright.com. Requests to the Publisher for permission should be addressed to the Permissions Department, John Wiley & Sons, Inc., 111 River Street, Hoboken, NJ 07030, (201) 748–6011, fax (201) 748–6008, or online at http://www.wiley.com/go/ permissions.

Limit of Liability/Disclaimer of Warranty: While the publisher and author have used their best efforts in preparing this book, they make no representations or warranties with respect to the accuracy or completeness of the contents of this book and specifically disclaim any implied warranties of merchantability or fitness for a particular purpose. No warranty may be created or extended by sales representatives or written sales materials. The advice and strategies contained herein may not be suitable for your situation. You should consult with a professional where appropriate. Neither the publisher nor author shall be liable for any loss of profit or any other commercial damages, including but not limited to special, incidental, consequential, or other damages.

For general information on our other products and services or for technical support, please contact our Customer Care Department within the United States at (800) 762–2974, outside the United States at (317) 572–3993 or fax (317) 572–4002.

Wiley also publishes its books in a variety of electronic formats. Some content that appears in print may not be available in electronic books. For more information about Wiley products, visit our Web site at www.wiley.com.

Library of Congress Cataloging-in-Publication Data:
Johnson, Bruce, 1947 Feb. 4-
    The hedge fund fraud casebook/Bruce Johnson.
        p. cm.
    Includes index.
    ISBN 978-0-470-56046-4 (cloth)
    1. Securities fraud–United States. 2. Securities fraud–United States–Cases. 3. Hedge funds–Corrupt practices. 4. Hedge funds–Corrupt practices–Cases. I. Title.
    HV6769.J64 2010
    364.16'3–dc22
                                                                2009041463

Printed in the United States of America

10 9 8 7 6 5 4 3 2 1

To my mother,

who passed away before this could be published

Contents

Hedge Fund Life and Death

ALL ROADS START SOMEWHERE ELSE

At the outset of this book, I had accumulated nearly 20 years of research experience in the financial industry, including work as a securities analyst, the head of a research department, chairman of all securities research for an investment bank, and as an independent research consultant. My work has spanned both sides of the philosophic divide that separates "fundamental" analysts from "quantitative" analysts as well as within both methodologies characterized as "top down" and "bottom up."

Chronologically, the first half of my career was devoted to Japan and the emerging markets and the second was dedicated to hedge funds. The first contact with the "hedgies" began in the mid- to late 1980s as a broker with hedge fund clients. It did not take long to observe that these folks were a strange tribe particularly for their near total lack of interest in the seemingly important facts that we analysts took so much trouble to produce and for the opacity of whatever it was that did interest them. In 1997, I set up my own institutional advisory company, with a focus on subjects related to index investment, an area in which I had gained expertise as a broker. Through this work, I became directly involved in the research strategies and management of hedge funds. Not long after that I "drank the Kool-Aid" and became a full-time hedge fund advisor in Hong Kong and, later, a hedge fund consultant in San Francisco.

In 2003, I returned to the United States to manage the U.S. office of an international hedge fund consultancy. The mostly young, bright, and hard-working professional staff there were engaged in activities that were familiar to me from my days as a fundamental company analyst, such as visiting hedge funds, asking a lot of questions, putting the results into analytic text and numbers and advising the client-investors on what to buy and sell. A smaller number of more quantitative people were responsible for aggregating the analyst data, along with broader top-down data on the economy and the markets to produce high-level strategic advice that went into performance assessment, asset allocation, and portfolio construction.

WHAT'S DOING IN DUE DILIGENCE?

Given an in-built aversion to repeating challenges and wishing to avoid competing with people half my age, I became a connoisseur of unpopular research topics. The more undesirable the topic, the more time I could spend in peaceful contemplation. After asking around for the ugliest and most tedious subject available, the universal response was *due diligence*.

So began six years of research that culminated in a book on hedge fund fraud. Work on my new research topic started inauspiciously enough, trying to understand why it was so unpopular and yet so important. Early observations established the fact that due diligence was an extremely labor-intensive and, therefore, costly activity, characterized by a lot of real and metaphorical shoe leather expended in visiting hedge funds around the country. Each visit entailed running through long lists of carefully constructed questions designed to catch lies and inconsistencies while harvesting as much useful information as possible. The gum-shoe tactics also included physical auditing of the workplace, or "kicking the tires" by inspecting the workplace, its people and practices in order to identify any "canaries that had stopped singing in the coal mine," the "red flags," the "gut-feelings"—indeed, anything that seemed odd or out of place.

However, spoiling this picture of the dedicated sleuth are the more banker-like salaries that hedge fund analysts are paid rather than the workmanlike wages of detectives. These high costs, long hours, and tedium are not sufficient to give due diligence its reputation as the least-loved subdiscipline. What guarantees its place in analyst ignominy are the lead shoes—not gum shoes—that are a standard part of the attire and signify the doom-laden mission of the wearer. For unlike the detective, who starts with the knowledge that there was a crime, the due diligence analyst begins and ends with no crime while having the certainty of its future possibility. The task is summed up by Cowper's dictum that "the absence of proof is not a proof of absence." A clean bill of health can never be determined. Fraud is probably the most alarming event that can befall a hedge fund and a hedge fund investor. Fraud not only taints the investment, but it poses real liabilities to the investor. Beyond the real liability and real monetary loss, there is also a range of collateral damage that can be sustained, including loss of job and undermining of the business franchise of the investor. It is a minefield, where after deploying every reasonable means of detection, one must proceed, with the suspicion that some mines must remain undetected. And, the situation can get immeasurably worse. A fraud, may never come to light or may surface enough to produce a lawsuit and civil or criminal fraud charges—charges that must be proven to a sufficient degree, which is a process that can take years.

In the long run, due diligence takes the prize as the most dreaded advisory service because of its poor cost–benefit ratio. The certainty of high cost and the uncertainty of results entail a potential negative payoff for those who undertake it. So, why is it there? Two reasons: Due diligence alone can immunize its purchasers from being charged with negligence in the event of a fraud, and there is no better alternative. Moreover, in the hedge fund world, there is no equivalent to the broker research that is the backbone of information for equity investors. The restrictions on hedge fund advertizing, too, mean that the equivalent coverage for mutual funds that companies such as Morningstar provide is not available for hedge funds. Due diligence is the meat and potatoes of hedge fund research. It is almost the only way to get detailed information about hedge funds.

With these impressions in hand, I set off on what became the long road that led to this book about fraud. However, there were several important waypoints along that road that put fraud last—not first—in the series of investigations that resulted.

My prior experience in the management of research—including a 50-person research team in Tokyo at the height of the "bubble" years—made me very conscious of research overheads, and desirous of ways to reduce them without diminishing the results. The principal means to accomplish this was through a combination of automation and unbundling of the analyst skill set. For this reason, the labor intensiveness of due diligence felt like a problem begging for a solution. Due diligence, however, had a more serious problem than its cost structure. Its most serious flaw was its lack of clear efficacy. While it protected its users from charges of negligence, it had no assessible track record of catching criminals or preventing previously honest people from becoming criminals.

My hopes for improving the cost–benefit of due diligence became stuck on the benefits side of the equation because it did not appear to have an objective measure of performance and had no obvious way to measure improvement. Instead, it was like a variant of Monopoly's "Get out of Jail Free" card—to be presented when things went wrong. (This was not to deny or denigrate the usefulness of due diligence as a means of gathering information about hedge funds.)

THE SUCCESS OF FAILURE

Having reached this first twist in the road, I put due diligence aside and focused on the circumstances that made due diligence a necessity in the first place. This shifted the investigation from the question of "What's wrong with due diligence?" to that of "What's wrong with hedge funds that they need due diligence?" In turning this question over, it gradually transformed into a more basic question: "Why do hedge funds fail?"

The hedge fund industry had long been prone to periodic "die-offs" where as many as 15–30 percent of all funds cease trading for a variety of reasons. Some, including the biggest and most successful, suddenly "implode" or "blow-up," losing a majority of their net asset value in a matter of days, or hours. Others voluntarily return investor funds and go out of business when they sense a lack of opportunity. Many suffer severe redemptions that force them to shut down, while a small number suffer the "unkindest cut" and fall victims to fraud.

This periodically churning sea of birth and death can cause a high degree of instability in an institutional investor's hedge fund portfolio. At one time I had likened it to stably managing a college football team when every year all of your seniors depart and there is a new intake of freshman. The hedge fund "bench" is similar in turnover, but it occurs in a more chaotic pattern, both with respect to the timing of arrivals and departures and the near randomness in the composition of the individuals that depart.

In the past, the subject of fraud and that of fund failure was often conflated, causing much confusion as to whether evil was widespread in the "hedge-sphere" or was it mostly the benign failures of largely honest folks. The broad study of failure was intended to answer these questions by examining the causes and frequencies of failure attributable to all causes and evaluated over all years.

Earlier in my career, as an index provider, I observed similar cycles of creation and destruction in the form of new companies entering and existing companies exiting an index during an index recomposition. In most cases, the companies leaving the index are those that have experienced a reduction in market cap while those coming in have had growth in market cap. To a great extent, the exiting and entering refreshes the success content of the index by rescreening for size. In a growing market and economy, stocks that cease to grow will eventually be flushed out of an index. Like scenes edited from a film, they end up on the cutting-room floor and are lost to index consciousness.

I had a hunch that while indexes illustrated the mechanics of success, the data of these exited "defunct" companies might be the best source for understanding failure, and, with a little bit of hunting around, I was able to find some index vendors that had and would share these data. Years later, thinking about the failure of hedge funds, I recalled the defunct data and acquired some that I recompiled into a database of failed hedge funds—and then structured that into what might be called a "failed funds index."

What was most surprising about this strange index was that no one, including quants, had an intuitive picture of how such a hedge fund failure index should look:

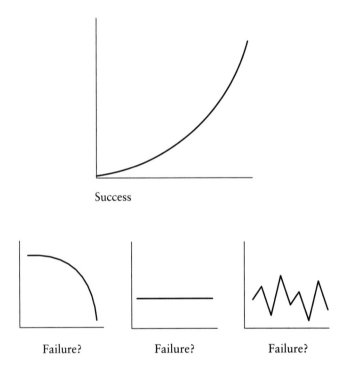

Success

Failure?   Failure?   Failure?

The surprising result was that the performance of the "failed funds index" looked a lot like that of the normal "live" hedge fund index, except that the performance was somewhat lower. If true, this implied that failure looked like success, only less so. Success and failure, as far as hedge funds were concerned, were not apples and oranges, but perhaps, first-rate apples and second-rate apples. Several months of more detailed analysis followed, breaking down the failed funds into subgroups having common causes of failure. In medicine, the procedures used for deceased subjects are different from those used in normal practice. It is much the same with dead funds. Their description and analysis require special forms of data. Normal funds data are continuous (runs from the beginning to the end) for any time period examined:

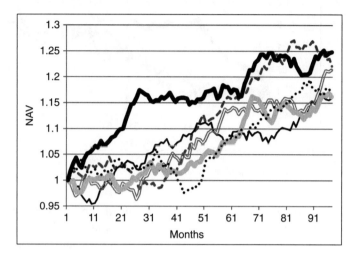

Five Normal Funds NAV Monthly, Rebased to 1.0

Sometimes a new fund is added to the index and starts to contribute its performance in the midst of a period, as per "Series 5" below:

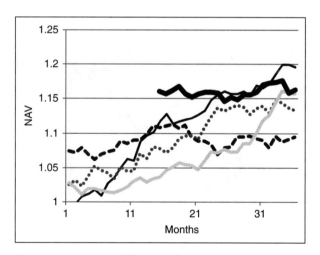

Five Normal Funds NAV, Including One with a Later Start Date

Sometimes, an existing fund experiences a performance blow-up and "dies," as shown again in Series 5:

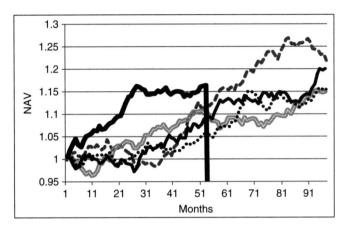

Four Live Funds, One Dead Fund NAV

In a database (or index) comprised of only dead funds, the performance data for each fund may begin and end at a different point in time, making the data discontinuous both within and across series. This means that it is not possible to vertically align all of the data to calculate averages. And, without this cross-sectional comparison, it is not easy to determine common characteristics between the time series. Moreover, the immediate period leading up to the "death event" may express unique behavior that would be lost in averaging it in with normal funds. The same is true at the start of the fund's life, its "birth" and the period immediately following the birth:

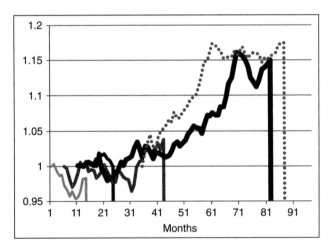

Five Dead Funds with Different Start and End Dates

I constructed two purpose-built sets of data to adjust for these dead fund attributes. One was referred to as "end-adjusted data" and the other as "start-adjusted data." As their names suggest, these data sets recompiled the dead funds values so that either their start points or end points line up vertically (coincidentally). The data in this form facilitated detailed examination of the various patterns of deaths or births. The drawback of this method was the loss of the characteristics of the actual time period; but, if one's intention is to study death, a death is a death is a death, to paraphrase Gertrude Stein. They are more comparable in place rather than in time:

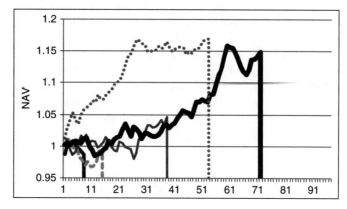

Five Dead Funds: Data "Start Adjusted"

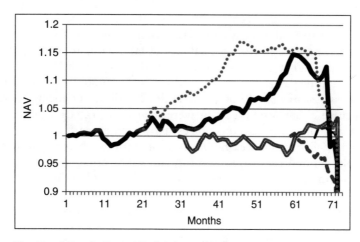

Five Dead Funds: Data "End Adjusted"

In the first case, it meant that one could compare all of the dead funds at the time they were, say, 11 months old, or, as in the second case, all funds in the six months before they died. With the second set I could, for example pose the question, "For all funds that appeared to die in a catastrophic collapse in returns, what was going on one month earlier or one year earlier?" Or, with the start-aligned data, "How many funds died at different ages in their lifespan, rather than in different months of the year or different years?"

Ultimately, this work resulted in comparative summary statistics of average fund life and allowed grouping of performance for subgroups that seemed to have died for similar reasons.

The foregoing analysis eventually led to the central conclusion that the majority of hedge funds expired as a result of a shortage of capital (a condition I call "capital insufficiency"). This main cause of fund death seemed to explain the relatively good aggregate performance of failed funds already seen in the failed funds index referred to earlier. The insufficiency of capital could have been due to slightly worse performance that had the effect of diverting capital to other funds, or, perhaps, the fund never attracted sufficient capital in the first place. Equally, the lack of capital could have been due to weak marketing (the corollary being firms that raise large amounts of money because of good marketing, but have lackluster performance.)

At the opposite end of the spectrum were a relatively small number of funds that died as a result of fraud. It was a comforting observation that crime did not appear to be a dominant factor in the failures (number of failures, rather than value of failures).

CREDIT IS THE PROBABILITY OF FAILURE

Having arrived at a peak of sorts, where the terrain of fund failure could be seen within its context, I reached another of those turns in the road where the research changed direction. Having started on the problem of due diligence a year or so earlier, the research had been transformed into an analysis of fund failure. Now enough perspective had been obtained to turn the question of failure on its head and ask, "If one knew the historic probability of failure due to any and all causes, did this not equate with a generic definition of hedge fund credit?"

There had never been a great need for hedge fund credit ratings. The funds were not issuers of debt (though some did distribute financial instruments and some of these either used credit or were themselves rated), nor was their equity acquired, except in rare circumstances. However, given the sums of money they controlled, their privacy-seeking business operations, their power in the hands of few people, limited regulatory scrutiny, no share price, and not a great deal of public domain information, some measure of their probability of failure would be a valuable tool to have as a parallel check on the health and safety of the funds.

One further reason for interest in hedge fund credit was the growth in demand for insuring hedge fund risks. Some hedge funds themselves were reportedly seeking to insure against so-called "rogue traders," and it might not be long before hedge fund investors might wish to insure against hedge fund failures due to a variety of causes. While this might not free the investors of the obligation to carry out due diligence, it might help to limit the exposure to any residual risks that remained after due diligence. And, as a practical point, I was still hoping to find a way to reduce the labor intensiveness of due diligence, which made it slow and expensive.

As both the number of hedge funds and hedge fund investors increased toward 10,000, the number of funds for which investors might want due diligence was in the hundreds and this had to be repeated at least once a year if not two or more times. If one analyst could hypothetically perform due diligence on five funds per week, and that is optimistic to be repeated week after week, it might work out to some 15 per month and around 150 per year. If each fund is seen twice a year, it would equate with covering 75 funds per analyst. (In reality, the limit is more like 50.) This would mean that providing due diligence coverage of just 10 percent of the funds universe would require 20 full-time analysts. This still does not solve the problem of clients wanting due diligence on some of the other 9,000 funds. Even another 1,000 to 2,000 funds covered would increase the number of analysts to 40 to 60. While it is certainly possible to manage this many analysts, the logistical problems increase geometrically and the ability to provide the coverage says nothing about the costs of doing so, which also increase at a linear rate.

For these reasons, great appeal was found in any research that could be "machine-driven"—as is much of the performance and risk analysis. In an effort to do just that, the ongoing investigation moved on to another track, pursuing a more automated calculation of hedge fund credit as the statistic for the probability of fund failure.

The credit phase of the project began with the supposition that if cash insufficiency was the prime cause of hedge fund failure, then a model of cash sufficiency was, to a large extent, a model of hedge fund credit, the probability that a hedge fund would fail. This work was eventually implemented as a computer program.

The key to the credit model is the fact that it combines hedge fund cash flows with performance, creating a larger picture of the forces operating on a given fund than performance alone. This helped to balance one of the conflicts faced by fund managers and indirectly by investors, which is the trade-off between cash under management, which earns a small but stable fee, and cash earned through positive performance, which earns a greater fee but is unstable.

Where the credit model (shown in the following figure on page xviii) becomes subtle and complex in its workings is in breaking down its basic elements and in the interaction between these elements, including:

Income Sources

- *Management fee income.* A function of funds under management and the level of the fee charged.
- *Actual performance fee income.* A function of performance, fee level, and high-water mark, all of which had to be calculated separately for each tranche of investor cash invested at a given point in time.
- *Option value of expected income.* The model also calculated the implied "in-the-money" or "out-of-the-money" option value of a performance fee during the interval prior to its next payment date. This model calculated the amount of money in each tranche of assets under management (AUM) that was currently above the high-water mark times the amount of time left until the performance fee was earned.

Costs

- *Fund manager overheads ("burn rate").* Could vary considerably from one type of operation to another, including numbers of staff and offices and locations.

Other

- *Lock-up period.* The cushioning effect of investor capital that could not be redeemed.
- *Accumulated earnings.* The flexibility afforded by having financial reserves.

- *Redemptions.* Investor withdrawals of cash.
- *Redemption cascade.* Occurs where redemptions reach a critical level, triggering an unstoppable outflow of assets.
- *Balance equations.* Several summations that netted out positive and negative values at different levels.
- *Credit.* Pegged to one of the balance level equations.

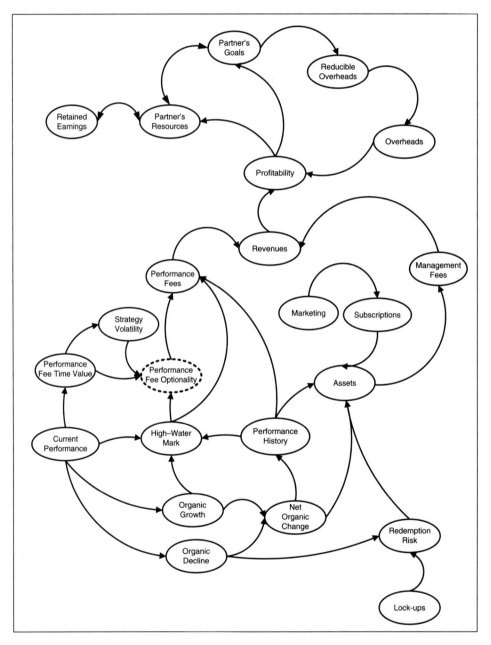

Schematic Diagram of the Principal Elements in the Hedge Fund Credit Model

The credit model made it possible to run an automated calculation over the data for hundreds or thousands of funds, revealing many of the internal value dynamics that were never before visible. The underlying data could be added at any time and by people other than analysts and they could be aggregated at many more levels than just performance and risk. As the model ran, it also generated large quantities of intermediate data that could go into a database and be used for further analysis, such as estimating new subscriptions and redemptions.

BAITING FRAUD

With the completion of the hedge fund credit model, there was an integrated analytical tool that could describe all of the general forms of hedge fund failure that had been witnessed to date, with the single exception of fraud. While one of the least frequent causes of failure, fraud seemed different from all of the other causes, and its analysis also appeared to be less amenable to quantitative methods. For this reason, it was left out of the previous work, and for the same reason it was the last aspect of fund failure to be tackled.

The first phase of the fraud research consisted of little more than creating files for every case that could be found. However, the first discovery was that relatively few cases could be found. While there is much talk about hedge funds and fraud, the examples quoted are usually the same handful. Prior to the recent case of Bernie Madoff, the most famous hedge fund scandal cited was Long-Term Capital Management (LTCM), which went under in September 1998. This was the classic and, perhaps, the first termed a "systemic risk" to the global financial system. The trouble with LTCM as an example is that fraud was never charged. It was certainly a failure, a "blow-up," and involved more than a small amount of naiveté and some degree of negligence—but not fraud. So, the biggest and best example, the most oft-quoted, is no example at all. Uncharacteristically, LTCM was also bailed-out by a consortium of large banks, which later reaped a large profit as a result.

Other big cases spoken of around the water cooler included: Askin/Granite (1994), Berger/Manhattan (2000), Smirlock/Laser (2000), Natale/Cambridge (2000), Lauer/Lancer (2003), Strafaci/Lipper (2003), Bayou (2003), and Amerindo (2008). With additional effort, a few others could be dredged from the collective memory, such as Yagalla–Ashbury, Hoover, Hegarty–Hyannis, Amaranth, and Millennium. After collecting this "low-hanging fruit," one is struck by the fact that there are not that many and that the majority are so recent that few have completed the legal process and had final judgment rendered. And, prior to the mid-1990s, the archives are pretty bare. All of this was puzzling after starting this book with the misconception that hundreds of cases and case documents existed going back decades.

It was little short of a disaster to find that comprehensive documentation of hedge fund frauds were either nonexistent or just were very hard to come by. Most frustrating was the fact that no complete authoritative list of cases had ever been compiled. As a result, one never knew how many cases there really were or when you were finished searching for new ones. There seemed no alternative to hunting for needles in a haystack.

The U.S. Securities and Exchange Commission (SEC) Web site (www.sec.gov) contains thousands of enforcement actions, but they are not categorized to identify hedge funds. If you go through the cases one by one, you can find the keywords "hedge fund" in the text of some, which, once compiled, does produce a decent list of hedge fund frauds. However, the vast majority of these SEC cases do not involve hedge funds, but rather corporations and corporate executives, brokers, accountants, and mutual or fixed income fund managers as well as individuals purporting to be such.

The case universe was substantially further expanded with the inclusion of commodity trading advisers (CTAs) and commodity pool operators (CPOs), which again meant screening all of the CFTC enforcement actions for other key phrases. A third major source of cases is newspaper archives, especially for cases where the two main regulators (SEC, CFTC) were not involved. These included both private actions and those pursued by state and federal law enforcement. Finding cases at the state level, for example those private actions that are filed in state or county courts and cases filed by state regulators in state courts, may be found by checking each state's court records, but some are certain to be missed, either because of a lack of available records or just the inability to mount a complete search.

Once there was a near complete list of cases, each case was dissected into its component data, and the storyline of each fraud was worked out, including the principal actors and actions. There were often substantial differences in documentation and detail available.

The intention at the outset was to publish every known case, though this proved to be an unrealistic goal given the high proportion of cases that have not yet been decided. A further reason for 100 cases is that it is generally considered to be a minimally sufficient set for statistical analysis. Lastly, it has established the history of the crime from its earliest days, the most difficult part to document.

The final leg of this journey involved the compilation of aggregate statistics of the full set of cases and an analysis of this aggregated data in order to put the cases into subgroups based on type. And there it ends.

The work stands as a substantial casebook, a near-complete historical record, a quarry of facts, figures, plots, people, and punishments. It is the first extensive book wholly dedicated to this subject and provides the first comprehensive attempt to draw conclusions as to the nature of fraud in the hedge fund industry, its reasons, its methods, the outcomes, and some insights into ways to prevent, or predict, the crime in advance.

This book is devoted to the subject of hedge fund fraud. Its purpose is educational and its structure follows its purpose. The method is scientific in three senses: fact-based, comparatively organized, and statistically meaningful. While the subject dictates that it is also substantially concerned with legal matters, this book is not intended to be about the law or for the purpose of training lawyers. Instead, the educational message has been directed to the investment community, those who seek to risk their capital on a rational basis and want to better understand some of the outer reaches of what constitutes rational risk.

The book is divided into two parts. The first is a broad appraisal of the context of fraud and hedge funds. The second is a compendium of 100 cases, each laid out in an identical format for comparison.

Part One, Life, Death, and Degeneration, consists of three introductory chapters providing general explanation of the subject matter and approach.

Part Two, Cases and Conclusions, consists of Chapters 4 and 5. Chapter 4, the heart of the book, features the casebook—100 chronologically arranged case studies beginning with the first known case. Each case involves a hedge fund participant and a formal allegation of fraud. All cases have been disposed within U.S. jurisdictions: civil, criminal, or administrative. An identical page format of facts, charts, tables, and summarized texts has been employed for each case in order to facilitate case comparisons. Chapter 5 follows with an analysis and functional grouping of cases.

Acknowledgments

Part of the strategy in choosing this topic was to select an "unloved" area of research, where there was freedom to pursue the subject over a long period in an uncompetitive environment. Careful selection paid off to such an extent that, not only were curious observers almost entirely absent, but even friends and family appeared to be calling less often. The normal look of interest one gets when you say you are writing a book soon evaporated when you explained that it was about hedge fund fraud, and hedge fund death. (Some of my best friends are hedge fund managers.)

As a consequence, the writing of this book proved to be a fairly solitary endeavor. That, in turn, makes the job of writing an acknowledgments page a simpler task than usual. There is no need for a Stadium of Heroes or Hall of Fame. In their place, a Bench of Acknowledgment will do to say thanks to those that suffered and sweated alongside me.

In the genesis of the idea and its circuitous evolution, I received a great deal of support and encouragement from Simon Ruddick. His long-term interest in unique data and the interface of qualitative–quantitative information were shared subjects over many years, as was my excursion into hedge fund life and death. Thanks, pal.

My lawyer, Karen Frank, was instrumental in putting me together with the folks at John Wiley & Sons and getting me established as a writer.

My wife, Shoko, not the long-suffering type by nature, had to make major adjustments in her life to put up with the difficult person she married, a forbearance pushed to the limit during the long years it took to research and write this book. She also knows that I'd be lying if I said I will not do it again.

My editors at Wiley were the magic that transformed my files into a commercial book. I would especially like to thank Tim Burgard and Stacey Rivera for their tireless efforts and apologize for my excessive questions.

The last one on this little bench of acknowledgment is my lovely little nephew "Bertie," who kept me company, watched over my shoulder, stretched and yawned, and hopped about in the sheer pleasure of living.

Introduction

Hedge Fund Fraud and "the Appliance of Science"

The available means for dealing with hedge fund fraud have been relatively unproductive, unscientific, expensive, and time consuming. There is now a basis for altering and improving the current practice to make it more productive, more scientific, less costly, and more expeditious.

The current discipline—a combination of investor due diligence, law enforcement, and judicial procedure—has not served anyone well. Yet there are no credible alternatives. Given the small number of hedge funds that were operating until recent times, hedge fund fraud had been too infrequent a crime to justify compiling specific class data from which statistical inferences could be drawn regarding actual rates of risk. Moreover, even within the larger case set of all investment fund frauds, where a sufficient body of statistical data exists, the approach has been no different because of the legalistic bias of the regulators and the securities statutes they administer.

There is now the prospect of a more scientific methodology for better understanding and controlling this crime, which brings it in line with other applied sciences such as criminal forensics, actuarial science, investment finance and risk control and is also the logic used by most institutional investors in managing their portfolios. The first step in this transition has been taken in this book by compiling a sufficient statistical history of the occurrence of the crime within the narrower hedge fund case set. For the first time, a more scientific approach to hedge fund fraud analysis can take place with the expected result—a more effective means of dealing with the crime.

FINANCE IS SCIENCE

Most of today's institutional investment is undertaken on a substantially scientific basis. Despite the evidence of recent market crashes and the malfunctioning of large swathes of the economy and financial system, most institutional investors employ some form of logical or empirical analysis to determine when and how to invest. Most of these analyses could also be described as the "scientific method," or its quasi-scientific form. (There are also large areas of pseudoscience and nonscience coexisting and interacting daily with the more rational methods.)

These analytic approaches have increasingly accommodated differences between normal market behaviors, such as exist within a "normal distribution" of probabilities, and exceptional market behaviors, often referred to as "events," sometimes more specifically as "bubbles" and more popularly as "crashes." There is generally an accurate perception, too, that these exceptional periods are discontinuous with normal periods when the normal rules do not seem to apply. However, even these nonnormal market periods are examined with the same scientific lens that is applied to the normal behaviors.

For investors, nonnormal conditions can mean excess returns but more often result in substantial losses. This is also true for hedge fund investors, but much less so for a variety of reasons:

- Many hedge funds hedge event risks.
- In their hedging of normal risks most hedge funds operate at lower volatility than the markets (though their leverage may just as often make them more vulnerable to certain market factors).
- Some hedge funds specifically engage in strategies that profit from events.
- Some macro funds correctly call the coming crashes and short the markets instead of going to cash.

Nevertheless, many hedge funds will suffer heavier losses when markets "tank." Also, because hedge fund hedging is more complicated than long-only investing, some hedge funds simply get their risk management wrong ("model risk") and suffer catastrophic loss ("blow-up"). Also, because at any given time, a large number of hedge funds are young funds with limited capital, including some with decent performance, they still fail to raise sufficient capital, or they have overheads too high to be profitable and have to close their business. Finally, a portion of funds close down for a variety of other reasons, anything from disagreement among the partners, loss of a major investor, merger or acquisition, or just a long spell of subpar performance.

Thus, despite their superior performance, large numbers of hedge funds shut down all the time. During periods of market upheaval, the numbers can rise to 15 percent per annum or more of all funds.

All of the negative outcomes in the life of hedge funds are contained within the same continuum of *risk assessment*. When funds close down for business reasons, it is an event that breaches the logical–scientific environment within which investment operates—but just barely. Most funds that close down have not had enormous losses, and many others are very small funds with few, if any, outside investors. Even in the extreme circumstances of a fund "blow-up," it is viewed in the same way that a market-crash would be—an investment loss under nonnormal conditions.

These boundary cases that result in funds closing down are "one-zero" or life and death events, and they are provided for in the investment contracts, articles, and other corporate founding documents.

FRAUD IS LAW

When there is a suspicion of fraud in a hedge fund, and that suspicion leads to charges or investigation, then the entire edifice of logical–scientific method falls away. The investor no longer has any calculations to make (unless they invest in legal outcomes). Nor, once the matter enters the legal system, will there be a quantifiable chance of determining whether a fraud actually took place.

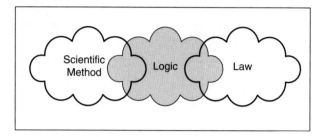

Scientific Method: Logic and Law

Once the fraud enters the legal system, the pattern of events that follows is what is sensible and efficacious for the legal system.

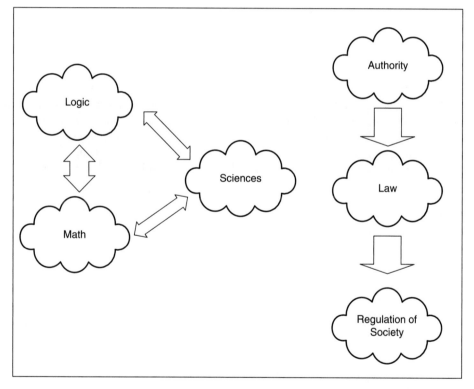

Science, Math, and Logic vs. Law, Order, and Society

What is lost in this breach of science is the opportunity to determine what did take place and, perhaps more importantly, how to reduce its occurrence.

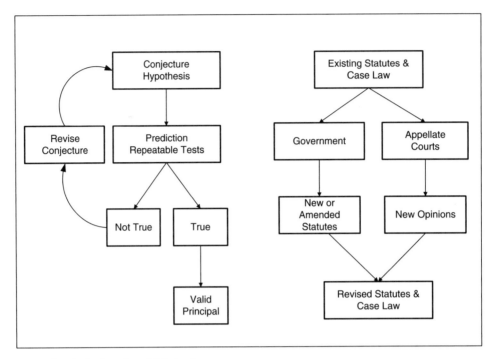

Scientific Method vs. Legal Method

This takes us back to the beginning of the process, to the initial vetting of funds, the *due diligence* procedure. Ideally, due diligence should be a scientific method to determine the probability of fraud, but it is not. Instead, it is a legal strategy to avoid a charge of negligence. How would you get to the moon if your process for getting there was designed to protect you from being charged with not getting there? And, as an alternative, if you ended up in Philadelphia as a result of a plea bargain?

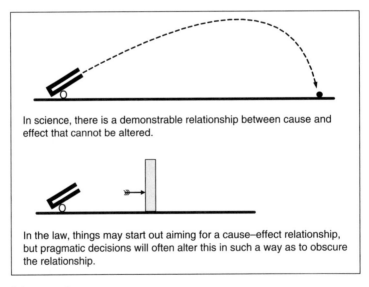

Science vs. Law

Up until recently, the scientific method could not be employed with hedge fund fraud because there were too few cases from which to draw meaningful conclusions, but now it is just possible to attempt this and thereby to alter how we perceive and deal with fraud. Part of this is to accept that fraud occurs and that the goal is to minimize it, not to avoid it 100 percent. It is part of the unalterable distribution of possible outcomes, even if a nonnormal part. The probability of fraud should—and can hopefully—be reduced and the residual risk that remains should be insured or accepted as loss.

ONE

Life, Death, and Degeneration

For decades, hedge funds have been the dream factories of finance where fortunes were made in mysterious ways, and occasionally lost. For those few who found hedge funds to be a school of hard knocks, it is probably apparent that the hedge fund life cycle can include a high "infant mortality rate," that hedge funds seem to die off in large numbers and, now and then, succumb to fraud.

Part One, Life, Death, and Degeneration, runs through three parallel strands of analytical development. Chapter 1 is an historical narrative of how laws continued, largely unsuccessfully, to grapple with the control of fraud. Chapter 2 looks at why current laws make it easier to discover—and bring to justice—perpetrators of fraud. Finally, Chapter 3, shows the unique structure of hedge funds how can contribute to the creation and continuation of fraud.

Historic Roots of
Prohibitions against Fraud

Hedge fund fraud is a conjunction of an ancient crime and a modern application. Fraud itself is a composite crime conjoining theft with deception. The earliest legal codes had clear proscriptions against theft ("thou shall not steal"), but a more ambiguous response to deception in general, focusing instead on false accusation ("thou shall not bear false witness").

FRAUD IN THE EARLIEST LEGAL SYSTEMS

In ancient history, laws that directly addressed commercial behavior tended to lag behind those that ensured the power of rulers. There are exceptions, however. The Code of Hammurabi and the Twelve Tables of the Roman Republic directly address fraud. The Code of Hammurabi dictated the death penalty for many crimes including theft and for "fraudulent sale of drink." The law 265 states that if "a herdsman, to whose care cattle or sheep have been entrusted, be guilty of fraud and make false returns of the natural increase, or sell them for money, then shall he be convicted and pay the owner ten times the loss." Romans were liable under the stricture of Tablet VIII, law 21, which stipulated that if "a patron shall defraud his client, he must be solemnly forfeited ('killed')."

However, despite the threatening tone of the early statutes, most were ineffective in their implementation and, until modern times, *caveat emptor* was the main defense against fraud. Most of the efforts to control fraud were applied to the sale of food in public markets, though here too the concern may have been more about preserving social order than protecting the rights of individuals. The regulation of food markets in post–Medieval England illustrates these early efforts. A number of specific selling practices were outlawed, with variable success. These included proscriptions against "forestalling," "regrating," and "engrossing," all of which concerned exploitative or deceptive practices by market sellers of food.

England's first chartered joint-stock company, the Muscovy Company, was founded in 1555, in part based upon the earlier model of medieval shipping joint ventures, which enabled the collective funding and sharing of risks. Over the next hundred years, the number and scope of these companies expanded rapidly—by 1696 there were over 150 traded—and with them, the scale and complexity of the market for shares and the emergence of brokers, jobbers, and dealers, and along with them, the numbers and types of market abuse. One such early abuse was the "corner," where investors colluded in the use of options to gain effective control of the market for a particular security or commodity.

Another financial innovation that greatly expanded the scope of fraud was the creation of a market for government debt. In England, the first such issue was in 1693. The Bank of England was established the following year and it assumed the responsibility for funding the government by debt issues, further expanding the scope of the investing public.

Within a very few years of these new markets getting underway there was a growing chorus of opinion and ridicule calling for controls to be put in place to limit abuse. Bills were debated by Parliament in 1694 and 1696, and in 1697 a bill was passed to limit the number of brokers to 100 and requiring that they be licensed by London's Lord Mayor. The Lord Mayor took the initiative by putting in place a number of regulations for brokers to follow.

In 1720 the exponential growth in the value of the South Sea Company and its subsequent calamitous collapse ultimately caused a seismic shift in legislation and the regulation of markets culminating in the passage of the "Bubble Act" by Parliament, often referred to as the "first securities law." The act banned the sale of stock in unchartered companies and specified four forms of sanction: fines and other punishments related to public nuisance offenses, imprisonment, and forfeiture, the right of investors to sue for treble damages, and the loss of license for brokers who engaged in such sales. Unfortunately, the Bubble Act was little used in the following decades, with one case prosecuted in 1722 and the next not until 1808, despite the proliferation of unchartered companies.

The next big legal innovation in England was Barnard's Act, which sought to regulate widespread abuses caused by stockjobbers. This act restricted their activities in three areas: restricting the use of options, contracts for differences, and naked shorts. But Barnard's Act proved as ineffective in enforcement as the earlier Bubble Act.

The growth and sophistication of the U.S. economy progressed more or less in parallel with that of England and with it so did the financial innovations and attempts to control them. Actions to combat fraud in securities advanced on two fronts: in private actions under common law and in state and federal statutes. State courts recognized the right of private actions as early as 1790. A decision in Connecticut (*Bacon v. Sanford*) was based on a case where the buyer of a security sought damages against the seller who apparently knew the correct value but chose to deceive the buyer, who did not. Many such cases of intentional misrepresentation and false statements in selling followed. Some of these cases reached criminal courts.

Over the years leading up to the mid-nineteenth century, English and American courts extended the interpretation of misrepresentation in common law cases to include statements made by sellers in public documents (as opposed to specific documents given to the buyer). This gave buyers of securities the general form of redress against fraudulent sellers that exists in modern times.

Progress at the state and federal level continued in parallel. Massachusetts issued public debt bonds in 1751 and was soon copied by other states. The national government in the form of the Continental Congress issued its first debt bonds in 1776. Patterns of trading closely followed English models as did market abuses. The onset of the Revolutionary War exacerbated the abuses and led to public calls to curb them. A number of speculators were arrested in Pennsylvania in 1779 for forestalling and engrossing.

Perhaps the earliest effort to regulate trading at the national level in the United States were provisions against insider trading that were included in the act that established the U.S. Treasury in 1789. This was the first statute to specifically address this crime in the United States or England and arose because of bad experiences with corruption and speculation in prior government debt issues, especially during the war period.

After a severe market crash in 1792 various states considered enacting versions of England's Barnard's Act, restricting stockjobbing. Pennsylvania tried to pass a weaker version, but even this failed; however New York later passed an act nearly identical to the failed Pennsylvania one. The statute was reenacted in 1801 and again in 1812. Some provisions were eased in a subsequent version, though a ban on selling shares that one did not own (short sales) remained until 1858 when the act was repealed.

Over the next few decades, the individual states legislatures and courts were active in efforts to rein in stock speculation. These efforts included acts to license stockbrokers, ban time trades, establish maximum settlement times, specify minimum holding periods for bank stocks, restricting banks from speculating in stocks, and applying ad hoc stipulations in the issuance of initial offerings.

In a then-famous 1862 case involving the Parker Vein Coal Company, officers of the company were found to have issued a $1.3 million tranche of fraudulent stock as part of a larger bona fide issue. This led the states of New York and Michigan to criminalize fraud in the issuance of securities. However, these findings only applied to misstatements and did not impose any obligations on issuers or sellers to make disclosures.

In 1882, New York State convened a special committee, the "Boyd Committee," to investigate the operation and use of stock market corners. "Do evils exist in the methods of the operators?" Chairman Boyd asked of a subpoenaed witness. "Not only do evils exist," the witness responded, "but they shall entail a public calamity." "Do you think it is the duty of the Legislature to remedy the evil?," the chairman asked another witness. "In every aspect of the case," he answered, "it is just as much the duty of the Legislature to remedy this evil as any other evil affecting the material and moral welfare of the people."[1]

The Boyd Committee concluded:

- A tax should be placed on futures trades where no physical delivery takes place.
- Futures sales for physical delivery are legitimate.
- Puts and calls and bucket shops are gambling and should be treated as such.

In 1887, the state of Illinois put into effect a law banning bucket shops. A similar New York state law followed two years later.

---

[1] *New York Times,* "The Speculative Curse," April 9, 1882, p. 7.

MODERN DEVELOPMENT OF SECURITIES FRAUD REGULATION AND ENFORCEMENT

With the arrival of the twentieth century, the evolution of securities fraud regulation and enforcement became more coherent and cohesive. The first 35 years of the new century swept the nation from a long history of fragmented efforts by different states to stamp out an array of ill-defined evils to a concentrated national program to establish a comprehensive regulatory infrastructure for securities. Progress during this period was driven by three stock market panics, in 1907, 1914, and 1929, and a progression of state and federal investigative commissions to determine the causes of each as well as attempts to rid society of the evils that undermined it and hampered the economy. By the beginning of the new century, the list of interrelated evils plaguing the markets included:

- Bucket shops
- Combinations
- Corners
- Gambling
- Short selling (without physical delivery)
- Speculation
- Stock gambling
- Stockjobbing
- Time trades
- Trusts

In tackling these evils, the United States had to find a way to overcome the jurisdictional duality embedded in its legal system, comprised as it was of states and a federal government. It was not entirely clear who bore the responsibility for crimes within the securities markets, though the states had possession of the physical exchanges and therefore had to control them, but with national industries and nationwide investment it was hard to see how some 40-odd states each with their own laws and many with their own exchanges could function as effective enforcement.

On top of this, there was the deep divide that exists to this day over the need to protect the public from all manner of theft and corruption versus the need to maintain free and open markets. Caught within these challenging and conflicting frames of reference the easiest solution was to do nothing, and that sufficed for most of the time, but the devastating drumbeats of crashing global markets and in the middle of this period the first war to be fought on a global scale kept up the pressure for action.

THE MONEY TRUST AND THE PANIC OF 1907

From the late 1880s, the myriad evils that were perceived to be plaguing the markets began to coalesce in the public's mind into a super evil called the "money trust." This was seen as a nexus of power and money under the control of a relatively small number of rich industrialists who, through "interlocking directorships," controlled most of American industry, finance, energy, and transportation. The Democratic

Party, under the leadership of William Jennings Bryan, took up the challenge of opposing the money trust and, along with it, the debasing of the currency that was the result of going off the gold standard. The Panic of 1907 seemed to confirm the public's and the politicians' anxiety.

A failed attempt to corner copper was blamed as the immediate cause. This resulted in a run on several banks that were thought to be involved and had the knock-on effect of contracting credit generally. New York's third largest trust bank, Knickerbocker Trust, failed at this time. New York City was only saved from defaulting on its debt by the personal intercession of J. P. Morgan in purchasing its bonds.

The following year (1908) then President Theodore Roosevelt called for action against the vices of the market:

> *There is no moral difference between gambling at cards or in lotteries or on the race track and gambling in the stock market. One method is just as pernicious to the body politic as the other in kind, and in degree the evil worked is far greater. (However) The great bulk of the business transacted on the exchanges is not only legitimate, but is necessary to the working of our modern industrial system and extreme care would have to be taken not to interfere with this business[.]*[2]

Roosevelt called for the Congress "to prevent at least the grosser forms of gambling in securities and commodities," such as making large sales of what men do not possess and 'cornering' the market.[3]

Roosevelt's plea went largely unanswered. However, in 1909, the governor of New York, the state in which the nation's largest stock exchange, the New York Stock Exchange (NYSE), established the Hughes Committee along the very lines called for by Roosevelt "in view of the evils incident to speculation and of the importance of sound business methods in connection with our vast transactions in securities and commodities[.]"[4] Speculation was defined as "forecasting changes of value and buying or selling in order to take advantage of them."[5] The Hughes Committee went on to examine many of the specific speculative practices observed at the NYSE, in particular those involving manipulation. Distinctions were made between some forms that were acceptable (e.g., in support of a new issue), and others that were not (e.g., pushing up prices in order to dump shares).

BLUE SKY LAWS

In March 1911, Kansas broke new ground with the enactment of its "Blue Sky" law designed to prevent the fraudulent sale of securities by making it a felony crime. It also clearly set some standards for corporate disclosure and required licensing of

---

[2] Steven Thel, "The Original Conception of 10(b) of the Securities Exchange Act, *Stanford Law Review* 42, no. 2 (January 1990): 396.

[3] Ibid., 397.

[4] Ibid

[5] Ibid.

brokers. (The text of these laws can be found at the Web site of the Kansas Office of the Securities Commissioner at www.securities.state.ks.us/edu/bluesky.html.)

Section XII

Any person who shall knowingly subscribe to or make or cause to be made any false statement or false entry in any book of such company, or make or publish any false statement of the financial condition of such company or the stocks, bonds or other securities by it offered for sale, shall be deemed guilty of felony; and upon conviction thereof shall be fined not less than two hundred dollars nor more than ten thousand dollars, and shall be imprisoned for not less than one year nor more than ten years in the state penitentiary.

Section XIII

[A]ny agent who attempts to sell the stocks, bonds or other securities of a company that has not complied with the act, or any agent who attempts to sell stock or bonds without having received a license from the bank examiner, shall be fined not more than five hundred dollars or imprisoned in the county jail not more than ninety days, or both.

Of more than 500 applications received for licensing as brokers, the state only approved 44. This act is credited with driving many corrupt operators out of the state. It is not surprising then that over the next several decades every state with the exception of Nevada passed a similar "blue sky" act. New York State passed its blue sky law in 1921, the Martin Act, which remains a formidable and still sharp weapon against fraud.

THE PUJO COMMISSION

In May 1912, a Senate Congressional subcommittee, the Pujo Committee, was formed to investigate the "money trust," blamed for the panic of 1907. As a secondary objective the Commission was also to investigate the control of the nation's stock exchanges. Much of the substantive debate picked up where the Hughes Commission had left off and frequent reference was made to its findings regarding the New York Exchange, speculation, and manipulation.

Many of the top industry and finance leaders of the day were called in to answer questions, including J. P. Morgan and John D. Rockefeller. Among other things, the Pujo Committee exposed the monopolistic practices of the "combines" and the web of interlocking directorates by which a few at the top could control the resources and workings of many companies across all of finance, industry, and transportation.

The findings led to proposals for amendments to the national banking laws and, more pertinent to the subject of this book, a bill that prohibited the use of interstate communications—mail, telegraph, and telephone—in the commission of a securities fraud. The interstate feature gave the federal government a basis for jurisdiction in fraud cases, whereas the blue sky laws did the same for the individual states within their own boundaries.

Both the Hughes and Pujo committees were important and influential in defining and forming public attitudes to specific areas of market abuse however, little or no effective legislation was enacted between the time of the Pujo findings and the 1929 stock market crash. Nevertheless, one precedent-setting development that came out of the World War I years (1917–1919) was the Capital Issues Committee, a wartime agency that functioned for just six months, during which time it effectively regulated securities issuance and served as a model and precedent for the later Securities and Exchange Commission (SEC). Also during this period, a number of bills were debated in Congress, at least one of which, proposed by Congressman Dennison, helped to move the regulatory thinking forward, in this case with respect to linking the various state blue sky laws with a federal interstate commerce provision to create a seamless jurisdiction, though none of these were enacted.

Another landmark of this time was the appearance of the first mutual fund in 1924, the Massachusetts Investors Trust.

THE GREAT CRASH AND THE PECORA COMMITTEE

The Great Crash of 1929 was the defining event on the road to regulation. It significantly raised the temperature on legislators to get some effective laws enacted. Within the government there were two main pathways to accomplish this end: one was yet another committee to investigate and recommend and the other was the executive office itself, with the accession of Franklin Delano Roosevelt as the nation's president.

The Pecora Committee, empaneled in March 1932 by the Senate Banking and Currency Committee, initially at the behest of President Hoover, who believed manipulators were responsible for market declines. This committee followed a path similar to its 1912 predecessor, the Pujo Committee, calling in for public questioning the heads of the large banking houses, including Otto Kahn (Kuhn, Loeb), Charles Mitchell (National City Bank), and J. P. Morgan Jr. as well as the head of the New York Stock Exchange, Richard Whitney.

By January 1934, the Pecora Committee had reached the main recommendations it wished to incorporate into a bill comprising four main points:

1. Stock exchanges to be licensed by the federal government.
2. Establishment of an administrative authority to assure fair dealings.
3. Authorities given the powers to revoke an exchange license or impose other penalties.
4. Authorities also given discretionary powers over rules governing transactions that could take place within exchanges.

ROOSEVELT'S MEN

Before Franklin D. Roosevelt became the 32nd president, one had to go back to Woodrow Wilson to find a similar champion of financial reform. In 1911, as Governor of New Jersey, Wilson strongly came out against the "money trust," saying,

"The great monopoly in this country is the money monopoly. So long as that exists, our old variety and freedom and individual energy of development are out of the question." These words were quoted in an influential book, *Other People's Money* written by Justice Louis Brandeis, who, with Wilson, was very active in promoting and fostering new financial legislation and, along with the Pecora Commission, formed a conceptual foundation and reservoir of talent when Roosevelt took office in 1933. More than any chief executive before and since, with the possible exception of President Obama, Roosevelt injected himself directly into the process of crafting both the general objectives and specific words of the acts that would regulate the financial world for the next 75 years.

Before becoming president, Roosevelt had been governor of New York State (1929–1932), an office that put him in one of the best possible vantage points to observe the unfolding of the Great Crash of the stock market as well as the opportunity to know many of the people that would be instrumental in designing the new legislation that would be needed to fill the vacuum left in its wake. In addition to Samuel Untermyer, chief counsel to the Pecora Commission, the key talent enlisted by Roosevelt was Felix Frankfurter, a Harvard Law School professor and through him some of his most gifted students including James Landis, Benjamin Cohen, and Thomas Corcoran. Years later, Landis went on to become head of the U.S. Securities and Exchange Commission (SEC). All of these, now Roosevelt people, were lawyers who had cut their teeth in antitrust cases and were supporters of the work of the Pujo Committee.

THE SECURITIES ACT OF 1933

Roosevelt's "MO" in getting bills drafted was to secretly put several teams to work in parallel and then switch between them as the merits of each emerged in Congressional debate. He was like a single jockey riding three or four horses in a race, switching mounts as the race progressed, determined to be on the winner when it crossed the line.

In the final version of the Securities Act, the first of Roosevelt's securities bills, the final drafting team (Landis, Cohen, and Corcoran) chose the most recent revision of the English Companies Act (1908) as a model for their work. In particular, what became Schedule A of the Securities Act, detailing the content of any prospectus issued to the public, drew much of its form and content from this earlier English act.

In introducing his legislative proposals to Congress on March 29, 1933, Roosevelt stated "This proposal adds to the ancient rule of caveat emptor the further doctrine: 'Let the seller also beware.'" This statement clearly illustrated the new government thinking on market regulation—that issuer's would now bear a regulatory risk to offset some of the credit risks faced by the buyers.

The act's main weapon against securities fraud was enshrined in Section 17, Fraudulent Interstate Transactions, subsection (a), Use of interstate commerce for purpose of fraud or deceit:[6]

---

[6] *Securities Lawyer's Deskbook*, University of Cincinnati, College of Law, Securities Act of 1933, Section 17 (Interstate Commerce).

a. It shall be unlawful for any person in the sale of any securities by the use of any means or instruments of transportation or communication in interstate commerce or by use of the mails, directly or indirectly—

   1. to employ any device, scheme, or artifice to defraud, or
   2. to obtain money or property by means of any untrue statement of a material fact or any omission to state a material fact necessary in order to make the statements made, in light of the circumstances under which they were made, not misleading; or
   3. to engage in any transaction, practice, or course of business which operates or would operate as a fraud or deceit upon the purchaser.

Another section with teeth to fight fraud is Section 5(a) relating to the need to be registered to engage in interstate trading of securities[7]:

Section 5—Prohibitions Relating to Interstate Commerce and the Mails

a. Sale or delivery after sale of unregistered securities Unless a registration statement is in effect as to a security, it shall be unlawful for any person, directly or indirectly—

   1. to make use of any means or instruments of transportation or communication in interstate commerce or of the mails to sell such security through the use or medium of any prospectus or otherwise; or
   2. to carry or cause to be carried through the mails or in interstate commerce, by any means or instruments of transportation, any such security for the purpose of sale or for delivery after sale.

At the time the Securities Act was enacted there was no SEC. Instead the provisions of the act were to be supervised by the Securities Department of the Federal Trade Commission (FTC). The shift to the new regulator would not take place until the following year.

THE SECURITIES AND EXCHANGE ACT 1934

The next important piece of legislation to be drafted was the Securities and Exchange Act of 1934. This act was initiated by yet another committee, this one established by then Assistant Secretary of Commerce John Dickinson in October 1933. Where the Securities Act addressed disclosure and issuance, the main focus of this committee was the regulation of the stock exchange and ultimately the creation of the Securities and Exchange Commission. A report was produced in January 1934. For the work on drafting the bill, Landis reunited with his two colleagues, Cohen and Corcoran. The bill was introduced to Congress as the Fletcher–Rayburn bill after its sponsors in the Senate and House, respectively and over the next few months, after much revision, "morphed" into the Exchange Act. One of the revisions was the creation of the new securities regulator, the Securities and Exchange Commission.

---

[7] *Securities Lawyer's Deskbook,* University of Cincinnati, College of Law, Securities Act of 1933, Section 5.

The new act, passed in May 1934, also contained new provisions to enforce antifraud measures, among them the combination of Section 10(b) and its companion Rule 10b-5, which together are, by far, the most frequently used antifraud weapon in the securities arsenal:

Section 10—Manipulative and Deceptive Devices

"It shall be unlawful for any person, directly or indirectly, by the use of any means or instrumentality of interstate commerce or of the mails, or of any facility of any national securities exchange—

To use or employ, in connection with the purchase on a national securities exchange or any security not so registered, any manipulative or deceptive device or contrivance in contravention of such rules and regulations as the commission may prescribe as necessary or appropriate in the public interest or for the protection of investors."

Rule 10b-5— Employment of Manipulative and Deceptive Devices

It shall be unlawful for any person, directly or indirectly, by the use of any means or instrumentality of interstate commerce, or of the mails or of any facility of any national securities exchange,

a. To employ any device, scheme, or artifice to defraud,
b. To make any untrue statement of a material fact or to omit to state a material fact necessary in order to make the statements made, in the light of the circumstances under which they were made, not misleading, or
c. To engage in any act, practice, or course of business which operates or would operate as a fraud or deceit upon any person, in connection with the purchase or sale of any security.

The reason for the peculiar duplication of content in 10(b) and Rule 10b-5 reflects Congress' view that it could not, or should not, determine the fact of securities fraud, but should delegate that responsibility to the SEC.

THE INVESTMENT ADVISER'S AND INVESTMENT COMPANIES ACTS OF 1940

With all of the Congressional committee investigative work of the early 1930s, resulting in the passage of significant legislation such as the Securities Act (1933) and Securities Exchange Act (1934) and others such as the Public Utility Holding Company Act (1935), the regulation of the principal financial participants had been determined. So, from the middle of the decade committee research turned to the roles of several of the remaining participants, including investment companies and investment advisers.

It is thought that the first dedicated investment advisory firm, A. M. Clifford, commenced operations around 1915. Having started in 1911 as a broker, the company decided to specialize in order to manage the assets of one of its clients. From that time, Clifford referred to itself as an "investment Counselor and Financial Analyst." Scudder Stevens & Clark started up in 1919 with the sole purpose of selling investment advice for a fee for the amount of assets under management. By

1934, when legislation was being debated, the number of investment counselors had grown to 394. At that time most states required no registration or professional competency standards for these firms. The provisions in the act were derived largely from consultations with industry. The act became effective in November 1940.

The two sections of this act most cited in the hedge fund fraud cases in this book are 206(1) and 206(2), below[8]:

Section 206—Prohibited Transactions by Investment Advisers

It shall be unlawful for any investment adviser, by use of the mails or any means or instrumentality of interstate commerce, directly or indirectly—

1. to employ any device, scheme, or artifice to defraud any client or prospective client;
2. to engage in any transaction, practice, or course of business which operates as a fraud or deceit upon any client or prospective client;

COMMODITIES REGULATION

The first known commodities trading market was established in Osaka, Japan, in 1650. The first commodity exchange in Chicago, the Chicago Board of Trade (CBOT), started trading in 1848, some 56 years after the Buttonwood Agreement that served an equivalent purpose for stock trading in New York.[9] Another Chicago exchange, the Produce Exchange, opened for trade in 1874. And where the CBOT concentrated on grain, the produce exchange traded produce, eggs, lumber, and livestock. In 1898, a group representing the Produce Exchange Butter and Egg Board split away from the Produce Exchange.

As early as 1858, the CBOT issued guidelines for grain quality, and in the following year the exchange received a charter from the State of Illinois, giving it the power of law. The CBOT followed with a ban on options trading in 1865 and the setting of regular hours of trade in 1873.

The Civil War years (1861–1865) were generally prosperous for grain traders and, while the exchange appreciated the role of speculation in fostering liquidity, the markets were frequently plagued by cornering operations, resulting in what turned out to be only a one-year ban on short selling in 1866. As with the equities markets in New York and other cities, Chicago was also besieged by bucket shops. A *Chicago Daily Tribune* article in 1879 expressed the frustrations of the time: "The fraud, cheat and swindle are so transparent that it seems to be a libel on common intelligence to admit that these establishments do an immense business every day."[10]

The exchange made strenuous efforts to stamp out the bucket shops by disconnecting the Western Union telegraph lines that they used to receive prices and at one time whited-out the windows of the exchange to stop information getting out.

---

[8] *Securities Lawyer's Deskbook,* University of Cincinnati, College of Law, Investment Advisers Act 1940.

[9] David Greising and Laurie Morse, *Brokers, Bagmen, and Moles: Fraud and Corruption in the Chicago Futures Markets* (New York: John Wiley & Sons, 1991), 41, 45.

[10] Ibid., 48.

In a 1904 U.S. Supreme Court case against the bucket shops, the exchange won the right to control the flow of its information and, in the Chief Justice's opinion also legitimized options trading. In 1919, the Chicago Mercantile Exchange opened its doors, offering futures and forward contracts in butter and eggs only. Cheese was added in 1929 and potatoes in 1931.

The Federal Trade Commission, which at that time had responsibility for oversight of the exchanges carried out an extensive study of grain trading, including grain futures. In August 1921, the Future Trading Act was passed which regulated trading in grain. This act incorporated the unusual feature of a 20-cents-a-bushel punitive tax on options and futures trades not executed on a designated market contract. However, the following year the U.S. Supreme Court in *Hill v. Wallace* declared the Future Trading Act to be unconstitutional because of its use of Congress' taxing powers.

In September 1922, the Grain Futures Act became law. Unlike its predecessor, the Future Trading Act, the new bill utilized interstate commerce as the basis for the government's jurisdiction (rather than tax). The act prohibits trading outside of the market contracts. It also called for the establishment of a Grain Futures Commission as an agency under the Department of Agriculture. Another Supreme Court Case (*Board of Trade v. Olsen*) in February 1923 upheld the constitutionality of the new act.

THE COMMODITIES EXCHANGE ACT OF 1936

On June 15, 1936, the Grain Futures Act was superseded by the Commodity Exchange Act. The new act expanded the number of commodities traded to include: cotton, rice, mill feeds, butter, eggs, Irish potatoes, and grain. In a similar vein, the Grain Futures Commission was superseded by the Commodity Futures Commission. From time-to-time over the coming years, several commodities were added to the list of those traded and several were also dropped.

Within the new legislation the most oft-cited section in the hedge fund fraud cases is Section 6(b) Fraud, false reporting, or deception prohibited:

U.S. Code: Title 7 (Agriculture),

Chapter 1 (Commodity Exchanges)

Section 6b Fraud, false reporting, or deception prohibited

(a) "Contracts designed to defraud or mislead; bucketing orders

It shall be unlawful

   (i) to cheat or defraud or attempt to cheat or defraud such other person;

   (ii) willfully to make or cause to be made to such other person any false report or statement thereof, or willfully to enter or cause to be entered for such person any false

The Commodity Futures Commission was overhauled once again with its powers expanded in 1974 and renamed as the Commodity Futures Trading Commission (CFTC) as it stands today. In September 1975, the reformed CFTC approved the first futures contract based on a financial instrument— "Ginnie Mae" certificates futures. And in November the CFTC approved the first futures contract linked to U.S. government debt.

The CFTC rules were amended again in January 1979 to address the operation of commodity pool operators (CPO) and commodity trading advisers (CTA). This is the area that directly governs the equivalent of hedge fund managers/advisers within the commodities sphere.

BRIEF HISTORY OF FRAUD IN THE DIFFERENT TYPES OF INVESTMENT COMPANY

Like the big market crashes, the big investment frauds have had a permanent fascination for the public who never seem to tire of hearing of them: the Tulipmania, the South Sea Bubble, Credit Mobilier, the Mississippi Company …. But just below the scale of these national obsessions are hundreds of serious investment frauds that are more circumscribed in scope, generally involving fewer victims (even though these can number in the thousands) or having a shorter life in the press.

INVESTMENT TRUSTS

According to some industry claims, the first investment trust was the Foreign & Colonial Investment Trust, established in 1868, by the eponymous Foreign & Colonial Company. While this may have been the first such fund in the English-speaking world, it appears that earlier examples can be found in the Netherlands (including one created by King William I in 1822), at least as far back as 1774, credited to a merchant named Adriaan van Ketwich. There was apparently also an investment trust established in Switzerland in 1849. The first of these funds in the United States was possibly the American Investment Trust Co. noted in 1885, followed by others including the Boston Personal Property Trust, which was founded in 1893 and was also the first closed-end fund in the United States.

Perhaps the first (English language) evidence of fraud involving an investment trust was the case of the Land Investment Trust, part of the greater failure of the London and General Bank in 1892. This famous case occurred some 24 years after the founding of the Foreign & Colonial Investment Trust. Ultimately, a former Member of Parliament, Jabez Balfour, and several others were found guilty of the fraud and committed to prison.

MUTUAL FUNDS

In the case of the mutual fund, the generally acknowledged "first" in the United States was the Massachusetts Investors' Trust in 1924 (though the Alexander Fund in Philadelphia, founded in 1907 is an earlier prototype); however, the greatest growth came after the Funds Act of 1936, which granted "mutuals" exemption from corporate tax. Evidence for a "first" mutual fund fraud may not be extant until the early 1960s, when investors filed suits against several funds alleging unreasonable levels of fee payment to advisers, with the implication that fraud was involved.

This case bears similarities to the "market timing" cases of 2003 in that the suits were directed at a relatively broad industry practice rather than specific individual culprits and resulted in changes in industry practice (and in this case in new legislation).

A more clear-cut case of outright mutual fund-related fraud may be as late as 1973 (49 years after the appearance of the first U.S. mutual) in the case against Robert Vesco (who ended up controlling the sprawling and corrupt IOS funds empire discussed in the final section, "Funds of Funds"). Certainly by the early 1980s, there are records showing the SEC taking action against mutual funds. The first of these was the suspension of investment adviser Richard Bartoli for self-dealing and misconduct and, in February 1983, its revocation of the registration of Investment Adviser CMC Funding Ltd for fraud.

Using any of the preceding examples as a baseline, it appears that there was a lag of around 40 to 50 years between the emergence of mutual funds and the emergence of a recorded case of mutual fund fraud.

INDEX FUNDS

Index funds have exhibited a more peculiar pattern. The earliest index fund is thought to have been developed and managed by Wells Fargo, apparently for a single client pension fund (Samsonite Corp.) around 1971. The first multiclient index fund was probably launched in 1974 by Batterymarch Financial Management. Oddly, there is a record of an Index Fund, Inc.—a registered open-ended investment company that was a plaintiff in a civil bribery and stock manipulation case in which federal indictments were handed down as early as August 1972 (see Case 4). Among the defendants in the case, which commenced around June 13, 1973, was Robert Hagopian, president of the Index Fund and president and chairman of that fund's investment adviser.

The odd thing about this case is the fact that the dates ascribed to these actions (i.e., 1972 and 1973) would make this obscure fund among the earliest index funds created (believed to include Wells Fargo, American National Bank of Chicago, and Batterymarch Financial Management). Another curious conjunction is the fact that this fund was a Boston-based company, as was Batterymarch Financial Management, whose principals, Jeremy Grantham and Dean LeBaron, created the first multiclient commercial index fund in Boston between 1972–1974. Mr. Grantham had put the concept in the public domain by speaking of it at a seminar at the Harvard Business School in 1971. If the Index Fund, Inc., was a genuine fund, it would suggest that its president, Robert Hagopian, probably had some contact with Grantham and LeBaron, perhaps even having attended the seminar chaired by Grantham at Harvard.

Apart from the above legal footprints, the only other known case involving an index fund to date occurred in November 2001, at which time criminal charges and later civil charges were brought against a Steven Adler, who was the principal of a company called Vector Index Advisors. In fact, this company did not manage any index funds, but had a two-stage strategy fraudulently deployed, in which a tactical switching between the one strategy and the other was based on whether the equity index was rising or falling. This manager was ultimately jailed for 60 months and his company was deregistered by the SEC.

Other than these two cases—one puzzling due to its extremely early date, the other with only the most tangential relationship to an index fund—there have been no other cases of index fund fraud to this day. One potential explanation for the scarcity of index fund frauds is simply due to the fact that there were never very many index funds until recently. A count of current index funds, however, seems to dispel this argument. At present there appears to be more than 2,500 funds, and over 300 fund groups (or management companies). So perhaps the answer has something to do with the nature of index funds; in particular, their objectively determined performance and the limited number of methods of achieving it. There have been articles from time to time criticizing index funds for practices the writer's have claimed or implied are exploitative, unprofessional, or dishonest, but the same could be said for other forms of investment, and such criticisms are not the same as there being grounds for pursuing a legal case.

FUND OF FUNDS

The fund-of-funds product either was or was not invented by Bernie Cornfeld. In 1962, his offshore mutual fund management company, IOS, launched the Fund of Funds, which would go on to become his most successful fund. Certainly he pioneered the general concept and was responsible for lodging that concept into the minds of investors worldwide. Unfortunately, for all concerned, IOS was a thoroughly corrupt organization and this first "fund of funds," if not wholly corrupt from the start, became substantially so as time went on. So, whether the Cornfeld product can justifiably be called the first fund of funds is debatable. The later honest funds would understandably claim that it was not, that the IOS Fund of Funds was something different than today's fund of funds.

On the assumption that Bernie Cornfeld did not create the fund of funds product in 1962, then the credit for the launch of the first fund of funds should go to the March 29, 1985, inception of the Vanguard Star Fund. In Europe, a clutch of funds were launched in October 1985 when the United Kingdom's Department of Industry approved the product, including Abbey Life, Britannia, Grieveson Grant, Henderson, and, Save And Prosper.

The earliest example of wrong doing at the fund of funds dates to September 2002, with the case of Nathan Chapman Jr.'s Domestic Emerging Market Minority Equity Trust's fraud against the State of Maryland pension system. Also convicted and sent to prison in this case was Alan Bond of Albriond Capital Management. The apparent time interval between the launch of the fund of funds in 1985 and the presumed first fraud was 17 years.

HEDGE FUNDS

According to available facts and industry folklore, the first hedge fund was created in 1949 by Alfred Jones. The earliest fraud in relation to a hedge fund was in August 1968. This case accused the senior executives and salesmen of the then, Merrill Lynch, Pierce, Fenner and Smith, with providing insider information to several of its investment clients. These included five hedge funds. The hedge funds named were among the earliest hedge funds, one of which was none other than A.W. Jones & Co. (and A.W. Jones Associates), the very first hedge fund (see Case 1 in the next chapter).

Assuming no earlier cases are found, it would mean that 19 years elapsed before a hedge fund fraud case had materialized. See Table 1.1 for a summary of years of the first known frauds and intervals.

TABLE 1.1 Financial Product Appearance and First Known Fraud

	A: 1st Known Example	B: 1st Known Fraud	Interval (B-A)
Investment Trusts	1868	1892	24
Mutual Funds	1924	1973	49
Index Funds	1971	1973	2
Fund of Funds	1985	2002	17
Hedge Funds	1949	1968	19

CHAPTER 2

Assumptions Regarding Events and Uncertainties in the Mortality of Hedge Funds

While hedge funds may just be the latest victims of securities fraud, they also differ in some important respects from the older fund types and in ways that have a bearing on how fraud perpetuates within them.

Hedge funds are more complex in the number and range of asset classes in which they invest and in the strategies they use to capture their investment profits. Their legal structures are often more complex than other funds due to their use of offshore and onshore entities. Administering and auditing hedge funds are more demanding for these same reasons.

One of the distinguishing features of hedge funds is their dual fee arrangement: a combination of a management fee based on assets under management, like mutual funds, plus a unique performance fee based on a percentage of investment profits earned over a specified period, usually quarterly. The performance fee is generally subject to conditions, chief among them, a "high water mark," which operates like an upward-only ratchet, fixing the minimum threshold for earning a performance fee. Returns are measured as absolute rather than relative to a benchmark.

Also, laws designed to exclude retail investors have greatly limited the availability of research on hedge funds. This, in turn, has given rise to an entirely unique process of vetting them. It also reinforces the tendency for hedge funds not being very communicative, an aspect further enhanced by their practice of periodically closing to new investors. Finally, up until recently, the majority of hedge funds were not registered with a regulator. Even now many remain unregistered or have a mix of registered and unregistered entities in their organizational structure.

A simplified diagram of the dual fee structure operation and relationship to other basic management functions is shown in Figure 2.1.

INCENTIVIZATION OF HEDGE FUNDS

Even with the dual fee structure, the basic revenue cash flows and their implied incentives are relatively simple: The hedge fund manager is positively incentivized by both the amount of assets under management (AUM) and absolute gains derived from performance. However, there are deeper layers of interaction between performance past and present and management policies. For example, management has the option of

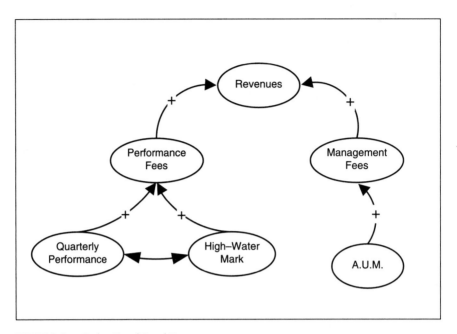

FIGURE 2.1 Hedge Fund Dual Fees

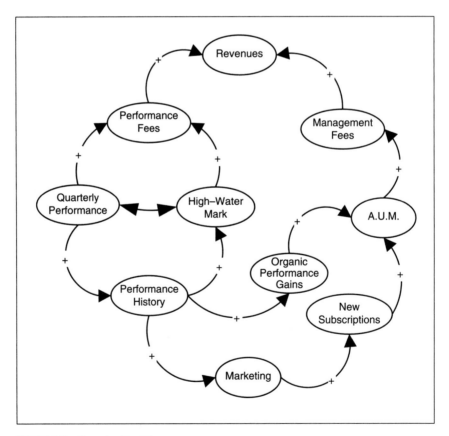

FIGURE 2.2 Broader Fee Picture

promoting aggressive marketing or not. Skillful marketing, or a deal with a marketing agent, can bring in more subscriptions, which, in turn boosts assets and management fees. If past performance has been good, that can also spur marketing. And increased subscription assets will also raise the amount earned from performance fees. Figure 2.2 shows the broader effects of interaction between the two types of fees.

Figure 2.3 shows the introduction of a hypothetical corruptive element into the fee revenue flows, in this case a manager overvaluing an illiquid asset and how this feeds through and corrupts the other factors.

A more complete diagram of the performance and fee revenue flows is shown in Figure 2.4. This richer array of interactions indicates that there is considerable scope for differences in the behavior of funds and their manager's, due to changes in the balance of incentives that are available at any given time. Many of these finer distinctions are not visible from the investor's vantage point.

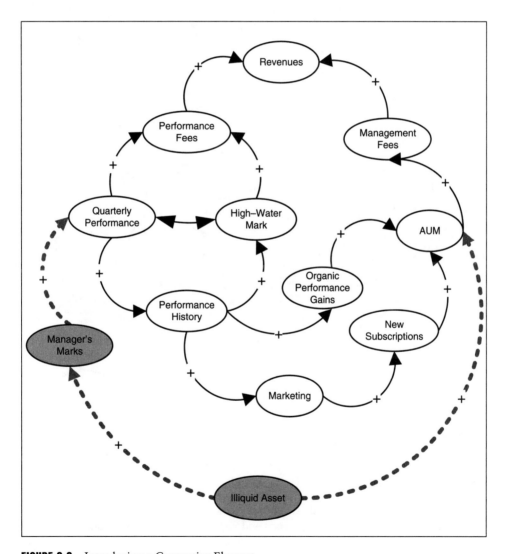

FIGURE 2.3 Introducing a Corruptive Element

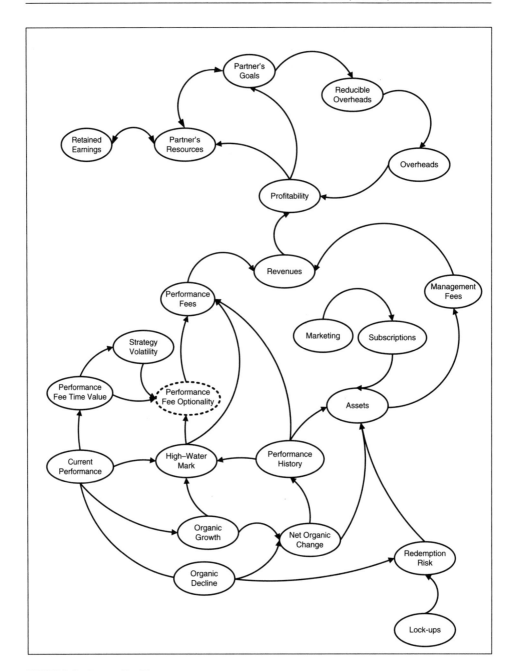

FIGURE 2.4   Large Fee Picture

MORTALITY CALCULATIONS

When a fund fails catastrophically, as shown in the Figure 2.5 example of a "blow-up," the owners/managers do not need a pencil and paper to know if they are still alive; but at other times, a life or death call is just that, a call or determination of circumstances as they

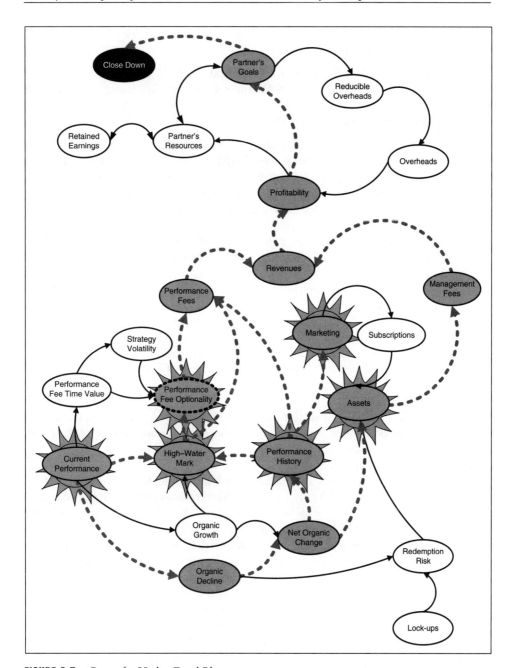

FIGURE 2.5 Case of a Hedge Fund Blow-up

are likely to be in the near future. In most of these cases, where the business viability is at or near its critical values, the owner/manager will estimate the odds of achieving a level of revenue required for survival. For hedge funds, this concept is more complex than for other businesses. For the numerical majority of funds that do not have billions of dollars under management, the performance fee is the faster road to revenue; and the performance fee has an optionality that makes its value at any given time a probabilistic calculation.

The probability of the manager receiving a performance fee at the end of the performance quarter is a function of:

- Time remaining in the performance fee period
- "Distance" between the current NAV and the current high-water mark (HWM)
- Volatility of the NAV
- Assets under management (AUM)

In an extreme case, where, the end of the performance fee period is just days away and the current NAV is far below the HWM, the odds are very much against the manager earning a performance fee for that period. As the time remaining becomes longer and the NAV gets closer to the high-water mark, the odds are improved. However, even where the current NAV is above the HWM, there is still a chance it could be lost before the end of the period.

For the manager who has been running an operating loss at the business level for some time, burning through seed capital and, perhaps, exhausting corporate and personal assets as well, missing a performance fee can tip the scales in favor of winding up the business. Similarly, where the distance between the NAV and the HWM has widened into the equivalent of a year or more of volatility, the manager may come to the same "game over" conclusion. Some amelioration of these circumstances can be achieved, at least short term by cutting overheads and drawing upon retained earnings or other partnership resources. A manager can also shift to higher volatility strategies or increase leverage to try to get better odds of triggering a performance fee. Another, darker practice could be to obtain illiquid assets where the value can more easily be overstated.

Several other mortality calculations may also be made at this time. If fund performance has been poor for some time, there is a rising risk of redemption. However, like the performance fee, this is often not a straight-line or single-variable calculation. One reason for this is that many funds have "lock-up" periods for incoming money. These locked-up assets are not redeemable, for a specified period of time stated in the prospectus. Many funds also have various terms in their prospectus that can be used as a basis for deferring redemptions, such as notice periods and maximum percentage of holdings that can be redeemed at one time.

Another factor is the composition of the investors. Some funds, especially start-ups, have only a handful of investors and can be greatly impacted if any of these "foundation investors" leave. Many investors also place restrictions on the maximum percentage of AUM they wish to represent, often a limit of 10 to 20 percent. So, when sizeable redemptions do occur it can push some of the other investors beyond their maximum percentage of AUM. This, in turn, can cause the equivalent of a redemption avalanche or cascade, where some redemptions trigger an unstoppable rising tide of redemptions that consume the entire fund en masse. This is, in effect an implosion of the fund, resulting in dissolution.

Where funds have strong performance, they can grow NAV "organically," and this organic growth can help to offset some redemption pressure. Also, where AUM is large, the management fee on its own can be substantial enough to fund a profitable business, without the contribution of any performance fees. A billion dollars of AUM on a "two-and-twenty" fee formula would mean $20 million per year of management fees. A $10 billion fund would yield $200 million per annum on the same basis. Some funds that have strong marketing operations or some form of captive clients can run for years in this way.

Why these calculations are important in the context of a book on hedge fund fraud is because a substantial proportion of frauds and perhaps those most dangerous to investors begin as legitimate businesses. These cases of "funds gone bad" have likely had managers that made similar fund mortality calculations. But they did not limit their choices to the business alternatives outlined thus far and allowed themselves to consider unconventional solutions that included criminal behavior as shown in Figure 2.6.

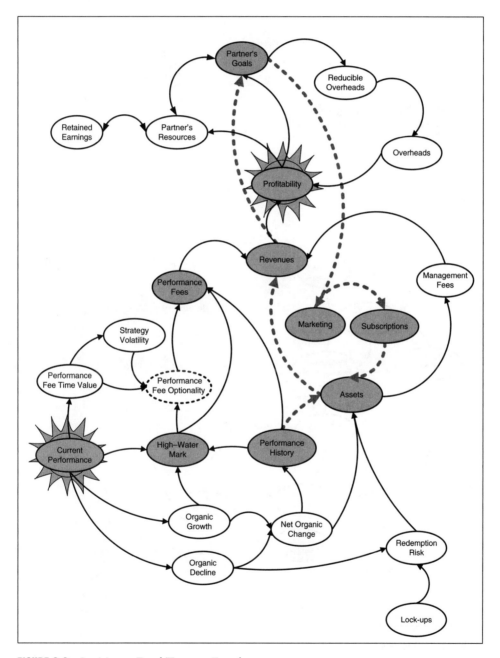

FIGURE 2.6 Legitimate Fund Turns to Fraud

Start-up hedge funds have a very high mortality rate due to their small size and often very limited start-up capital. In this respect they more resemble start-up restaurants in terms of their odds of survival, than other financial start-ups. The vicious circle (shown in Figure 2.7) illustrates the negatively reinforcing interactions of poor performance, or weak marketing, high-water mark and limited odds of getting a performance fee.

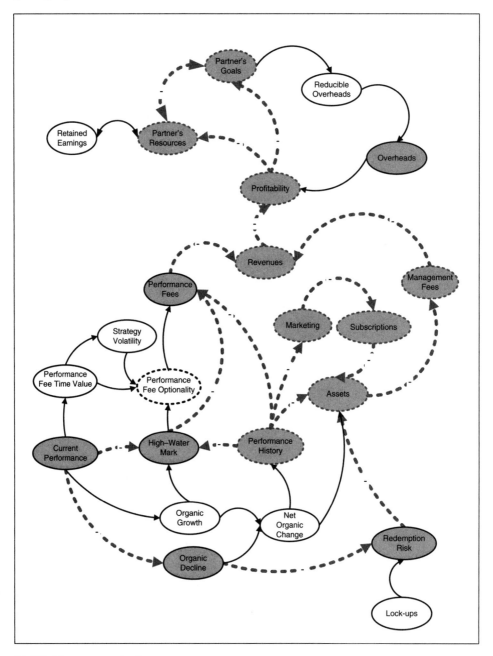

FIGURE 2.7 Vicious Circle

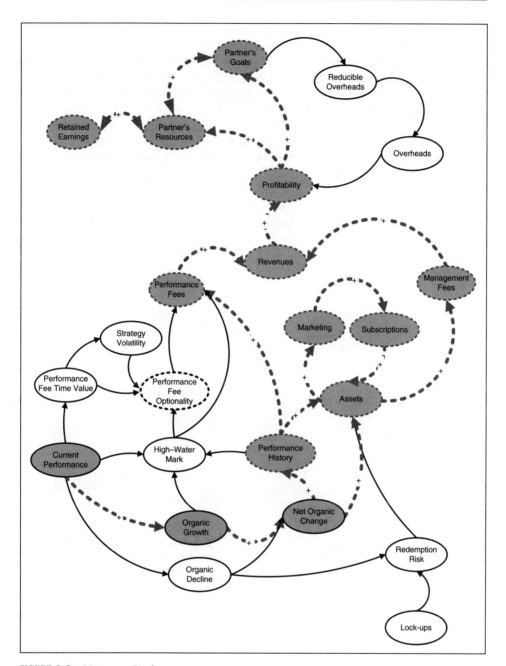

FIGURE 2.8 Virtuous Circle

The opposite set of positive interactions of a virtuous circle is shown in Figure 2.8.

The dominant mode of hedge fund failure is undercapitalization. Most start-up funds are little more than a "one-man-band" or "two guys in a boat." Because fund management is, in effect, a self-funding business it does not require much start-up capital to get going. If it is to be a regulated entity it does require a basic administrative overhead and generally imposes some additional requirements for regulatory capital. A highly quantitative firm may need extra overhead for programmers and hardware, while fundamentally driven managers may require specialist analysts. To a great extent, however, one or two ex-brokers or investment bankers, with a few years of decent earnings and bonuses behind them, can fund a start-up and keep it going for a year or two.

The problems start to mount after that point if the mechanics of the virtuous circle do not get going, especially if a poor performance period moves them too far from their high-water mark. The start-up can then begin to suffer the terminal effects of capital insufficiency as shown in Figure 2.9.

If a fund survives its start-up phase, it can still suffer a catastrophic collapse or "blow-up" at any time due to unforeseen circumstances. These circumstances may be externally driven, as from a suddenly changing market environment, or internally driven, from weak administration, faulty risk models, or a combination of both (see Figure 2.10).

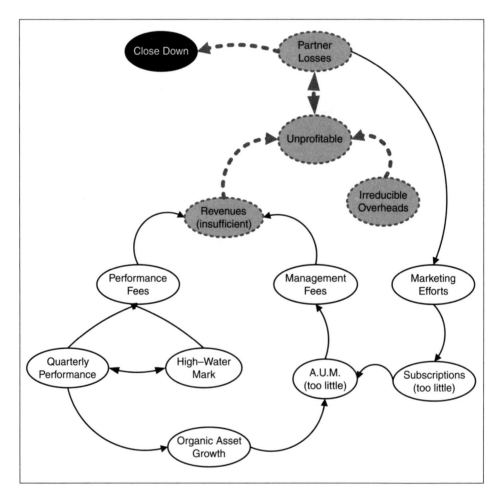

FIGURE 2.9   Capital Insufficiency

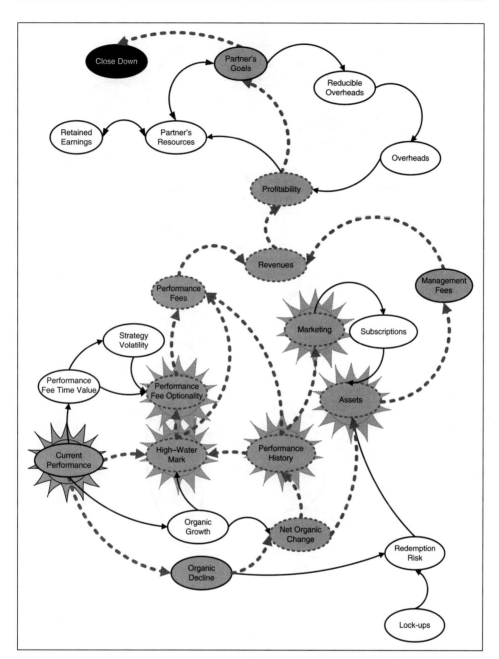

FIGURE 2.10 Blow-up: Sudden Catastrophic Performance Decline Ripples through Profitability Components to Destroy Fund

A blow-up can also result from fraud, as in the case of a "rogue trader." But in an opposite form of outcome, the problems can smolder, out of sight for years as in a Ponzi scheme. The structure of this type of scheme is shown in Figure 2.11.

This chapter illustrated some of the ways in which the unobservable dynamic interactions of fees, performance, and marketing can affect and often determine the

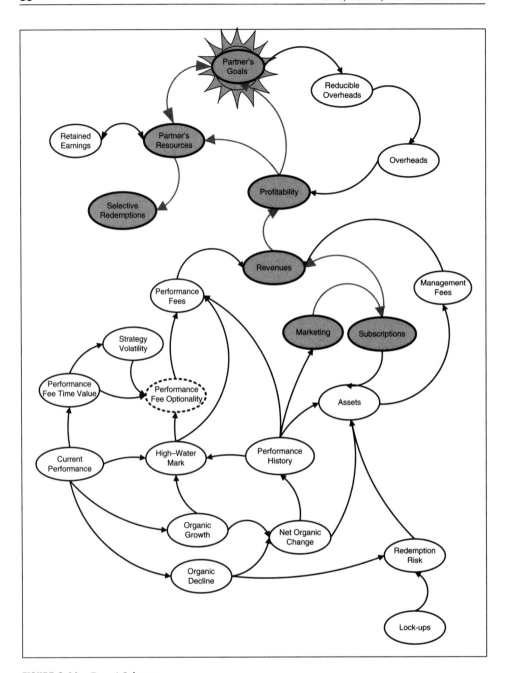

FIGURE 2.11   Ponzi Scheme

mortality of a hedge fund, and, by extension, lead to fraudulent means to avert it. It also demonstrates that the unseen does not have to be completely unknowable. With a more hedge fund–specific analysis, the internal workings that can give rise to fraud can be better understood.

The next chapter deals with uncertainties in the enforcement environment that can affect how a suspected hedge fund fraud will be adjudicated.

CHAPTER 3

Uncertainties and Events within the Law Enforcement System

ENTERING THE BELLY OF THE BEAST

From birth to death, hedge funds activities are observed, recorded, and judged by the marketplace of hedge fund investors. Occasionally, like bumper cars hedge funds sometimes knock into a regulatory obstacle and get bounced momentarily backward. However, when law enforcement or regulators sense the merest sniff of criminality in the air, they cause an enormous trapdoor to materialize beneath the hedge fund and all of its activities. That door starts to creak open when there is news of an investigation or pending suit. But, if fraud charges are filed, the trapdoor drops full open, exposing a cavernous maw, capable of swallowing the biggest fund, its related companies, staff, and all their resources and relations. The odds are that once this happens, the principal defendants will never be seen again, certainly not as they were before. When hedge funds drop through that trapdoor, they depart from the world we know, the world of markets and investors and enter a parallel universe where there are forces of gravity, rules of physics, logic, and proportion, but "not as we know them."

The goals and methods of law enforcement are substantially different from those of investment or of finance. For investors, all changes are part of a continuum of events and values. Even when there are unforeseen events that cause discontinuities in value and market practice, they can be accommodated within the confines of financial understandings. Bankruptcy, one of the most severe of discontinuities, is provided for with collateral, insurance, and the hierarchy of creditors. Although bankruptcy places the courts at the head of the table, it does so in a limited and specific way, because bankruptcy is a functional process governed by the financial principles of maximizing the enterprise value for the benefit of the creditors in the order of their status.

The same cannot be said for the adjudication of fraud. When fraud is alleged, most of the equilibrating mechanisms of the marketplace are swept away. Most of the subjects that are open to debate between managers and investors are largely set aside or altered by the legal process.

THE GAME OF SNAKES AND LADDERS

The well-known English children's game of "Snakes and Ladders," like "Chutes and Ladders" in the United States, was allegedly based on an ancient forerunner in India that represented the often whimsical nature of fate and salvation. It includes a sequence of paths (the "ladders") by which one can make progress by steady orderly steps paralleled by an intermittent series of more rapid courses of descent (the "snakes"). The two paths intersect in a manner determined partly by chance. The movement of the players in this game is a good model for the fate of perpetrators and victims alike once an alleged fraud becomes a legal concern.

Beyond the disorienting effect of the "trapdoor," the vista of the twisting pathways that track across the legal terrain not only makes cause and effect difficult to keep clear, but can make it taxing to figure out where one is in the process and why. Figure 3.1 shows this complex terrain from one perspective, the branching of the civil and criminal processes.

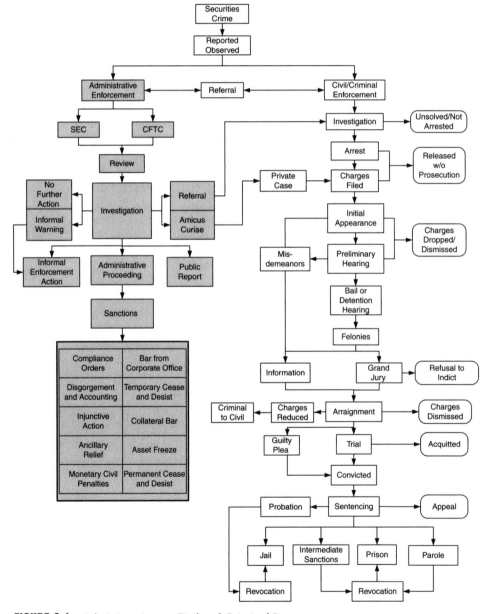

FIGURE 3.1   Administrative vs. Civil and Criminal Processes

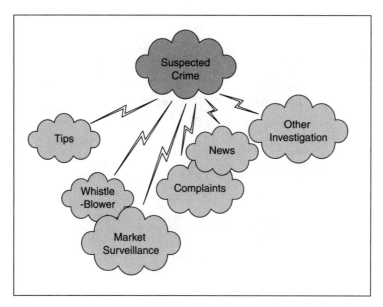

FIGURE 3.2 Enforcement: Sources of Information

The point of entry to the enforcement system is a suspected or alleged crime. In an extreme case, such as Bernie Madoff, the existence of the crime may become known from a confession by the perpetrator. In most cases, however, it will be by more indirect and, therefore, less certain means—even though a confession could also be false or inaccurate and, therefore, no more certain in value. There are a number of alternative channels for transmitting awareness of a possible crime to an enforcement agency, including those shown in Figure 3.2.

Information about potential crimes can be received by any number of enforcement entities, regardless of their relationship or relevance to the case or crime. This results in a good deal of cross-referencing of potential enforcement actions between agencies that, because of differences in investigative resources, often leads to ongoing cooperation in a case as shown in Figure 3.3.

No one would want the legal system to be any simpler than needed to determine guilt or innocence and to administer fair justice in righting wrongs. Equally, few would wish it to be any more complex than required to serve these same purposes. Our system appears to lean heavily in favor of the more complex. Much of this added complexity is a product of unavoidably imperfect laws being enacted or regulatory/enforcement bodies established to meet a perceived need at a point in time and becoming less relevant with the passage of time. On top of this, the federal system of government in the United States imposes the need for an intrinsic duplication in the machinery of state and often causes conflicts or ambiguities in the objectives and responsibilities of the two levels of government authority. As a result, investigations and case filings may be made at the state level or federal level. In some cases, a number of states will have some jurisdictional claims due to the location of the hedge fund's offices, its investors, or the markets in which it trades. Our legal system generally does not preclude or inhibit the bringing of multiple cases in different jurisdictions and by different parties, including by the states in their own right, on

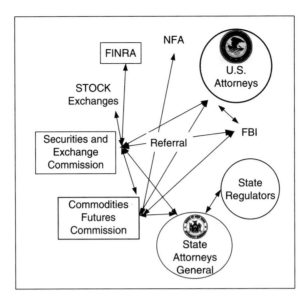

FIGURE 3.3 Enforcement Agencies Interaction
Note: FINRA is the Financial Industry Regulatory Authority.

behalf of others, or by others, though, over time the logic of adjudication of cases tends to cause a diminution in their number due to cases being combined, settled, dropped, or dismissed (see Figure 3.4).

The fact of separate parallel civil and criminal codes adds another duality to our system of justice. While the distinction undoubtedly serves a purpose in differentiating types of legal charges, processes, and punishments, it can also create separate lines of inquiry into what is essentially the same legal matter. Fraud is a crime with a footprint in both civil and criminal law. With securities fraud there is also the option of adjudicating within the confines of administrative law, by the regulatory agencies at the federal and state levels.

Another of the bifurcations in our legal system as it applies to hedge fund fraud is that a case may be brought by either a public or private entity, though, in the latter case limited to civil actions. In hedge fund fraud cases, the first filing is often by the private party victims who can react more quickly to perceived injury. However, the government's greater investigative resources just as often result in private filings following upon the release of investigative reports where the private parties can benefit from publicly funded research as well as the credibility of existing charges being filed by public authorities.

Class actions are a further variant of private filings given the large numbers of investors and sums of money involved.

More duplication is added to the justice system in hedge fund fraud cases due to the historical differences between the scope of authority of the Securities and Exchange Commission (SEC) and the Commodity Futures Trading Commission (CFTC). The differences between securities and commodities is generally clear and relevant, except in the context of hedge funds, entities that can and do invest in a wide range of assets including listed futures and options and over-the-counter

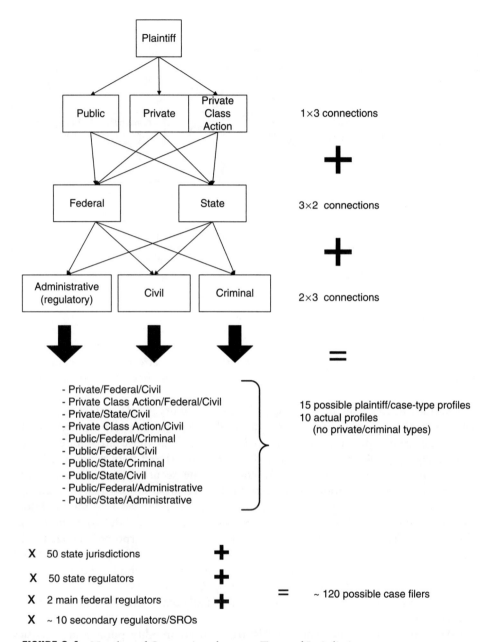

FIGURE 3.4   Number of Connections between Types of Jurisdictions

derivatives. Hedge funds also invest in assets that are traded in numerous markets inside and outside the United States as well as assets traded outside of markets.

A number of studies of hedge funds and their commodities counterparts: commodity pools and commodity trading advisers (CTAs) have been carried out by the SEC and the CFTC and as of several decades ago they concluded that similarities and/or overlaps between these investment entities were such that they were more or less the same thing and, in fact, many of the largest entities operated as both.

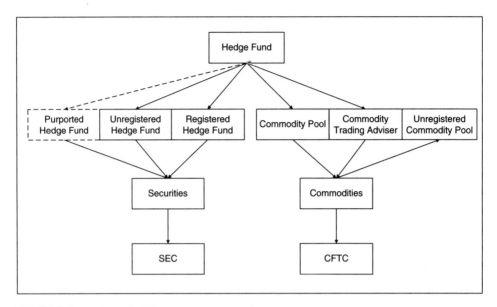

FIGURE 3.5 SEC vs. CFTC Registration Entities

However, this acknowledgement has had little practical effect on the operation of two separate streams of justice, except for the fact that they often cooperate (see Figure 3.5).

Another dichotomy in the hedge fund–commodity pool context is in their somewhat different and parallel treatment of unregistered and purported funds. Under the Commodity Exchange Act (CEA: Article 7 of the United States Code), all commodity pools must be registered, so an unregistered pool is an illegal pool that is implicitly guilty of fraud. By contrast, the securities statutes do permit exemption from registration under certain criteria (a situation that may change in the near future), though case law precedent has determined that the SEC does have jurisdictional authority over all U.S.-based hedge funds and some non-U.S.-based funds. One result of this difference is that so-called "purported" hedge funds, essentially entirely fake funds, do effectively comprise a class of SEC hedge fund fraud cases. However, there is not an exact equivalence on the commodity pool side, such as a purported commodity pool, since, under the CEA, it would be indistinguishable from an unregistered commodity pool, that is, a real commodity pool that has failed to register properly.

Ambiguities also arise where funds are both commodity pools and securities investment advisers (as many are) as to which agency should lead an investigation and/or act as plaintiff in a case. Hedge funds, by definition, tend to "hedge" long positions with short positions that can be options as well as short equity. (More confusingly, many ETFs, which are classed as commodities, are in essence, a security that is itself representing an index of securities, and these index securities can be equal to long or short [inverse] index returns.)

If the link between the cause and effect of the crime of fraud had not been obscured by the legal process up to this point, then the stage where plea bargaining occurs would likely do the job on its own. First, it should be pointed out, as with

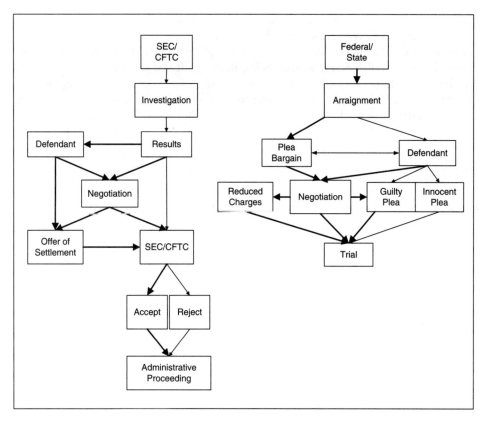

FIGURE 3.6 SEC and CFTC vs. Federal and State Plea Systems

the other parallel tracks of hedge fund justice, the plea bargaining procedures differ, as does the overall legal process between the agencies employing administrative law, such as the SEC and CFTC, and those following civil and criminal law. And, while differences also exist within these divisions, there is enough similarity to say that SEC and CFTC administrative procedure does it one way and the federal and state civil and criminal courts do it another way (see Figure 3.6).

Both methods have the same underlying goals and results—reducing the burden of trials, costs, and time generally, by agreeing to a compromise between prosecution and defense. From the point of view of obfuscating cause and effect, the prime aspect of this compromise is that the defendant will have his or her charges reduced, which often means that the most serious crimes they were initially charged with, will be taken off the docket and the charge(s) that remain may have the least to do with the initial character of the crime. This is despite the fact that the devastating commercial effects of the initial charges on the target companies and people will have occurred around the time of the first filing of charges and are not readily reversible. In other words, for a financial company the charge is as punishing as a verdict and even more so where there has been a verdict that has been reversed on appeal (see Case 14 PRINCETON-NEWPORT in Chapter 4 for an example).

In the civil and criminal procedures, the defendant will actually agree to plead guilty, thereby entirely bypassing an objective or scientific determination of innocence or guilt. In the administrative procedures, the pleas appear to work the other way around, with the defendant neither being found guilty or innocent, while agreeing to the publication of an SEC and CFTC account of events as well as agreeing to sanctions. Here too, the ultimate answer to "Did they do it or not?" is formalized as a fundamental nonconclusion.

Cases and Conclusions

Part Two consists of Chapters 4 and 5. Chapter 4 is the "casebook," containing 100 case studies arranged in chronological order from the first known case of fraud. Each case is set out in an identical format, the core of which is an expository summary of the case as well as tables, facts, and figures detailing numbers of victims, sums of money lost, cases brought, and punishments meted out. There follows an accompanying chart that shows the main characters, actions, interactions, and results in diagrammatical form.

Chapter 5 summarizes the case material in aggregate. It focuses on the identification of defining factors of fraud and descriptions of fraud subgroups that illuminate some basic differences in the types of fraud committed.

CHAPTER 4

Cases

The *case* is the basic unit of organizing the subject matter of this chapter. Here, the term has a meaning similar to that of other casebooks used for educational purposes in various disciplines—that is, some historical circumstance used as an example for educational purposes. This should be distinguished from the narrow usage in the law, where *case* refers to specific legal actions (as in *Smith v. Jones*). That said, there are many such legal cases referred to in this casebook.

Every case in this casebook involves a hedge fund and, with few exceptions, one or more persons who are functionally related to it and have been accused of fraud in a U.S. state or federal court or U.S. regulatory administrative proceeding. Some cases involve foreign entities that have had court actions filed against them in the U.S. The victims of the alleged fraud are, by and large, hedge fund investors and, in some instances, the hedge fund itself (e.g., defrauded by its manager or a trader). This is true even though a number of the cases involve crimes that involve no specific victims but rather against the operations of specific markets, exchanges, or simply against the "public interest."

HEDGE FUNDS

As used in this casebook, the term *hedge fund* tends toward all-inclusiveness, aiming to capture all hedge fund-related frauds. Given this aim the qualifying entities include:

- Hedge funds, hedge fund managers, hedge fund advisers
- Hedge fund partnerships
- Hedge fund trusts
- Registered hedge funds (SEC or state)
- Private hedge funds (registered or unregistered)
- Purported or alleged hedge funds or promoted as hedge funds
- De facto hedge funds (absolute return benchmark, ability to go short, charging a performance fee)
- Cited as being "hedge funds" by regulators, judicial or enforcement agencies, or by financial press of record
- Commodity pool operator (CPO), commodity pool (CP), and commodity trading adviser (CTA)
- Commodity pool or trading adviser partnerships

- Registered CPOs, POs, CTAs (CFTC or state)
- Unregistered CPOs, POs, CTAs
- Private CPOs, POs, CTAs

FRAUD

The meaning of the term *fraud* is that used in law. Simply put, fraud is theft by deception. By extension, *hedge fund fraud* is theft by deception involving hedge funds (as broadly defined in the previous section) as perpetrators or victims. The casebook has adopted the convention of recognizing hedge fund frauds on the basis of the filing of charges rather than the deciding of convictions. The reasons for this distinction are that:

- Charges better reflect the time when the alleged crime was committed; convictions often lag by years.
- Cases are often resolved by settlement rather than conviction, leaving the question of guilt unanswered, and the details of these settlements are generally not made public.
- In SEC administrative proceedings the respondent's "Offer of Settlement" is frequently proffered in exchange for permitting the defendant to neither admit nor deny guilt.
- In judicial proceedings that result in a conviction, the plea-bargaining process often obscures the true nature of the crimes.
- Convictions may be fully or partially overturned in subsequent appeals that may be years in the future.
- Cases are sometimes split or merged, shuffling defendant companies and individuals in an indeterminate manner.
- Any number of cases can be filed against an alleged fraud defendant in a wide range of jurisdictions, making it unclear whether guilt in any, all, a majority, only in the most senior jurisdiction, or only on the most serious charges, should be the measure of guilt.
- In civil fraud actions, where the pursuit of restitution for damages is the main objective, plaintiffs pragmatically seek to file charges against defendants that have recoverable assets, rather than those most involved in committing the crime. The tendency to sue hedge fund auditors is one indicator of this bias.

Fraud represents a very broad class of crimes, only a tiny fraction of which has anything to do with hedge funds or investments in general. The frauds covered in this casebook mainly comprise those classified as "securities fraud," a domain regulated by the Securities and Exchange Commission. Within the SEC ambit, the violations that are grouped together with fraud, for the purposes of this casebook include:

- Failure to disclose material information
- Filing of a false report
- Insider trading
- Market manipulation
- Misappropriation
- Misinformation

- Record-keeping violations
- Registration violations
- Short-selling violations

Beyond these securities violations additional federal crimes associated with fraud include:

- Conspiracy to defraud the U.S. government
- Mail fraud
- Money laundering
- Racketeer-influenced and corrupt organizations (RICO)
- Wire fraud

CASE NUMBER AND CASE NAME

The title line for each case lists a case number representing the approximate chronological order of the filing of fraud charges. The number is followed by a one or two-part title name derived from the main defendant parties involved in the case. The convention has been adopted of capitalizing the name of the hedge fund or related corporate entity and placing that first, followed by the last name of the principal person defendant in upper- and lowercase letters. The two names are separated with a forward slash (e.g., GOTHAM/Berkowitz). Where there is only one entity or the corporate name and personal name are essentially the same, only one name is used and it is capitalized (e.g., LAMAR).

CAPSULE: GENERIC SUMMARY

A very brief summary of the central circumstance of the fraud is laid out in generic terms (i.e., devoid of contextual aspects). This provides a quick sense, the "gist," of the case and makes it easier to compare the "broad strokes" of one case versus another.

BULLET POINTS

The bullet points outline the key contextual elements in the case such as its being the largest or first in some important aspect; the main enforcement agencies involved; the nature of the principal offenders; and other remarkable, unusual, or unique facets that played a role in the case.

FRAUD FACTS

A standardized list of pertinent facts that apply to most or all cases:

- **Alleged Acts Date.** Approximate time when the alleged crimes were committed.

- **Enforcement Date.** Date of filing of the first or main or most authoritative charges against the hedge fund–related defendants. Where there are multiple filings, the order of precedence generally followed for choosing the enforcement date was:

  - SEC
  - CFTC
  - State securities regulators
  - Other federal and state market and securities regulators
  - Federal criminal
  - State criminal
  - Private class actions
  - Private individuals and/or corporations

- **Main Defendants.** Persons and other entities charged. In administrative cases these parties are referred to as *respondents*. Those that are related to hedge funds are shown in **bold type**.

- **Most Serious Charge.** The most serious charges alleged in complaints, or indictments for all of the defendants in all of the legal actions attached to the case. In general, criminal charges are regarded as more serious than civil, and civil more serious than administrative. Within the criminal law, those occurring in the hedge fund fraud cases taken to be the most serious include those related to organized crime, bribery, embezzlement, conspiracy, and mail and wire fraud. Within the civil law the crimes taken to be the most serious include: misappropriation, manipulation, commodities and securities fraud.

- **Damages.** Damages are the total dollar amount of monetary losses attributable to the fraud and related crimes within the case. For the perpetrator the damages correspond to "ill-gotten gains." Damages are expressed in both the U.S. dollars of the time and in U.S. dollars based on the year 2005 (**in bold**); the latter provides a uniform measure of losses due to fraud across the full time span of all the cases and adjusts for all of the inflation from the date of the crime to 2005.

- **Number of Investors.** The number of investors is the number of individual entities that invested in the hedge fund or group of funds involved in the fraud. The number does not necessarily represent all of those that actually lost money as a result of fraud. Where the number of investors is not known, a range is provided where possible. Some cases involve "victimless" crimes, where the victims are taken to be the "public interest," or the markets or all investors generally.

- **Highest Court.** Identifies the most senior judicial level to have heard any significant aspect of the case. In this order the appellate courts rank highest, followed by criminal civil and administrative. Also federal courts are interpreted as senior to state courts.

- **Most Severe Sentence/Sanctions.** Criminal prison sentences are at the top of this scale and at the bottom are censures and injunctions handed out by administrative courts. Also, permanent sanctions (e.g., injunctions, suspensions) outrank temporary or term sanctions. The ranking includes:

  - Prison
  - Home confinement, halfway house, community service
  - Supervised release, probation
  - Disbarment

- Monetary fines
- Restitution, disgorgement
- Revocation of registration
- Suspension
- Censure, injunction, cease-and-desist order

- **Sentences/Sanctions.** A list of all main defendants and the key elements of the sentences and/or sanctions they have received in relation to the given case.
- **Cases.** A list of the main actions filed in relation to the case. The format includes the following details:

  - Title of Court Action (*Plaintiff v. Defendant,*—e.g., *SEC v. Jones*)

- Code number of case (e.g., 02cr0379):

  - Last two digits of year (e.g., 02)
  - cr or cv denoting criminal or civil, respectively
  - A sequential number issued by the court where the action was filed

- A word describing whether the case was criminal, civil, or administrative
- The judicial district in which the court is located, normally designated by a cardinal point (e.g., SDNY is Southern District New York S. Dist. N.Y.)
- Administrative cases are designated in a different manner

CASE SUMMARY

This is one of the main sections of the casebook pages and is the largest in size and content. Occupying a page or more, the case summary provides an expository description of the case and generally includes a description of the main:

- Defendants
- Victims
- A precise or approximate sequence of events that covers the background, course, and aftermath of the fraud
- Modus operandi (MO)
- How/why the fraud came to light
- Actions taken by enforcement
- Results

CASE DIAGRAM

Another of the major sections of the casebook pages is devoted to a graphic depiction of the case generally illustrating:

- Flow of money from investors to hedge funds
- Flow of money from hedge funds to advisers, general partners (GPs), limited partners (LPs), principals, and other professionals
- Provision of false or inaccurate information to investors

- Interactions between enforcement and perpetrators
- Key dates
- Sums of money invested, lost, and misappropriated
- Main defendants, aiders and abettors, and coconspirators
- Investor victims
- Counterparties to trades
- Enforcement agencies involved in case
- Sentences/sanctions meted out to main defendants
- Money recovered

The diagrams for the cases have been standardized to the extent possible in order to facilitate comparisons and all of the diagrams make use of the same limited set of symbols shown in legend in Figure 4.1.

The basic structure of all of the case diagrams is similar. For example, time runs from the top of the diagram to the bottom; the innocent, aggrieved, or accusing parties (mainly investors and enforcement) are on the right side; while the accused are on the left. The parties are connected by arrows that illustrate actions, including the transfer of information and money. Dates and sums of money, where known and relevant, are between the party and the action. Figure 4.2 illustrates some of the basic flows common to the cases.

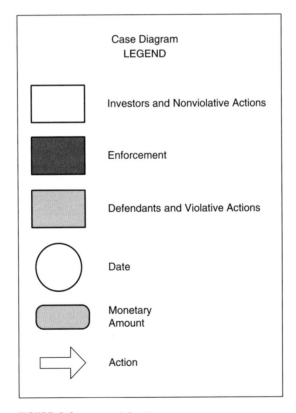

FIGURE 4.1 Legend for Cases

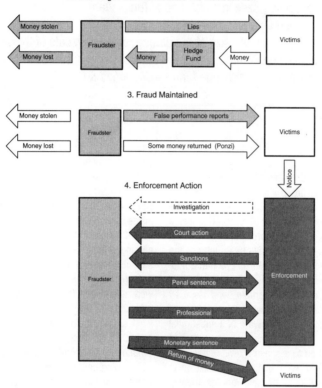

FIGURE 4.2 Case Diagrams Basic Elements

The corporate finance department of an investment bank passed client-confidential, price-sensitive information to its institutional brokerage clients, including mutual funds and hedge funds. Key highlights:

- SEC case
- Administrative action
- Earliest known enforcement case involving hedge funds
- First insider trading case in which hedge funds were implicated
- First class action against a hedge fund
- Light sanctions given the size of the damages and the scale of the violations
- Included a significant proportion of the earliest hedge funds extant at that time
- Included the world's first hedge fund—A.W. Jones & Co.

Case Summary

On August 27, 1968, the SEC filed charges in what was the first known case of fraud involving hedge funds in the United States. The case concerned insider trading by a group of investment institutions, including seven of the earliest hedge funds, in the common shares of Douglas Aircraft. The inside information comprised a lowered earnings forecast issued by Douglas and provided by Douglas to the underwriting department of Merrill Lynch at a time when it was being considered to lead a syndicate for a new $75 million convertible bond issue by Douglas. Prior to the issue and final appointment of Merrill, Douglas became aware of a substantial reduction in its estimated earnings and passed this information on to a senior Merrill underwriter on the West Coast, who, in turn, passed it on to a research executive in the New York institutional sales office. From there the information was relayed to a number of Merrill's institutional clients, including seven of the earliest known hedge funds. The SEC filed these charges just two weeks after it received a favorable decision in a landmark insider trading case (*SEC v. Texas Gulf Sulphur*, 65cv1182) in which the SEC pursued injunctions against the company and individuals under section 10(b) of the Securities and Exchange Act of 1934 and Rule10(b)5.

In contrast to the civil case, the SEC pursued its case as an Administrative Proceeding, pressing charges against Merrill Lynch and 14 of its executives and salesmen as well as 14 investment institutions.

The seven hedge fund defendants included A.W. Jones, the world's first hedge fund, and several other early spin-offs from the Jones operations, such as Fairfield Partners and City Associates. It was alleged that the institutions benefited from the inside information by selling or shorting 153,000 to 190,000 shares of Douglas stock on the NYSE and earning or avoiding losses on some $4.5 million as a result. Most of the parties were censured and two of Merrill's operations and several of its executives were suspended for periods of 15 to 60 days. In parallel with the SEC action, there were also at least six private civil actions filed between 1968 and 1971: *Sanders v. ML, Hirsh v. ML, Baehr v. ML, Smachlo v. ML, Shulof v. ML,* and *Shapiro v. ML,* all pursuing damage claims based upon the same events and facts of the SEC case. The first five were dismissed for not having an actionable cause under the "Birnbaum Rule," which maintains that (1) the fraud be of the type usually associated with the purchase and sale of securities; and (2) that the protection of SEC Rule 10(b)5 be applied to the purchaser or seller of the stock. *Shapiro v. Merrill Lynch* (70cv3653) was more successful. It was a class action and included defendants that had purchased and/or sold Douglas shares during the period of the alleged fraud. An appeal court held that Shapiro had an actionable case as a class action, however the final outcome of this case is not clear and it is likely that the parties reached a settlement.

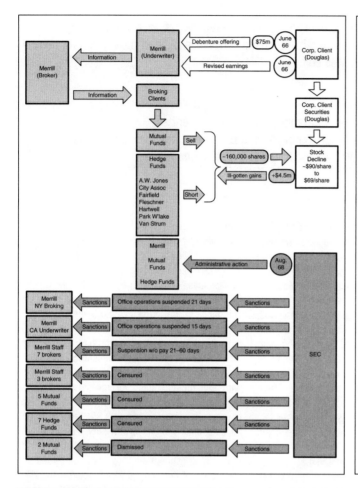

Fraud Facts

- Alleged Acts Date: June 20, 1966
- Enforcement Date: August 28, 1968
- Main Defendants **(hedge fund-related)**: Merrill Lynch (ML execs), **A.W. Jones Associates, City Associates, Fairfield Partners, Fleschner Becker Associates, Hartwell Associates, Park Westlake Associates**
- Most Serious/Dominant Charge: Insider trading
- Hedge Fund Role: "Tippees" (receipt and use of inside information)
- Damages $actual **($2005): $4.5 million ($27 million)**
- No. of Investors: NA
- Highest Court: Administrative
- Most Severe Sentence: 21-day suspension of regional business activities

Sanctions:

- A.W. Jones & Co.: Censured
- A.W. Jones Associates: Censured
- City Associates: Censured
- Fairfield Partners: Censured
- Fleschner, Becker Associates: Censured
- Hartwell Associates: Censured
- J.M. Hartwell & Co.: Censured
- Park Westlake Associates: Censured

Cases:

- *SEC v. Merrill Lynch* (administrative)
- *Sanders v. Merrill Lynch* (68cv3522, civil, S. Dist. N.Y.)
- *Hirsh v. Merrill Lynch* (68cv5183, civil, S. Dist. N.Y.)
- *Baehr v. Merrill Lynch* (69cv1418, civil, S. Dist. N.Y.)
- *Smachlo v. Merrill Lynch* (70cv1202, civil, S. Dist. N.Y.)
- *Shulof v. Merrill Lynch* (70cv4819, civil, S. Dist. N.Y.)
- *Shapiro v. Merrill Lynch* (70cv3653, civil, S. Dist. N.Y.)

Precedents:

- Use of term "tippees" to denote parties that receive inside information

The defendant, a hedge fund adviser, misdirected orders to a broker in return for commission kickbacks. It was also accused of misuse of fund money to pay certain overheads of the adviser. Key points:

- SEC case
- Administrative action
- First case with a hedge fund manager as main defendant
- Central charge was order-routing for the purpose of commission kickbacks
- Hedge fund manager required to compensate hedge fund

Case Summary

The Hubshman Fund was founded around 1966 when it entered into prolonged negotiations with the SEC to register a "mutual fund," but one that would be offered to the public and that would utilize hedging and leverage. The minimum investment was $1,000 (around $6,500 today).

In November 1966, after registering with the SEC, 10 million shares were offered at $10 per share. The Hubshman Fund was managed by the Hubshman Management Corporation. Louis Hubshman, Jr. served as both president of the Fund and manager of the Management Corp. Hubshman Management Corp. also served as the investment adviser and underwriter to the fund. The weaknesses of this overlapping authority would show up three years later as a contributing factor to the legal problems the Hubshman companies encountered.

In March 1969, the SEC initiated Administrative Proceedings against the Hubshman Management Corp. and Louis Hubshman for violating the antifraud provisions of the federal securities laws. Specifically, the manager was charged with receiving kickbacks on its brokerage transactions, and with having the fund pay for some of the expenses of the management company. In an "Offer of Settlement" agreed with the SEC, Hubshman Management Corp. had its broker-dealer registration suspended for 30 days and Louis Hubshman Jr. also received a 30-day suspension from associating with any broker, dealer, or investment adviser. Hubshman Management Corp. also agreed to pay the Hubshman Fund $63,351 and to forgo an additional $36,000 of advisory fees from the Fund. The terms of the agreement also provided that the Hubshman entities were permitted to neither admit nor deny any wrongdoing—a fairly standard clause in SEC administrative settlements.

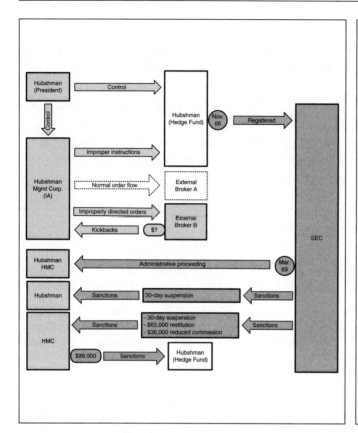

Fraud Facts

- Alleged Acts Date: November 30, 1966
- Enforcement Date: March 22, 1969
- Main Defendants **(hedge fund-related): Louis Hubshman, Hubshman Management Corp.**
- Most Serious Charge: Receiving kickbacks from brokers
- Hedge Fund Role: Improperly directing brokerage business in return for kickbacks
- Damages $actual **($2005): $99,351 ($430,000)**
- No. of Investors: Approximately 4,000
- Highest Court: Administrative
- Most Severe Sentence: 30-day suspension plus $99,351 disgorgement

Sanctions:

- Louis Hubshman: 30-day suspension
- Hubshman Management Fund: 30-day suspension plus $99,351 restitution

Cases:

- *SEC v. Hubshman* (administrative action)

Precedents:

- SEC-registered hedge fund—seemingly open to retail investors

A husband and wife, who were limited partners in a hedge fund, alleged that the general partners, caused them to incur losses by failing to inform the investors of a substantial increase in the holdings of risky, unregulated securities. Key points:

- Private action
- A second action in two years against Fleschner Becker Associates (see Case 1 MERRILL LYNCH)
- The appeal decision recognized the SEC's right to regulate hedge funds as well as the right of investors to bring private actions under the Investment Advisers Act
- Damages based on paper losses, despite the investors having realized absolute gains at the time after redemption

Case Summary

Fleschner Becker Associates (FBA) was one of the hedge funds charged in the Merrill Lynch Douglas insider trading case (see Case 1) and was censured by the SEC for its role in those events. The events in this private case took place at roughly the same time as the Merrill Lynch case, though any direct links are unknown.

The private suit was brought by two of the limited partners (a husband and wife) of the Fleschner Becker Associates hedge fund, charging the General Partners and their accountants (Goodkin) with failing to disclose the accumulation of what became a majority holding of unregistered securities while claiming a "most conservative" investment strategy.

According to legal documents, holdings of unregistered securities increased from around 15 percent to around 72 percent between September 1967 and 1968 and over the next 12 months ranged as high as 88 percent. Monthly reports to the limited partners made no mention of unregistered securities. When the limited partners received their annual statements for the year ending September 1969, prepared by a new accounting firm, they included a footnote stating that unregistered securities comprised approximately 77 percent of securities investments.

The plaintiffs redeemed their investments with the partnership at the first opportunity after hearing this news. And, despite having earned a profit overall on their investment in the fund, they filed a suit for damages in excess of $1 million on the basis that they would have earned higher returns had they redeemed at an earlier date when the substantial increase in unregistered securities should have first been disclosed.

In a summary judgment, the court found in favor of the defendants. The judgment was based on the facts that the plaintiffs could not show that they had suffered any real damages from the actions of the fund or its accountants. A subsequent appeal court partly reversed this judgment, finding that while there was no basis for a suit under the Securities Exchange Act (Section 10(b) and Rule 10b(5)), there was a basis under the Investment Advisers Act of 1940, Section 206. The appeal was important in establishing the right of investors to pursue private actions against investment advisers.

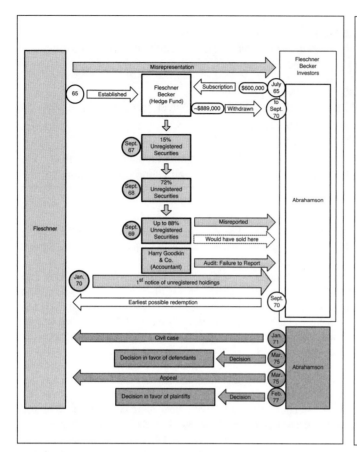

Fraud Facts

- Alleged Acts Date: September 1968
- Enforcement Date: January 30, 1971
- Main Defendants **(hedge fund-related): Malcolm Fleschner**, **William Becker,** Harry Goodkin & Co., **Fleschner Becker Associates**
- Most Serious Charge: Failure to disclose material information
- Hedge Fund Role: Defendant in private fraud case brought by limited partners
- Damages $actual **($2005)**: $1.3 million **($6.3 million)** (2 investors)
- No. of Investors: 66
- Highest Court: Civil, private
- Most Severe Sentence: (Final outcome not known)

Sanctions:

- The final outcome of the case is not known, nor is the disposition of any awards for damages or other sanctions upon the plaintiff hedge fund general partners and their accountants.

Cases:

Abrahamson v. Fleschner (71cv00344, civil, S. Dist. N.Y.)
Abrahamson v. Fleschner (appeal 75–7203, No. 212)

Precedents:

- Appeal established the right of the SEC to regulate hedge funds
- Right of investors to bring private actions against investment advisers

Two hedge funds and a number of mutual funds were defrauded by an extensive criminal conspiracy in which bribes were paid to get the funds to purchase overvalued or worthless securities. Key points:

- First criminal case against a hedge fund entity
- Biggest case to date and one of the most extensive ever
- Hedge fund use of unregistered securities
- Violations included the U.S. Conspiracy Statute
- Included the first hedge fund-related SEC case against an accounting firm
- Galanis subsequently re-offended again and received a long prison sentence

Case Summary

This was a major case in terms of the scale and complexity of the fraud and was likely the biggest case involving a hedge fund during a 10-year period or more. The case ultimately involved some 50 individuals and companies including several banks, hedge funds, mutual funds, and their investment advisers and legal counsels, as well as more than one group of penny-stock promoters. It also illustrates how multiple violator networks can work together opportunistically to accomplish broader criminal aspirations.

The foundation for the immediate case was Ramon D'Onofrio, a well-established penny-stock promoter, and a network of his accomplices, individuals working for at least two stockbroking firms and one Swiss Bank, one or two law firms, and executives of several small companies. Onto this well-oiled criminal base a separate and more credible organization had been established by the two principal defendants. John Galanis had been an investment analyst with Merrill Lynch and portfolio manager with Neuwirth Fund Inc., while Akiyoshi Yamada was formerly an assistant vice president with Kuhn, Loeb. Together they created: Armstrong Investors, SA, and Armstrong Capital, two offshore funds for investment in U.S. securities, Everest Management, Armstrong's investment adviser, and Takara Partners, an unregistered hedge fund.

While it is possible and perhaps likely that the initial investment objective was not criminal, it is clear that it became so within a year of commencing business. Having raised around $3.9 million from a roster of blue chip, high-net-worth investors, including G. Keith Funston, former head of the New York Stock Exchange, Galanis and Yamada had become attracted to the potential returns from unregistered stocks and needing assistance to manipulate the securities of some small companies, they came into contact and began collaborating with the D'Onofrio network in several manipulation schemes that are the primary subjects of this case.

Enforcement action commenced no later than January 25, 1970, when the SEC suspended trading of one of the penny stocks and started an investigation. By June 1971, there were at least two private lawsuits filed including one prospective class action (Delfino, et al.). On November 11, 1971, the SEC charged 44 individuals and companies with fraud. The core of the SEC complaint was that Everest (a Galanis/Yamada entity) had misappropriated $1.5 million from Armstrong Investors S.A., and additional sums from the Takara hedge fund.

First National City Bank and its subsidiary First National City Trust (Bahamas) were charged with falsifying information, and several mutual funds and their managers were charged with having aided and abetted the scheme, such as Robert Hagopian, a fund manager who received a bribe to induce the Index Fund of Boston to purchase overvalued shares. Another hedge fund implicated in the allegations was Tudor Hedge Fund, via charges brought against its then president, Stephen Sanders.

Galanis became a fugitive until he was extradited several years later. He was sentenced to five years in prison, but was probationed after six months because of his cooperation. Yamada was sentenced to two years. These were probably the first hedge fund managers to be imprisoned for fraud. In another precedent, Takara's auditor, Laventhol, Krekstein, Horwath & Horwath was disciplined by the SEC for having allegedly accepted a $17,000 bribe and for distributing false or misleading financial statements. Ramon D'Onofrio also received an 18-month prison sentence. Many of the others involved faced administrative sanctions, one lawyer was disbarred, and one or more brokerage companies were closed down.

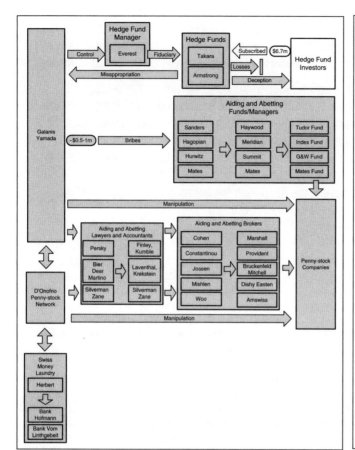

Fraud Facts

- Alleged Acts Date: Late 1969
- Enforcement Date: Early 1970
- Main Defendants **(hedge fund-related): John P. Galanis, Akiyoshi Yamada, Takara Partners, Everest Mgmt. Corp., Armstrong Investors, Takara Partners, Tudor Hedge Fund**
- Most Serious Charges: Criminal fraud, bribery
- Hedge Fund Role: Duped by their advisers into buying overpriced or worthless securities
- Damages $actual **($2005)**: Circa $4.0 million **($21.3 million)**
- No. of Investors: NA
- Highest Court: Criminal
- Most Severe Sentence: Multiyear prison terms

Sanctions:

- Indictments (main SEC case): 44
- Permanent Injunctions Ordered: 32
- Criminal Actions Filed to 1975: 14
- Prison Sentences Ordered: 4

Cases: Criminal Cases: (U.S. v. . . .

- *D'Onofrio, Galanis, Hagopian (72cv00884 S.D.N.Y.), Herbert (73cr00654 S.D.N.Y.), Stoller (74cv00159 S.D.N.Y.), Strub (73cr00654 S.D.N.Y.), Van Aken (72cr01221 S.D.N.Y.), Yamada, Zane (73cr00192 S.D.N.Y.)*

Civil Cases: (SEC v. . . .

- *D'Onofrio (72cv3507 S.D.N.Y.), Everest (71cv4932, S.D.N.Y.), Laventhol*

Civil Cases: (Private)

- Del Fino Class Action, *Armstrong v. Galanis (70cv5315 S.D.N.Y), Competitive v. Yamada (72cv1986 S.D.N.Y), Index Fund v. Hagopian (73cv2665 S.D.N.Y.)*

Precedents:

- First SEC case against a hedge fund auditor
- Galanis became a fugitive and had to be extradited

The principal and fund group, which included one hedge fund, were involved in more than 20 years of litigation with the SEC, centering on two cases concerning disclosure and reporting and ultimately an unsuccessful de facto effort to remove the principal. Key points:

- An SEC administrative action reached the U.S. Supreme Court on appeal
- Precedent-setting case that defined the SEC's burden of proof in establishing fraud in administrative cases to "preponderance of evidence" rather than the previous more stringent standard of "clear and convincing evidence"
- Steadman fought the SEC for 30 years with enough success to remain at the head of his funds group for all but a few months
- Over this extensive period, the Steadman funds group ranked as one of the worst-performing group of funds ever tracked

Case Summary

Steadman Funds was a small mutual funds group first established in 1952 by William Steadman. Following his death in 1964, management of the funds passed to his brother Charles, a Harvard Law School graduate. At that time the single Steadman Investment Fund Inc. had $3.2 million in assets under management. In June 1971, the SEC ordered administrative proceedings against Charles Steadman and five of the group's companies extant at that time, one of which, Steadman Amerifund, N.V., was described as a hedge-type fund by the *New York Times*. The other funds named were: Steadman Security Corp. (investment adviser to the funds), Steadman Investment Services Corp. (a registered broker-dealer), Steadman International Capital Corp. (a Panama company acting as Manager of the "hedge-type" fund, which was a Netherlands Antilles company), and Republic Securities Corp., a registered broker-dealer.

The SEC charged Steadman with a conflict of interest resulting from depositing fund's money in noninterest-bearing bank accounts where Steadman was also seeking loans unrelated to the funds. The SEC ordered that Steadman should be permanently banned from the industry. However, what should have been the end of the enforcement process turned out to be the beginning of a 30-year legal wrangle, which, surprisingly, the SEC basically lost. In a series of appeals, which in 1981 got as far as the Supreme Court, it was ruled that the SEC had to provide more justification before imposing its most severe sanction. The SEC reduced Steadman's sanction to 180 days suspension, with the imposition of the sanction waived.

Despite the lack of victory over Steadman, the Supreme Court decision was valuable in defining the level of proof the agency required to prove fraud in administrative proceedings. This decision effectively lowered the SEC's burden of proof to the "preponderance of evidence" rather than the more demanding "clear and convincing evidence" standard. This precedent (*Steadman v. SEC*, No. 79–1266) is cited to this day. The SEC terminated its case against Steadman on January 5, 1982, a case it had commenced on January 25, 1971, 11 years earlier.

By 1989, the SEC again had Steadman in its sights, this time for not registering his funds in other states (i.e., Blue Sky laws) where it was doing business. Steadman had obtained a legal opinion that he did not need to register since he had converted his out-of-state business to mail order and his resident state (District of Columbia) did not require registration. As matters progressed, the SEC demanded that Steadman create a legal reserve fund to cover the cost of any litigation that might be brought as a result of not being registered. Steadman countered that the SEC had no right to require this reserve. In July 1989, the SEC filed *SEC v. Steadman* (1:89cv02026), a civil securities fraud suit from which it sought and won a permanent injunction against Steadman. However, before the regulator could close the file on Steadman, most of the ruling was reversed on appeal (June 26, 1992) and the injunction was set aside. Steadman died in 1997 still in control of funds that were often judged to be among the worst performing mutual funds. To this day, the story of the Steadman funds remains the gold standard for poor performance and the unshakeable faith or foolishness of some investors.

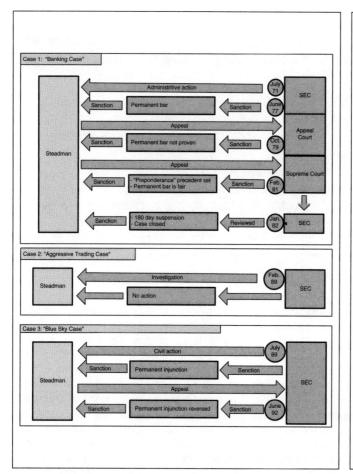

Fraud Facts

- Alleged Acts Date: 1965
- Enforcement Date: June 26, 1971
- Main Defendants **(hedge fund–related): Charles W. Steadman, Steadman Amerifund, N.V**, Steadman International Capital Corp.
- Most Serious Charge: Insufficient capital to meet potential liabilities
- Hedge Fund Role: Named defendant in one of the cases
- Damages $actual **($2005): $240,000 ($700,000)**; 1st case in 1988$, $694,020 **($1.2 million)**
- No. of Investors: 26,000
- Highest Court: Civil (U.S. Supreme Court on appeal)
- Most Severe Sentence: Barred from industry (reversed on appeal), suspension

Sanctions:

- Charles W. Steadman: Barred (reversed on appeal)
- Charles W. Steadman: 180-day suspension (waived after appeal)
- Charles W. Steadman: Other stipulations, adopted by defendant

Cases:

- *SEC v. Steadman (Investment Co. Act Rel. No. 9830, SEC Admin)*
- *Steadman v. SEC (77–2415, appeal, USCOA 5th Circuit)*
- *Steadman v. SEC (450 US 91, USSC)*
- *SEC v. Steadman (89cv02026, civil, USDC Dist. Columbia)*
- *SEC v. Steadman (91–5130, appeal, USCOA Dist. Columbia)* . . .

Precedents:

- Supreme Court decision defined the SEC's burden of proof in administrative law cases

This case involved a private civil suit filed against GPs after the hedge fund had "blown-up." Limited partners (LPs) charged General partners (GPs) and fund accountants with failure to notify of withdrawal of principal capital and investment in risky, unregulated securities. Key points:

- Private action by fund LPs after fund blow-up
- No enforcement action taken
- Alleged GPs knowingly withdrew personal capital prior to collapse, violating partnership agreement
- GPs invested in unregistered securities beyond agreed limits
- Allege fund's accountants negligent in not informing LPs of withdrawals
- On appeal, court upheld the right to sue the accountants, though the case was withdrawn with unknown results

Case Summary

Guarente-Harrington Associates, LP, a hedge fund founded in 1968, ended its life catastrophically three years later in October 1971. It had lost about 72 percent of the estimated $7 million that 35–40 limited partners had invested. However, unlike other blow-ups, some of the limited partners decided to pursue a private suit and—unique at the time—the main target of the suit for damages was Arthur Andersen, the fund's auditor. In doing so and in subsequent appeals, which included the Supreme Court, the case established a new precedent in defining the liability of accountants to parties other than direct clients that are affected by their decisions.

The key allegation of the plaintiff's case was that the general partners, Guarente and Harrington, had violated the terms of the partnership agreement in withdrawing $2 million of about $2.6 million of their initial capital from the fund without giving the limited partners proper prior notice or disclosure after the fact. Other allegations concerned valuations and portfolio allocation of restricted stock held in the fund's portfolio. The partnership agreement had stated the objective of "investing and trading in marketable securities and rights and options relating thereto." When the fund collapsed the investors found that much of the remaining assets were comprised of restricted stocks for which a marketable value was misleading.

Over the course of the proceedings, the case against Arthur Andersen was separated from that against Guarente and Harrington: the latter apparently having little prospect of obtaining results. Arthur Andersen's defense relied on the concept of "privity"—whether certain of the investors had a right to claim negligence and contract breach when it was the partnership as a whole that were counter-parties to the contract with Andersen. However, the earlier precedent, *Ultramares v. Touche*, had established that there was an "indeterminate class of persons . . . who might deal with the (debtor-promisee) in reliance on the audit." On appeal, the court held that "here, the services of the accountant were not extended to a faceless or unresolved class of persons, but rather to a known group possessed of vested rights, marked by a definable limit and made up of certain components" and also that "the duty of reasonable care in the performance of a contract is not always owed solely to the person with whom the contract is made . . . it may inure to the benefit of others" (as per *Rosenbaum v. Branster Realty*).

Having won the right to sue, the plaintiff investors were free to pursue the allegations that the general partners had built up a large position in restricted stock, contrary to the partnership agreement, and had also failed to notify the investors of the fact. Furthermore, plaintiffs maintained that when the general partners became aware that the fund was likely to fail, withdrew the bulk of their own money from the fund, contrary to the partnership agreement and here too, failed to provide notice of the fact to the investors as well as attempting to disguise the fact via accounting maneuvers. The investors maintained that Arthur Andersen as auditors should have known these things and should have incorporated them in their auditor's report for the year ending October 31, 1969.

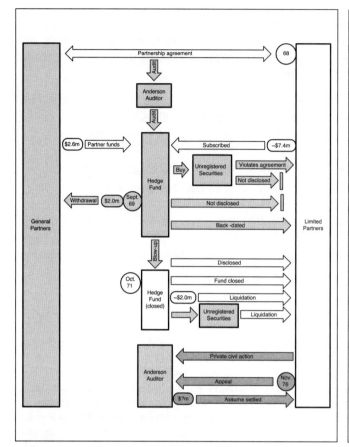

Fraud Facts

- Alleged Acts Date: 1969–1970
- Enforcement Date: Approximately 1972
- Main Defendants **(hedge fund–related): William E. Guarente, George F. Harrington,** Arthur Anderson & Co., **Guarente-Harrington**
- Most Serious Charge: Accountant's negligence
- Hedge Fund Role: General Partners defendants in private suit, later dropped
- Damages $actual ($2005): Not specified ($10 million fund lost 72 percent of value) ($10 million investment loss in $ '05)
- No. of Investors: 40
- Highest Court: Civil (Supreme Court appeal)
- Most Severe Sentence: None

Sanctions:

- William E. Guarente: No grounds for action
- George F. Harrington: No grounds for action
- Arthur Andersen & Co.: Ground for action, outcome unknown

Cases:

- *White v. Guarente* (43NY356)

Precedents:

- New ground in establishing the culpability of accountants of hedge funds to suit by investors

The defendants were limited partners in a hedge fund that held a minority position in a listed family-controlled company in which the defendants were also directors and substantial shareholders. The listed company was also charged with failure to disclose other material facts to shareholders. Key points:

- New York State attorney general investigation foreshadowed concerns, including new issues and analyst incentives, pursued by Eliot Spitzer 30 years later.
- Illustrates risks of price manipulation in closely held family companies with limited free float.
- While not a defendant, a hedge fund was directly implicated in a conflict of interest in the roles played by two of its limited partners and its own investment actions.
- With all of the investigation of this company, that of the SEC was both the most stringent but also the least well-founded.
- The basis for enforcement action to halt a share offering concerned lack of disclosure of discussions with a labor union.

Case Summary

Levitz is a well-known, family-managed furniture company that pioneered the discount warehouse–style store in the early 1960s. At that time, the company was busy raising capital by floating more shares, while also rearranging some of the family holdings in the company. Some of this rearranging was allegedly done via a hedge fund, Kaplan & Nathan & Co., through which two of the Levitz brothers, the chairman and president, were then partners, owned 125,000 Levitz shares.

Trouble started when *Barron's* published an article, "All in the Family—Some Business Dealings by Levitz Look a Bit Too Cozy." There was an appearance that the number of nonfloating shares tied up by the family as well as by hedge funds and other institutions, amounted to a corner in the stock. In early February, the SEC, the New York attorney general, and NYSE began an investigation into the volatile behavior of the stock. On February 22, 1972, the company announced a 3:1 stock split. On June 1, the SEC suspended trading in the stock, stating that the action was related to findings of its investigation. Levitz postponed the issue of new shares and stock-split. When the SEC did bring charges on June 3, these charges were connected with the company's allegedly not informing shareholders of a pending new agreement with the Teamsters Union.

On June 28, 1972, Levitz submitted a settlement proposal to the SEC, which the SEC accepted. It called for suspension of the registration of new shares and the publication of facts with Levitz conceding certain facts without admitting or denying any guilt. That agreement terminated the SEC case, but it did not terminate the separate investigation being carried out by New York State Attorney General Louis Lefkowitz, which went on for another seven months. By February 24, 1973, the state attorney general's office had completed a 495-page study of trading in Levitz stock based upon which it decided to charge certain unnamed "stock brokerage firms, security analysts, mutual funds and hedge funds and other institutional investors, with having engaged in securities dealings in Levitz stock that were contrary to the interests of the general public."

The latter charges focused on the alleged "rewarding" of analysts for favorable reports as well as engaging in "special favorable treatment" in the allocation of new shares. It does not appear that any parties were punished for this behavior but the report did influence the opinions of securities lawmakers and foreshadowed the IPO investigations by the then New York State Attorney General Eliot Spitzer some 30 years later.

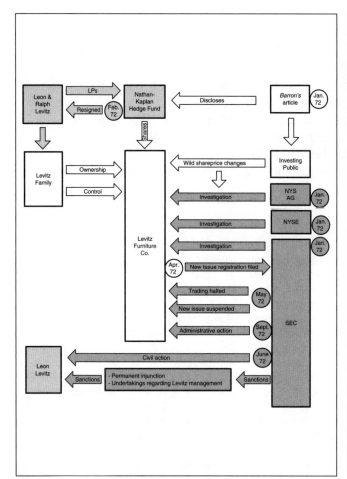

Fraud Facts

- Alleged Acts Date: April 1972
- Enforcement Date: May 1972
- Main Defendants **(hedge fund-related):** Levitz Furniture Corp., **Leon Levitz, Ralph Levitz, Kaplan-Nathan & Co.**
- Most Serious Charge: Failure to disclose material information
- Hedge Fund Role: Two defendants were LPs in a hedge fund that held a large block of shares in the defendant's family-controlled company
- Damages $actual ($2005): NA
- No. of Investors: Two hedge fund LPs, 2,130 equity shareholders
- Highest Court: Civil
- Most Severe Sentence: Permanent injunction, improved governance (i.e., resignation as president)

Sanctions:

- Levitz Furniture Corp.: Stipulations re: governance
- Levitz Furniture Corp.: Stop order against share offer
- Leon Levitz: Permanent injunction, resigned as president

Cases:

- *SEC v. Levitz Furniture Corp.* (72cv01099)
- *SEC Admin. Proceeding* (3–3739)

The hedge fund manager collaborated with a broker-dealer to manipulate the "hot issues" market by disguising short sales. Key points:

- An SEC and NASD case
- Part of SEC's efforts to control abuses of new secondary "hot issues"
- First known "hot issues" case involving a hedge fund
- Complex subterfuge to disguise nature and identity of short selling
- Goal to depress new issue prices via manipulative practices
- Broker and hedge fund in close collaboration
- Both broker and hedge fund principals had prior violations of a similar nature

Case Summary

Awareness of "hot" new issues emerged from about 1946, and, from around 1959, the first "hot issues market" (1959–1962), there have been increasing efforts by the SEC and NASD to rein in its distortive price effects through regulation and enforcement. Despite these initiatives, a second hot issues market developed during the period 1967–1971. Following that episode, the SEC pursued a number of enforcement actions against violators. In one such case (A.P. Montgomery & Co.: Securities Exchange Act Release No. 10636, 3 SEC Docket 540) on January 30, 1974, administrative proceedings were instituted against 27 entities for violations of antifraud, antimanipulative, short sale, margin and record-keeping regulations.

Seventeen of those charged by the SEC submitted "Offers of Settlement," which were accepted by the Commission. Proceedings against a further seven were discontinued and one other was dismissed. The two remaining respondents were Joseph Buongiorno, a broker, and JAB Securities, his brokerage company. Like Montgomery and the others, Buongiorno and JAB had been active in hot issues for some time. They employed a strategy of shorting the secondary issuer's equity after indicating interest in purchasing the same amount of the new issue, resulting in lowering the new issue price, enabling the short position to be closed out at a profit.

Prior to the 1974 proceedings NASD had inspected JAB's books around December 1971 and found short-selling and covering violations in relation to new issues and issued a warning to Buongiorno, who gave assurances that the violations would not occur in the future. (Buongiorno and JAB's predecessor had also been suspended for violations in January 1965.) However, within a month or two of proffering these assurances Buongiorno was in discussion with

Vincent Naddeo, a longtime friend and former broker about another scheme to manipulate new issues.

Naddeo himself had a record of past violations. Having established V. F. Naddeo & Co. a registered broker-dealer in 1960, the company was put into receivership by the SEC in 1970 for record-keeping and net-capital violations. (SEC v. V. F. Naddeo, 70cv613, USDC SDNY). At the time of his meetings with Buongiorno in early 1972, Naddeo was in charge of trading for another broker-dealer called Dixon Dolce & Co., though he had already set up a hedge fund, V.F.N. Associates, for the purpose of pursuing a new issue arbitrage strategy along similar lines to Buorngiorno and JAB Securities.

With Buongiorno's help and guidance Naddeo/VFN was able to register his intention to purchase a specified amount of a new issue with several brokers involved in the issue's distribution, a process known as getting "circled." With these future shares reserved, Naddeo proceeded, via Dixon, Dolce, to short the shares of the issuer in such a manner as to cause those shares to decline in value just before the issue price was fixed.

To obtain better results, the shares were often shorted on the downtick, or no tick, rather than after an uptick. The short sales were made to JAB, Buongiorno's company. JAB purchased them as a principal then sold long through one of the distributing brokers. Over the course of a few months, Naddeo and Buorgiorno had implemented this strategy in at least five new issues.

Buongiorno and Naddeo were both caught in the SEC's monitoring operations and they and their companies were the subject of administrative proceedings. JAB Securities had its registration revoked and Buongiorno was barred from the industry. Naddeo consented to a settlement and was sanctioned.

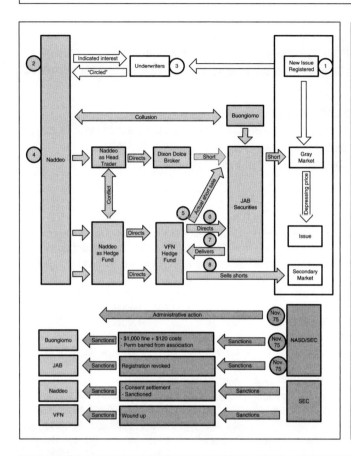

Fraud Facts

- Alleged Acts Date: January 1, 1972
- Enforcement Date: January 30, 1974
- Main Defendants (**hedge fund–related**): Buongiorno, **Naddeo**, JAB Securities (**VFN Associates**)
- Most Serious Charge: Market manipulation
- Hedge Fund Role: Party to manipulation of new "hot" issues
- Damages $actual ($2005): Not known
- No. of Investors: NA
- Highest Court: Administrative
- Most Severe Sentence: Registration revoked, $1,000 fine, industry bar

Sanctions:

- Joseph Buongiorno: Industry bar
- Vincent Naddeo: Consent agreement, sanctioned
- JAB Securities: Expelled from NASD, registration revoked
- VFN Associates: Firm wound up

Cases:

- *SEC v. Buongiorno* (3 SEC Docket 540, administrative)

Four hedge funds were subject of a class action prosecution for allegedly colluding with the author of a popular financial column to short stocks prior to publication of negative articles. An appeal court found that the prosecution was "malicious" and not warranted. Key points:

- Private civil case, later class action
- First case of alleged collusion between journalist and short sellers/hedge funds
- First case of "malicious prosecution" with verdict against plaintiffs
- Class action denied by court due to not meeting required criteria

Case Summary

The Nemeroff case was foreshadowed by a 1975 suit in which Dow Jones & Co. and Alan Abelson, a *Barron's* columnist sued *BusinessWeek* magazine and its publisher McGraw-Hill for an article that quoted an investor claiming to have profited from a "golden news leak," from Abelson's column before it was published. That suit was settled in June 1976 including a printed retraction from *BusinessWeek*.

Within one year *Barron's*, Dow Jones, and Alan Abelson were again on the receiving end of allegations of leaking information, this time to a group of hedge funds and short sellers who were allegedly shorting stocks that Abelson made negative comments on in his articles.

A shareholder of one of these subject companies and his lawyers sought to create a class action to pursue charges of conspiracy to manipulate the share price of Technicare Corp. Four hedge funds and their principals were named as defendants along with Dow Jones, its editor, and Alan Abelson, a columnist for *Barron's*.

A private civil suit was filed on March 25, 1977 (77cv1472, SDNY). The plaintiff of the suit was Robert Nemeroff, a dentist and shareholder of Technicare. On January 6, 1978, an amended complaint was filed that excluded Lawrence Bleiberg, Boxwood Associates, Marc Howard, and Marc Howard Associates, eliminating two of the four hedge funds and their principals. In the amended suit, the hedge funds were alleged to have solicited the media entities to publish negative reports.

The district court decided that the suit did not meet the criteria for a class action. It also found that the case was based on "unsupported gossip and inadmissible hearsay" and that the real objective was "the public airing of damaging allegations against the publishers . . . that constituted bad faith . . . (by parties) that should have known better[.]" The court ruled that the plaintiffs should pay $50,000 costs to the defendants. The case went to appeal, but the appeal was denied.

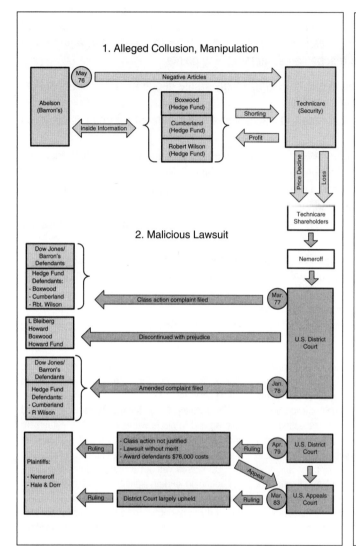

1. Alleged Collusion, Manipulation

2. Malicious Lawsuit

Fraud Facts

- Alleged Acts Date: May 3, 1976
- Enforcement Date: March 25, 1977
- Main Defendants **(hedge fund-related):** Alan Abelson, Meyer Berman, **Lawrence** and Robert **Bleiberg**, Dow Jones & Co., **Boxwood Associates, Cumberland Associates, Marc Howard Associates**
- Most Serious Charge: Collusion, conspiracy to manipulate share prices (dismissed)/Malicious lawsuit (upheld)
- Hedge Fund Role: Named defendants, coconspirators
- Damages $actual **($2005):** $76,000 legal costs (against plaintiffs) **($245,000)**
- No. of Investors: NA
- Highest Court: Civil, class action and appellate
- Most Severe Sentence: Plaintiff was assessed $76,000 to cover defendant's costs

Sanctions:

- Plaintiff: Nemeroff: $76,000 Defendant's costs

Cases:

- *Nemeroff v. Abelson* (77cv01472, civil, S. Dist. N.Y.)
- *Nemeroff v. Abelson* (appeal 82–7488, No. 559. 2C.)

Precedents:

- Imposition of counsel's fee upon plaintiff

The SEC charged a hedge fund and its manager with manipulative practices designed to create artificially high prices in listed securities in order to sell them at a profit. The SEC and the defendants reached an agreement. Key points:

- Marc Howard had been one of the most high-profile hedge fund managers of his time
- Howard Associates had reportedly achieved a 1,250 percent return in its six years of life
- Both Marc Howard and "Associates" had been named defendants in a "malicious class-action lawsuit" the previous year (see Case 9, Nemeroff)
- Both entities were also reportedly the subject of NYSE and SEC investigations at the time of the earlier abortive case
- SEC charged that Howard benefited by creating the appearance of actively traded stocks
- It does not seem that the SEC sought any monetary sanctions in the case
- Sanctions included an unusual requirement to observe a minimum holding period before selling shares.

Case Summary

On August 10, 1978, the SEC filed charges against Marc Howard and Marc Howard Associates for stock price manipulation. This case likely arose as a result of investigations the SEC and NYSE carried out in relation to the earlier Nemeroff class action suit. That action had included Marc Howard and Howard Associates as named defendants, though that case was ultimately judged to have no merit. The Nemeroff case documents refer to concurrent investigations of the same or related events by the NYSE and the SEC, though neither had taken any action at that time.

Up to the time of the Nemeroff case, Howard Associates, which was founded in 1969, was considered to be one of the most successful hedge funds, with eight-year performance of 1,250 percent (according to a report in the *Washington Post*) and Howard was included in a *Time* magazine feature story on "The New Rich."

In its complaint the SEC charged the fund with "creating actual and apparent active trading in . . . securities, and raising the prices of such securities for the purpose of inducing the purchase of such securities by others." Among the securities named as subjects of Howard's manipulations were Columbia Pictures, De Soto, and Pan American World Airways.

By January 10 of the following year, Howard had agreed to settle with the SEC. The settlement included a permanent injunction and a stipulation that required Howard not to sell blocks of more than 25,000 shares without waiting at least four days, excepting in certain specified circumstances. By the terms of his offer of agreement with the SEC, Howard was permitted to neither admit nor deny his guilt. Tellingly, Howard was also not ordered to make any restitution, which implied that there was not a clear case for imputing damages to any parties. Less than seven months later, Howard Associates announced that it had "a terrible year" and was winding down its business. Howard claimed that his "short positions went up . . . and long positions went down with a great degree of regularity . . . so I decided to close before we lost any more money." Any linkage that may have existed between the SEC action and the subsequent closure is a matter of conjecture.

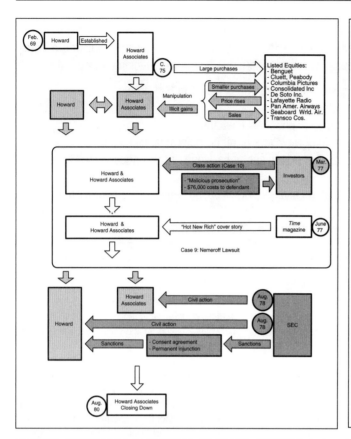

Fraud Facts

- Alleged Acts Date: 1975
- Enforcement Date: August 11, 1978
- Main Defendants **(hedge fund–related): Marc Howard, Howard Associates**
- Most Serious Charge: Market manipulation
- Hedge Fund Role: Defendant
- Damages $actual **($2005)**: (not specified)
- No. of Investors: 50
- Highest Court: Civil
- Most Severe Sentence: Permanent injunction

Sanctions:

- Marc Howard: Permanent injunction
- Howard Associates: Stipulations regarding future minimum holding period of shares

Cases:

- *SEC v. Howard* (78cv03865 civil, S. Dist. N.Y.)

The defendant, a CFTC-registered commodity trading adviser (CTA), created and raised money for an unregistered commodity pool, which after some time became a Ponzi scheme, that later collapsed when sufficient new funds were lacking. Key points:

- One of the largest cases handled by the CFTC up to that time
- Unregistered commodity pool
- First hedge fund/commodity pool Ponzi scheme
- First case based outside of New York or other major financial center
- Chilcott received a 12-year prison sentence—one of the longest ever meted out in a hedge fund case
- Chilcott was a recidivist, receiving another prison sentence for another fraud a decade later
- The main restitution came from Chilcott's broker, Shearson Lehman

Case Summary

Around 1977 Thomas Chilcott, then about 28-years old and a resident of Fort Collins, Colorado, formed a commodity pool (Chilcott Commodity Fund) and two commodity pool operators (Chilcott Commodity Corporation, Chilcott Portfolio Management, Inc.) and began soliciting for investors. From later accounts, it appears that he was very successful and had gathered some $30 to $40 million or more from investors numbering in the hundreds.

While Chilcott maintained client trading accounts with brokers Shearson Lehman and Boettcher & Co., and may have done some trading on their behalf as stated in his solicitations, most, if not all of the money was invested in unrelated ventures clearly outside the scope of his representations to the investors, and the majority of this money was lost. In reality, Chilcott was simply recycling money from new clients to old, in a Ponzi scheme. When the number of new investors did not keep up, the scheme began to falter and later became the subject of an FBI investigation of a Florida options scam involving a Chilcott investor. On June 17, 1981, Chilcott's offices were raided by its agents.

The CFTC filed a civil complaint, got some temporary injunctions shutting down or freezing Chilcott's operations, and had the court appoint a receiver, who sought to recover assets via a bankruptcy action. In the meantime, Chilcott was indicted by a grand jury and later sentenced to 12 years in prison in the resulting criminal action. He was released on parole early in 1987, but was soon back in jail for three years for another scam and was arrested again in 2005 while a fugitive in Mexico for another fraud scheme he masterminded with his wife in Fort Myers, Florida.

In the earlier 1981 case, the receiver took the action of suing Chilcott's broker, Shearson Lehman, on behalf of the Chilcott Commodity Fund (and its investors). Although Chilcott was not an employee of Shearson's, the court held that Shearson had violated its fiduciary and supervisory responsibilities in looking after the Chilcott investor money in the broker accounts. In January 1988, a jury awarded Chilcott Futures Fund $31.6 million plus $7.8 million in punitive damages. This amount was reduced to $33 million in a 1991 settlement after appeal, equivalent to 98.5 percent of investor losses and 93 percent of creditor losses.

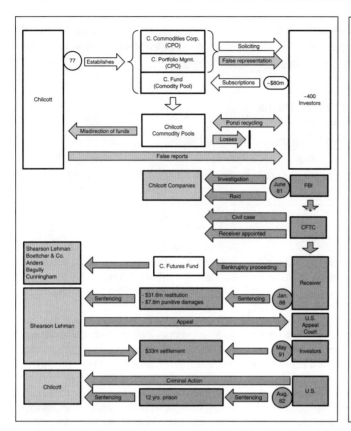

Fraud Facts

- Alleged Acts Date:
  1977–1981
- Enforcement Date:
  June 17, 1981
- Main Defendants
  (hedge fund–related):
  Thomas Chilcott,
  Chilcott Futures Fund,
  Chilcott Commodities
  Corp., Chilcott Portfolio
  Mgmt.
- Most Serious
  Charge(s): Wire fraud,
  misappropriation
- Hedge Fund Role:
  Defendant
- Damages $actual
  ($2005): $31.6 million
  ($75 million)
- No. of Investors:
  Approximately 400
- Highest Court: Criminal
- Most Severe Sentence:
  12 years' imprisonment,
  $33 million restitution

Sanctions:

- Thomas Chilcott: 12 years' prison
- Shearson Lehman: $33 million restitution

Cases:

- *CFTC v. Chilcott* (81cv999, civil, Dist. Colo.)
- *Johnson v. Chilcott* (82cv00889, civil, Dist. Colo.)
- *U.S. v. Chilcott* (81cr228, criminal, Dist. Colo.)

The defendant in this case failed to disclose prior sanctions and violated conditions on use of client funds and registration. When substantial losses appeared at an early stage, false reports were given to investors. Key points:

- SEC case
- CBOE broker-dealer and options trader
- Fraudulent use of client money
- False representation to investors and to regulators
- Lost all money in risky trading
- Appeal set a legal precedent arguing "constructive amendment" of the indictment

Case Summary

In July 1979, Steven Kuna and his associate, John DeLeeuw, began soliciting residents in Michigan to invest in a prospective "conservatively" managed hedge fund, Steven A. Kuna Associates, and raised some $1.3 million from around 30 investors. This money was placed in an escrow account that was barred from withdrawal until several conditions listed in the offering memorandum were met, including a minimum balance of $600,000, the securing of a broker-dealer registration with the SEC and the Michigan Securities Bureau, and approval granted for membership by the Chicago Board Options Exchange (CBOE).

In December 1979, the escrow account proceeds were transferred to another bank along with a letter from the original bank giving permission to release funds despite the fact that several of the conditions for release had not yet been met, including SEC registration and CBOE membership. On December 19, Kuna applied for CBOE membership but as a sole trader, trading his own money. Kuna commenced trading on January 30, in his own name but using his investor's funds. Kuna applied for SEC registration on February 19, again as a sole trader using his own funds.

The CBOE became aware of Kuna's trading of Kuna Associates funds in July 1980 as well as his failing to disclose that he had been previously sanctioned by the NASD. Kuna was told to inform his investors of these facts, which he did and reapplied for membership in the name of Kuna Associates. Kuna was then allowed to resume trading in October 1980. However, in the intervening months, the "liquidating balance" reported by Kuna's clearing broker, which showed a high of $2.16 million at end of June (implying a six-month gain of 66 percent), was almost $1 million less by the end of July ($1.21 million) and about $1 million by end of September. Within a month of allegedly resuming trading in the name of Kuna

Associates, this balance was stated as just $134,794, indicating a near complete wipeout in one or two months. These extreme changes in net asset value (NAV) were suggestive of highly risky trading, not the conservatism espoused in the solicitation.

During the period of sharply declining balances, Kuna's investors were receiving monthly reports from the firm's accountants that showed a slow but steady growth from $1.72 million in June to $1.90 million for October. However, at that point Kuna's options broker was impelled to freeze and then liquidate the account, thereby forcing Kuna to inform his investors, attorney, accountant, and partner of the then stark position of the fund, as well as the falsification of monthly reports. A grand jury indicted Kuna on 15 counts and he was ultimately found guilty on six of these counts. He was sentenced to two years' imprisonment on five of the charges and given a suspended sentence with five years' probation on one charge, conditional on his paying $1.2 million of restitution. He was also barred from practice as a broker-dealer.

As a footnote, an appeal to the case set a precedent that has been cited in other cases. In the appeal, Kuna charged that in the trial he was made a victim of a "constructively amended indictment" by the district court. This argued that while the indictment charged Kuna with a scheme to obtain money by false pretenses, the government had instead proven a case to prevent discovery of the false pretenses. The appeal court found that the defendant's conviction was correct (it was a "variation" rather than an "amendment" of the scheme charged), though it dropped the condition of restitution, requiring resentencing by the district court. The lower court re-sentenced Kuna to two years' imprisonment, with the probation starting concurrently with the prison term and it also reimposed the conditional restitution, albeit attached it to a different charge.

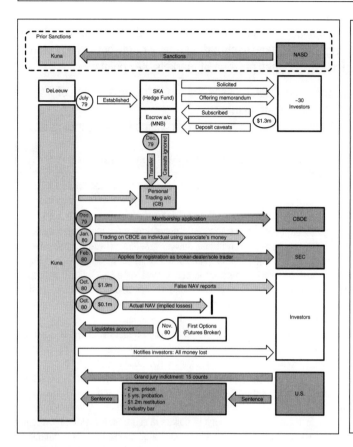

Fraud Facts

- Alleged Acts Date: 1979
- Enforcement Date: August 2, 1982
- Main Defendants **(hedge fund–related): Steven A. Kuna, Steven A. Kuna Associates**
- Most Serious Charge: Mail fraud
- Hedge Fund Role: Defendant
- Damages $actual **($2005): $1.2 million ($3.2 million)**
- No. of Investors: 30
- Highest Court: Criminal
- Most Severe Sentence: 2 years' imprisonment, $1.2 million restitution

Sanctions:

- Steven Kuna: 2 years' imprisonment
- Steven Kuna: 5 years' probation
- Steven Kuna: $1.2 million restitution
- Steven Kuna: Industry bar

Cases:

- *U.S. v. Kuna* (83cr921, criminal, N. Dist. Ill.)
- *U.S. v. Kuna* (84–2328, appeal, 7C)

Precedents:

- Constructively amended indictment

The defendant hedge fund manager ("risk arbitrageur") was at the center of a large and complex insider trading ring that was itself part of a larger network of high profile entities that engaged in widespread manipulation of markets. Key points:

- Part of an enormous network of related cases leading to the prosecution of Michael Milken and Drexel Burnham Lambert
- A large systematic exploitation of inside information on company takeover targets
- Record money penalties levied
- First hedge fund case to cite violations of SEA34 Sect. 14(e) Proxies

Case Summary

An anonymous letter received from a Merrill Lynch office in Caracas on May 25, 1985, sparked a complex set of insider trading prosecutions that would dominate headlines for the next six years, including scores of separate cases and more than a dozen indictments. The two main players in this now famous set of cases were Ivan Boesky and Michael Milken. Boesky, then labeled as an "arbitrageur," was, by present definitions, a hedge fund adviser. (Princeton-Newport, which described itself as a hedge fund, was another branch of this case, but has been treated here as a separate hedge fund fraud case, which is discussed in Case 14.)

In an eerie rehearsal of events to come, Ivan Boesky had been invited to speak at an SEC public hearing on market rumors and manipulation on February 19, 1986. Boesky's real troubles started on June 2 when Dennis Levine, a Drexel Burnham salesman, gave his name to government prosecutors in exchange for leniency in his own insider trading prosecution. Boesky completed a deal for himself on November 14, pleading guilty to one count of fraud, and consenting to $100 million in restitution and fines, the largest penalty levied by the SEC to that time, a three-year prison sentence, a permanent bar from the financial industry and his further active cooperation in the ongoing investigations.

The core charges against Boesky in the SEC case (*SEC v. Boesky*, 86cv8767) dated back as early as 1982 and related to his use of inside information in "arbitrage" trading of tender offers obtained from Levine and a network of other investment banker/corporate lawyer tipsters. These tipsters were either paid commissions for their information (e.g., Boesky agreed to pay Levine $2.4 million) or simply exchanged one tip for another. In some of the cases, the illegal trades were unknowingly copied by others in the order chain.

Unlike other inside traders who worked quietly in the shadows and took small positions in large companies, or large positions in tiny companies, Boesky operated openly as a risk arbitrageur and managed several companies and at least one large fund to carry out his strategies. With hundreds of millions of dollars raised from investors, he was in a position to take large stakes in large companies, the kind of companies that were the clients of top line investment banks. Boesky's trades and financial prominence put him in regular contact with credible, knowledgeable, and well-placed investment bankers that had access to the best information.

These ingredients built a large and effective, yet informal insider trading network that was able to manipulate dozens of large M&A deals over a number of years, but its success and informality also led to its uncontrolled overexpansion and eventual discovery. In all, the Boesky-related cases involved some 22 defendants and included at least six prison sentences amounting to an aggregate of more than 20 years together with fines and other payments of around $400 million.

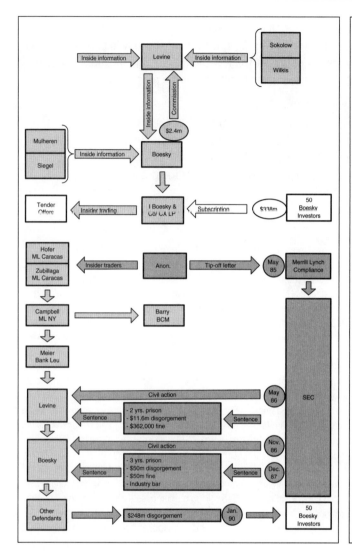

Fraud Facts

- Alleged Acts Date: 1985
- Enforcement Date: November 14, 1986
- Main Defendants **(hedge fund–related): Ivan Boesky (Ivan F. Boesky Corp.), CX Partners LP, Cambrian and General Secs. plc**
- Most Serious Charge: Insider trading
- Hedge Fund Role: Defendant
- Damages $actual **($2005): $50 million ($94 million)**
- No. of Investors: >50
- Highest Court: Criminal
- Most Severe Sentence: 3 years' imprisonment, $50 million restitution, $50 million fine, barred for life

Sanctions:

- Ivan Boesky: 3 years' imprisonment
- Ivan Boesky: $50 million disgorgement
- Ivan Boesky: $50 million civil penalty
- Ivan Boesky: Permanent bar

Cases:

- *SEC v. Boesky* (87cv0963, civil, S. Dist. N.Y.)
- *SEC v. Boesky* (87cr378, criminal, S. Dist. N.Y.)

The case, in which the hedge fund defendants were charged under the infamous RICO racketeering statute, was part of a high-profile government strategy to bring down what it perceived as a major network of insider traders and market manipulators. Ultimately, the case was dismissed with a good deal of criticism of the prosecution. Key points:

- Key part of the Boesky-Milken nexus
- A criminal prosecution led by then U.S. Attorney Rudi Giuliani
- First and last application of RICO statute against a hedge fund
- First hedge fund case focusing on the issue of "stock parking"
- Defendants acquitted on appeal, a major defeat for the prosecution

Case Summary

Princeton/Newport marked an historic low in the prosecution of hedge fund cases. Although an integral part of the greater government case against Michael Milken, the Princeton/Newport aspect was pursued separately and by the extreme means of the RICO, antiracketeering statute. The prosecutorial effort was led by then U.S. Attorney Rudolph (Rudi) Giuliani.

Princeton/Newport was probably one of the earliest hedge funds to employ a statistical arbitrage strategy and had a no less remarkable beginning. It had been founded in 1969 by James Sutton Regan and Edward Thorp, the latter, a gifted mathematician, who was once a junior associate of Bell Labs' Claude Shannon, the creator of communications (information) theory. Thorp had authored an insightful book on blackjack theory, *Beat the Dealer*, and later extended these insights to the stock market in *Beat the Market*. His work was read and admired by Fisher Black, of the eponymous Black-Sholes theory.

Princeton/Newport's thriving business came to a shuddering halt on December 17, 1987, when 50 armed federal marshals wearing bulletproof vests entered the hedge fund's New Jersey office and removed around 300 boxes of papers. The search warrants stated that the agents were looking for evidence of "parking" of securities and a "scheme to generate false and inflated federal income tax deductions."

The government held that the "parking" trades were sham trades to evade tax and, in consequence, were a form of racketeering, defrauding the U.S. government. Once a pretrial hearing concurred that the trades were tax frauds, the prosecution rolled out its big gun, the RICO statute. This would permit pretrial seizures and forfeiture of alleged ill-gotten gains,

designed to cripple a criminal enterprise and prevent criminal monies from disappearing well before a verdict. The problem with the application of RICO here was the implication of crippling and likely destroying a going concern before it had been found guilty.

The five senior partners/executives (excluding Thorp) were indicted by a Grand Jury along with one employee of Drexel Burnham Lambert (DBL) on August 4, 1988, and charged with 64 counts of conspiracy, racketeering, tax fraud, wire fraud, and mail fraud. At the time of the government raid, Princeton/Newport the collective entity had some 80 employees and was managing around $1 billion, of which $300 million were net partnership assets. The government was seeking to seize partnership holdings amounting to about 20 percent of the fund's assets. (The GPs had reportedly withdrawn $15 million of their assets after the search and then redeposited them under their wives' names).

In 1991, an appeal court found that the RICO statute was inappropriate for tax violations. In July of that same year, a federal judge dismissed the RICO convictions against all six defendants. In January 1992, the federal prosecutors decided not to retry the case, effectively dropping all charges. Later that year the same judge dropped the remaining three non-RICO charges that still applied to Newberg and Zarzecki. After the heavy cannon fire had stopped and virtually all of the enforcement actions had been reversed or dropped, a final, small caliber rifle shot was fired by the SEC that barred DBL's Newberg from the industry. That was all that remained of the entire enforcement effort. Princeton/Newport was, by then, long gone as a business, RICO was never used again in a securities case, and Rudi Giuliani was elected mayor of New York.

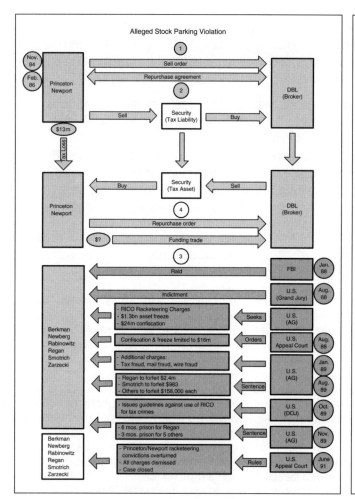

Fraud Facts

- Alleged Acts Date: 1984
- Enforcement Date: December 17, 1987
- Main Defendants **(hedge fund–related): James Regan, Jack Rabinowitz, Charles Zarzecki, Paul Berkman, Steven Smotrich, Princeton Newport, Oakley Sutton**
- Most Serious Charge: Racketeering
- Hedge Fund Role: Defendant
- Damages $actual ($2005): $13 million **($23 million)**
- No. of Investors: >10
- Highest Court: Criminal
- Most Severe Sentence: 6 months' prison, $1.6 million forfeiture

Sanctions:

- James Regan: 6 months' prison, plus $3.325 million penalties (reversed on appeal)
- Jack Rabinowitz: 3 months' prison plus $200,000 penalties (reversed on appeal)
- Steven Smotrich: 3 months' prison plus $1.246 million penalties (reversed on appeal)
- Charles Zarzeki: 3 months' prison plus $200,000 penalties (reversed on appeal)
- Paul Berkman: 3 months' prison plus $200,000 penalties (reversed on appeal)
- Bruce Newberg: 3 months' prison plus $200,000 penalties (reversed on appeal)

Cases:

- *USA v. Regan, et al.* (88cr00517, criminal, S. Dist. N.Y.)
- *USA v. Regan, et al.* appeal (89–1591, 2nd Cir.)

Precedents:

- RICO statute never to be applied again in a tax case

The defendant was a lawyer who created two unregistered hedge funds, raised money, and, when the funds started losing money, continued to misrepresent the fund's assets and performance. He also misappropriated escrow funds of his law clients in order to redeem fund investors. Key points:

- Like the Steadman case (Case 4), hedge fund manager principal was an attorney
- Unusually (and unlike Steadman), Pavarini's law clients were injured parties whose escrow funds were used to redeem investors
- The hedge funds were substantially wiped out in the market crash of October 1987
- Uniquely, the law clients sought preemptive rights of reimbursement based on there being a "constructive trust." Their case was decided against them
- All injured parties received 11 percent of their lost assets from a fund of $412,000

Case Summary

George Pavarini, a lawyer and real estate specialist living in Scarsdale, New York, established two unregistered hedge funds in 1981—Pavtec and Pavtec II. By 1982, the funds were losing money. However, instead of reporting this to investors, Mr. Pavarini resorted to the use of deceptive newsletters, statements, and tax forms. A February 1988 newsletter claimed that 1987 had been the "best year ever" and that the fund had gained 40 percent.

The SEC began investigating after receiving Pavtec newsletters and on July 14, 1988, it filed a complaint against Pavarini and his two hedge funds. An agreement was reached with the SEC in which Pavarini was permitted to neither accept nor deny the allegations but would accept a permanent injunction and monetary judgment against him. At the time the two hedge funds were wound up, there were some 290 investors who had lost around $3.3 million. Pavarini had also lost $455,957 of money that he had in trust for 12 of his law clients. The court documents claim that there was some commingling of investment and law client funds as well as indiscriminant personal use of both monies by Pavarini.

The liquidation assets of the two funds amounted to $420,000, comprised of $240,000 of liquidated personal and real property and around $172,000 of funds held by brokers used by the funds. The law client accounts held no money.

One aspect of the case sought to determine whether or to what extent law clients could be compensated by liquidation funds. The Clients' Security Fund of the State of New York had reimbursed the law clients and sought to partly offset this sum by claiming Pavarini's remaining assets. The Court decided that the law clients did not have a superior claim over the investors (nor vice versa) and that both sets of claimants would be compensated on a pro rata basis ($420,000/302 = $1,391 per claimant).

The result was that the 290 investor claimants, who lost $11,379 on average, got back around 12 percent of their losses, while the New York State Fund for the law clients, who lost approximately $37,996 on average, received less than 4 percent of the loss they reimbursed. However, the law clients were eventually made whole by New York State funds available for this purpose. In total, 15 awards were made to the Pavarini law clients, amounting to $543,165—a number of clients and sum of money suggesting 100 percent compensation. Pavarini was disbarred as a lawyer the following year after submitting his resignation to the Supreme Court.

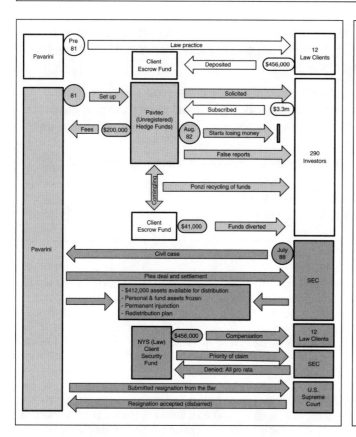

Fraud Facts

- Alleged Acts Date: 1982
- Enforcement Date: July 14, 1988
- Main Defendants **(hedge fund–related): George Pavarini, Pavtec Hedge Fund, Pavtec Hedge Fund II**
- Most Serious Charge: Mail fraud
- Hedge Fund Role: Defendant
- Damages $actual **($2005): $3.1 million ($6.3 million)**
- No. of Investors: 290
- Highest Court: Civil
- Most Severe Sentence: Disbarment

Sanctions:

- George Pavarini: Disbarment from the legal profession
- George Pavarini: Permanent Injunction
- George Pavarini: Disgorgement of $412,000

Cases:

- *SEC v. Pavarini* (88cv4897, civil, S. Dist. N.Y.)
- *In the matter of George F. Pavarini* (N.Y. Supreme Court Appellate Div. 2nd Dept., May 8, 1989)

The defendant was a mergers and acquisitions (M&A) attorney who passed or sold takeover information to a relative and a friend. The latter then resold the information to a hedge fund and to others. Key points:

- An insider trading case, with an M&A attorney as the main source of tips
- Information was traded within a network of family and friends, including brokers
- Jeffer Management Corporation, a hedge fund, received inside information from a broker
- Attorney received probationary prison sentence, monetary penalties, and disbarment
- Hedge fund principal faced criminal prosecution
- Most ill-gotten gains were recovered

Case Summary

The first case of the 1990s, Jeffer/Glauberman was an insider trading case. Steven Glauberman was a mergers and acquisitions specialist with prominent New York law firm Skadden, Arps, Slate, Meagher & Flom. He was charged with having sold inside information on 29 M&A deals involving companies that were clients of his firm, to a Smith Barney broker, Eban Smith, for $50,000. Some of the deals Glauberman tipped to Smith included: Bristol Myers' 1985 bid for Genetic Systems, the LBO of National Gypsum in 1985, Black and Decker's unsolicited bid for American Standard in 1988, Walt Disney's offer for Gibson Greetings, and Kmart's bid for Payless Drugstore Stores Northwest Inc.

Smith used this information for his own trading as well as passing it on to clients and/or prospective clients of his firm, including the firm of Jeffer Management Corporation (JMC), its principal, Peter Jeffer, and its trader, Stanley Patrick. JMC was an investment firm and likely a de facto hedge fund. Peter Jeffer is described as an "independent arbitrager," PMC traded, to some extent, on behalf of clients and Stanley Patrick, co-defendant and one-time employee of PMC is described as a former hedge fund trader.

Civil and criminal cases were files against Glauberman in New York District Court on August 9, 1990 (90cv05205, 90cr00517). On September 12, Glauberman changed his plea from not guilty to guilty, signaling that he had reached a deal with the prosecution and would, from that point, cooperate with the government against the other defendants. On June 1, Glauberman was sentenced to five years' probation on three counts and six months to be served in a halfway house, plus 200 hours community service for five years. He also had to pay $259,000 disgorgement to settle his civil SEC suit. Glauberman submitted a request to the court to resign from the bar, which was granted, an act that may have been a concession, rather than being disbarred.

Glauberman's cooperation contributed to the prosecution of his sister Lori, a broker at Bear Stearns, Eban Smith, a good friend, and Smith's wife and three children, for whom Glauberman was godfather. Lori Glauberman settled with the SEC and agreed to disgorge $38,271.84 and to be barred from the securities industry. Her illegal profits were deemed to be $19,135.92.

Smith was alleged to have made about $1.1 million from his illegal trades, from which he paid Glauberman $50,000. Smith also received $150,000 from the other codefendants, primarily the hedge fund defendants Jeffer and Patrick. Smith channeled his ill-gotten gains through accounts in the names of his three children (the godchildren of Glauberman). Smith's wife was also a trustee of the children's accounts. Smith's disgorgement demand in relation to these three accounts totaled $491,000.

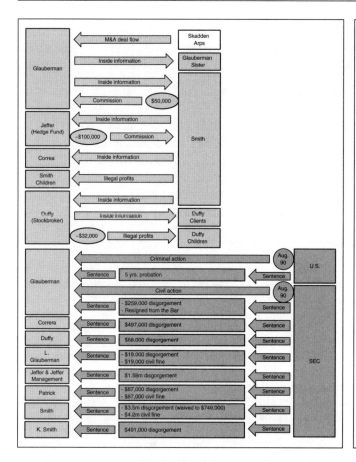

Fraud Facts

- Alleged Acts Date: 1985
- Enforcement Date: August 9, 1990
- Main Defendants **(hedge fund–related)**: Steven Glauberman, Eben Smith, **Peter Jeffer, Stanley Patrick, Jeffer Mgmt. Corp.**
- Most Serious Charge: Insider trading
- Hedge Fund Role: Defendant, tippee
- Damages $actual **($2005)**: $3.75 million **($5.6 million)**
- No. of Investors: NA
- Highest Court: Criminal
- Most Severe Sentence: 5 years' probation

Sanctions:

- Steven Glauberman: 5 years' probation, $258,778 disgorgement, resigned from bar
- Lori Glauberman: $38,271 disgorgement, barred from securities industry
- Eben Smith: $3.45 million disgorgement (all but $747,925 waived)
- Kathleen Smith: $491,227 disgorgement
- Stanley Patrick: 3 years' probation, $87,298 disgorgement, $87,298 penalty, barred from industry
- Anthony Correra: $496,842 disgorgement
- Peter Jeffer: $1.773 million disgorgement (doubtful)
- Jeffer Mgmt. Co.: $1.58 million disgorgement (joint and several with Jeffer)
- Thomas Duffy: $68,190 disgorgement

Cases:

- *SEC v. Glauberman* (90cv05205, civil, S. Dist. N.Y.)
- *USA v. Glauberman* (90cr00517, criminal, S. Dist. N.Y.)
- *In the matter of Glauberman* (181 A.D.2d207)
- *SEC v. Duffy* (92cv07492, civil, S. Dist. N.Y.)

The main defendant, a bulge-bracket investment bank, and three lesser defendant hedge funds faced prosecution for their part in masterminding the cornering of a U.S. Treasury market. Key points:

- Case concerned several instances of successful cornering of the U.S. Treasury market
- Salomon Bros. and the Steinhardt, Caxton and Soros hedge funds were named in some 50 lawsuits, including criminal prosecutions and a class action suit
- One suit was a successful U.S. prosecution under the Sherman Act antitrust law
- Hedge fund violations involved a cornering of the Treasury "repo" market
- Heavy fines were paid by Salomon and the two hedge funds
- Case became a Harvard Business School Case Study

Case Summary

This was a high-profile case centered on Salomon Brothers' role in perpetrating several short-squeezes or "corners" in U.S. Treasury auctions. Three prominent hedge funds, Steinhardt Management, Caxton Corp., and Soros/Quantum, were implicated in the actions, both in concert with Salomon as well as on their own. The hedge fund violations primarily concerned actions in the secondary Treasury "repo" market, in which short sellers were forced to deliver more expensive contracts because the "best-to-deliver" contracts were not available due to the cornering activities. In the April 1991 auction, SMC and Caxton held the equivalent of 158 percent of the $12 billion two-year notes.

The violations affected several Treasury auctions between February 1991 and June–July 1991 when the SEC and other enforcement agencies commenced civil and criminal investigations. Over the next several years Salomon and the implicated hedge funds, and their executives were subjected to about 50 lawsuits. Collectively, the firms and individuals paid over $400 million in disgorgement and fines, much of it in a "global settlement" with the SEC and Department of Justice (DoJ) Salomon's Chairman and CEO were forced to resign, one trader was imprisoned, and others were suspended or barred from the industry.

The hedge funds got off more lightly: no jail terms, no criminal prosecutions, and no termination of top management. However, they did pay proportionally large fines, around $100 million in aggregate, versus some $300 million for Salomon, and, reportedly for performance reasons, both Caxton and Steinhardt closed down their funds shortly after the legal actions.

The chief case against Salomon Brothers was that it had violated Treasury auction rules by purchasing in excess of a regulatory limit of 35 percent of bonds/notes offered. Salomon was also guilty of using client names to exceed regulatory limits and its most senior management for failure to supervise and failure to notify the SEC on a timely basis of violations.

Apart from the usual securities fraud–related charges levied by the SEC and DoJ, this case also had a separate antitrust prosecution, under the Sherman Act, as its centerpiece (*USA against Certain Property Owned by Salomon Brothers Inc*, Civil Action No. 92–3700, U.S. District Court, Southern Division, New York). Beyond the federal case, Salomon and the two hedge funds also settled a class action suit, which itself had consolidated 10 separate actions, on behalf of hundreds of thousands of Treasury market investors.

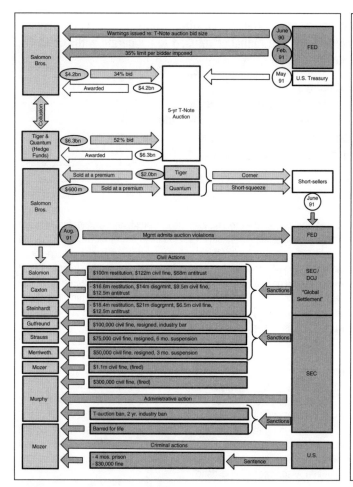

Fraud Facts

- Alleged Acts Date: May 30, 1991
- Enforcement Date: July 1, 1991
- Main Defendants (**hedge fund–related**): Salomon Bros., Mozer, Murphy, Gutfreund, Strauss, Merriwether, Steinhardt, Kovner, **Steinhardt Mgmt. Co., Caxton Corp.**
- Most Serious Charge: Antitrust violation, tax evasive trades
- Hedge Fund Role: Defendant
- Damages $actual (**$2005**): $203 million (**$300 million**)
- No. of Investors: In the thousands
- Highest Court: Criminal
- Most Severe Sentence: 4 months' prison

Sanctions:

- Salomon Bros.: $100 million restitution, $190 million penalties
- Steinhardt Mgmt Co.: $18.4 million restitution, $21 million disgorgement, $19 million penalties
- Caxton Corp.: $16.6 million restitution, $14 million disgorgement, $21.5 million penalties
- Paul Mozer: 4 months' prison, $1.13 million penalties, permanent injunction
- Thomas Murphy: $300,000 penalty, permanent injunction
- John Gutfreund: $100,000 penalty, resignation, industry bar
- Thomas Strauss: $75,000 penalty, 6-month suspension
- John Meriwether: $50,000 penalty, 3-month suspension

Cases:

- *U.S. v. Mozer* (93cr00006, criminal, S. Dist. N.Y.)
- *SEC v. Steinhardt Mgmt. Co.* (94cv09040, civil, S. Dist. N.Y.)
- *SEC v. Salomon* (91cv5442, 92cv3691, civil, S. Dist. N.Y.)
- *U.S. v. Salomon*
- *Three Crowns v. Salomon* (92cv3142, civil, S. Dist. N.Y.)

An unregistered commodity pool suddenly lost the assets of its one investor. Misappropriation was alleged, and the manager refused to cooperate with the CFTC, claiming no jurisdiction. Key points:

- An unregistered commodity pool
- All of pool's assets lost within a two-month period
- Defendant refused CFTC requests to inspect books and records
- Individual limited partner filed separate suit and won some restitution
- CFTC imposed harsh administrative sanctions

Case Summary

Daniel Clothier was the principal and an Associated Person of Collins Commodity Brokerage, of Wichita, Kansas, an entity registered with the CFTC both as a commodity pool operator and as an introducing broker. In 1984, Clothier/Collins organized the Heartland Futures Fund as a Kansas limited partnership (LP), for which Clothier acted as general partner. Heartland was an unregistered commodity pool that raised over $1 million from one individual, Dr. Martin Peskin, a local dentist, and his personal pension plan.

The investor's end-of-month statement for September 1991 showed a balance of just over $1 million. Not two months later, on November 22, Dr. Peskin received a letter from Clothier, which stated that: "I am embarrassed to advise you that the Heartland Futures Fund is essentially wiped out." Peskin's response to this notice included filing a complaint with the National Futures Association

(NFA), who commenced an investigation and, in January 1992, notified the CFTC. The CFTC visited Clothier's offices to inspect books and records, but received no cooperation on the grounds that it had no jurisdiction over the unregistered fund. The second week of February 1992 saw the filing of civil suits from both Peskin (on the February 7) and the CFTC (on the February 11).

Peskin's case received a favorable judgment and a restitution order for over $1 million to be recovered through asset sales and garnishing the wages of Mr. Clothier and his wife Kristin. The CFTC actions affirmed its rightful jurisdiction and imposed a number of sanctions including: Clothiers' disbarment, revocation of registration of Collins and Associated Person status for Clothier, as well as permanent injunctions for Clothier, Collins, and Heartland.

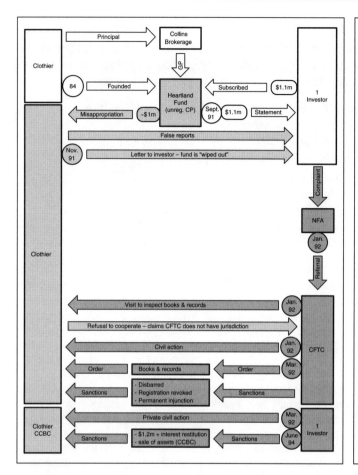

Fraud Facts

- Alleged Acts Date: September 1991
- Enforcement Date: February 11, 1992
- Main Defendants (**hedge fund–related**): **Clothier**, Collins Commodity Brokerage, **Heartland Futures Fund**
- Most Serious Charge: Misappropriation, Fraud
- Hedge Fund Role: Defendant
- Damages $actual **($2005)**: Approximately $1.2 million **($1.86 million)**
- No. of Investors: 1
- Highest Court: Civil
- Most Severe Sentence: $1.2 million restitution, disbarment, revocation of registration

Sanctions:

- Daniel Clothier: Permanent injunction, registration revoked, disbarred
- Collins Commodity Brokerage: Permanent Injunction, industry bar
- Kristin Clothier: Garnishee
- Clothier/Collins: $1.2 million restitution (joint and several)
- Heartland Futures Fund: Permanent injunction

Cases:

- *CFTC v. Clothier* (92cv01062, civil, Dist. Kansas)
- *Peskin v. Clothier* (92cv01151, civil, Dist. Kansas)
- *CFTC v. Clothier* (93–27, admin.)

Two internal hedge funds (commodity pools) managed by a commodities futures broker were coerced to make inappropriate loans to the parent to offset a shortage in regulatory capital. After a series of court actions, sanctions were meted out not only to the broker and fund executives but also to the auditor and to the exchange. Key points:

- Main defendant was one of the largest commodity brokers at the time
- SEC, CFTC, CBOT, and class action cases
- Broker shortage of regulatory capital
- Improper use of capital of internal hedge funds
- Broker's chief counsel sent to prison and disbarred
- Auditor held liable for largest award up that time
- CFTC named CBOT as a defendant for failure to supervise, CBOT paid a fine

Case Summary

Stotler and Company, a commodities futures broker, founded in 1962, was by 1987 the third largest clearing broker on the Chicago Board of Trade. Further boosting its prestige at that time, Karsten "Cash" Mahlmann, Chairman of Stotler, was elected as Chairman of the CBOT. There was also a major expansion of its infrastructure both domestically and internationally. To fund this ambitious expansion program, the parent Stotler Group Inc. launched an IPO of its Stotler and Company subsidiary in 1988.

Initial signs of trouble appeared in early December 1989, when SEC examiners arrived at the offices of Stotler subsidiary, R. G. Dickinson, to address an inadequacy of regulatory capital. At Stotler headquarters, senior management settled upon a desperate fix for the capital problem. They caused two Stotler-managed commodity pools to purchase $5.5 million of Stotler and Co. commercial paper—$4.5 million from Compass Fund and $1 million from Advanced Portfolio Management. Despite defendant Kolter's claim of having taken legal advice on these transfers, there were serious reservations about this and as to whether one or both purchases were in violation of the fund prospectuses, the terms of the offering, or the disclosure requirements of the funds.

In the early months of 1990, the National Futures Association raised questions about the commercial paper transactions regarding disclosure. By July, the CBOT imposed a deadline on rectifying the situation. At this time, Stotler urgently sought to locate a source of new capital, while actively moving its largest clients to other brokers in an effort to lower regulatory capital required. The stock was suspended on July 11. The CBOT deadline came and went on July 18, followed by the news that Stotler had withdrawn from its clearing status with the CBOT. Then, on July 24 and 25, the company defaulted on a $750,000 loan repayment and closed down. A class action investor suit, the first of a number of lawsuits was filed on August 9.

When the smoke cleared, Stotler was out of business; its registration revoked; its chief counsel (Kolter) was in jail; its chairman had resigned as chairman of CBOT; its accountant/auditor, Coopers & Lybrand, had settled one case for $500,000 (and a class action settlement may have cost it a further $2 million or more); other executives were suspended; and the CBOT itself was fined $300,000 by the CFTC for not adequately policing its exchange.

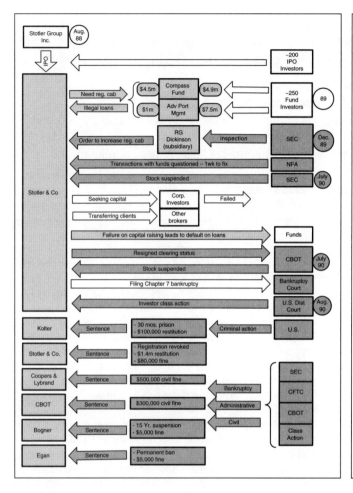

Fraud Facts

- Alleged Acts Date: December 31, 1989
- Enforcement Date: January 13, 1993
- Main Defendants (**hedge fund–related**): Bogner, Egan, Kolter, Mahlmann, Stotler & Co., Zarcone, **Adv. Portfolio Mgmt., Compass Future Funds**
- Most Serious Charge: Fraud
- Hedge Fund Role: Victim, internal hedge fund assets improperly allocated as loans to parent company
- Damages $actual (**$2005**): Approximately $5.6 million (**$8.7 million**)
- No. of Investors: Approximately 250 (Stotler commodity pools)
- Highest Court: Criminal
- Most Severe Sentence: 30 months' prison, disbarment

Sanctions:

- Eugene Bogner (CBOT): $5,000 civil fine, 15-year industry ban
- Thomas Egan (CBOT): $5,000 civil fine, lifetime industry ban
- Thomas Kolter: 30 months' prison, 36 months' supervised release, $100,000 restitution
- Chicago Board of Trade: $300,000 civil fine
- Cooper & Lybrand (CFTC): $500,000 civil fine
- Stotler & Co.: Permanently barred from registering

Cases:

- *Elson v. Stotler* (90cv04497, civil, N. Dist. Ill.)
- *SEC v. Egan* (92cv03480, civil, N. Dist. Ill.)
- *U.S. v. Kolter* (95cr00037, criminal, N. Dist. Ill.)
- *CFTC v. CBOT*

This case involved two separate but related Ponzi schemes that targeted hundreds of retirees. One of the schemes may have begun as a genuine investment, but both ended as pure embezzlement vehicles. Key points:

- Earliest Florida-based hedge fund fraud case
- Two separate but related commodity pools operated as Ponzi schemes
- Schemes targeted hundreds of retirees in a dental practice, a country club, and synagogue
- One scheme promoted with false promises of 20 to 40 percent returns and 25 percent stop loss
- Principals received stiff prison sentences

Case Summary

De Gol/Ericson is unusual in being a "twinned" Ponzi scheme. Dennis Golubowski and Robert Loehrmann of Coral Springs, Florida, were friends and former colleagues—and, from the early 1980s, both operated Ponzi schemes involving unregistered commodity pools that ultimately did little or no investing. Both faced criminal prosecution and both received lengthy prison sentences.

Loehrmann was the "manager" of Ericson Financial Group. Loehrmann's associate in this venture was Sidney Gutsin, a local dentist, who solicited amongst his patients for "investments" into their fraudulent scheme. They were able to raise $15 to $20 million from around 200 investors. Golubowski ran a separate but, perhaps, only just a slightly less phony investment scheme, De Gol Financial Group, which made many false statements regarding his investment strategy and raised as much as $20 million from some 200 other investors, many of whom were friends and/or members of his country club or synagogue. Adding to the twinning of these schemes was the fact that Golubowski apparently invested some of his investor's assets into the Ericson scheme, though

whether he did this expecting a return or on some other basis is not known.

This was the first Florida hedge fund fraud case. Up to this time, 12 of the prior 19 cases (63 percent) were New York-based. A further two (11 percent) were Illinois cases, reflecting the locus of the U.S. commodity trading markets. Combined, nearly three-quarters of the cases were in the two major market centers. Florida represents a shift in scene to an ideal target market of naïve, affluent, and ill-advised retirees.

Law enforcement shut down both operations in the same week in September 1992; however, by that time most of the assets were gone. Golubowski and Loehrmann faced criminal prosecution and prison terms—46 months for Golubowski and 86 months for Loehrmann. Gutsin reached an agreement in a civil case to disgorge $480,000 of ill-gotten gains and be banned from any association with the industry. He simply carried on with his dental practice as before. Golubowski and Loehrmann were ordered to make restitution of $8.1 million and $20 million, respectively.

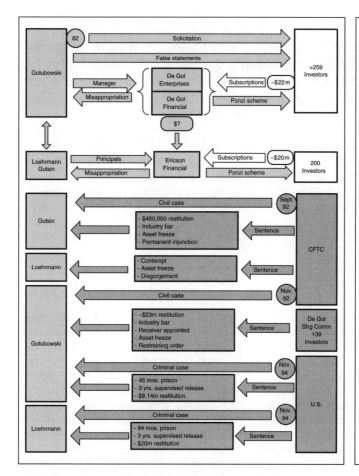

Fraud Facts

- Alleged Acts Date: 1982
- Enforcement Date: November 16, 1992
- Main Defendants **(hedge fund–related): Golubowski, Gutsin, Loehrmann (De Gol Enterprises, De Gol Financial Group, Ericson Financial Group)**
- Most Serious Charge: Mail fraud
- Hedge Fund Role: Operated as Ponzi schemes
- Damages $actual **($2005)**: Approximately $40 million **($57 million)**
- No. of Investors: Approximately 460
- Highest Court: Criminal
- Most Severe Sentence: 86 months' prison

Sanctions:

- Dennis Golubowski: 46 months' prison, 3 years' supervised release, $8.14 million restitution
- De Gol Enterprises: Restraining order, asset freeze, receiver
- De Gol Financial: Restraining order, asset freeze, receiver
- Sidney Gutsin: $480,000 disgorgement, industry bar, permanent injunction
- Richard Loehrmann: 86 months' prison, $20 million restitution, permanent injunction
- Ericson Financial Group: Disgorgement (joint and several), stop solicitation order

Cases:

- *CFTC v. De Gol Ent.* (92cv07158, civil, S. Dist. Florida)
- *U.S. v. Golubowski* (94cr06218, criminal, S. Dist. Florida)

The defendant advised a hedge fund group on takeovers and was appointed as a director of one of the targets to represent the fund's interests. While in this position, the defendant learned that the company was about to be acquired and passed on this significant inside information to two individuals—a friend and a family relation—both of whom purchased shares prior to the acquisition and profited once the news became public. Key points:

- SEC case
- Insider trading
- Main defendant was a consultant to the Soros Group on takeovers
- Defendant was given a seat on the board of Soros risk arbitrage target, Foxboro
- Defendant passed information on Foxboro acquisition by Siebe PLC
- Defendant did not purchase shares
- Defendant paid a fine but was not suspended or barred

Case Summary

The insider trading violations concern information relayed by Dr. Purnendu Chatterjee, a director of Foxboro Co., a maker of industrial controls, to his brother-in-law, Sukumar Shah, and another individual, Anjan Chatterjee. Around April 1990, the Soros Group acquired a 4.8 percent stake in Foxboro and placed Dr. Chatterjee, who had acted as a consultant to the Soros Group on takeovers, on the board of Foxboro as a director. On June 26, 1990, Foxboro announced that it had agreed to be acquired by Siebe PLC a UK company. The transaction was completed by September 1991. On January 13, 1993, The SEC filed a civil complaint charging Mr. Chatterjee with insider trading violations for his actions prior to the Siebe acquisition.

Dr. Chatterjee and his two coconspirators reached a settlement with the SEC and without admitting or denying their guilt they consented to the SEC publishing the charges and also agreed to pay disgorgements and civil monetary penalties totaling some $2.1 million. It was determined that Shah and Anjan Chatterjee profited in aggregate by $643,855 from the purchase of 52,500 Foxboro shares. While Purnendu Chatterjee did not purchase any shares, he agreed to pay an equal monetary penalty of $643,855. The SEC acting regional administrator in Boston stated: "This was a fraud. Mr. Chatterjee's actions as the director of a public company were a very serious abuse of the public's trust." The Soros group was not charged in any of these insider trading proceedings, although Soros, with the help of Chatterjee, had clearly been pursuing takeovers as part of his overall hedge fund strategy, of which Foxboro was a part. One of the other companies tackled by the Soros–Chatterjee team was Perkin-Elmer, which, at the end of 1991 would have been the third largest holding ($60 million) of the then $1.43 billion Quantum Fund. Other targets, including Tektronix and T-Bar Inc. filed private suits against Soros and Chatterjee. Other takeovers included Pansophic Systems, Computer Associates, and Beckman Instruments.

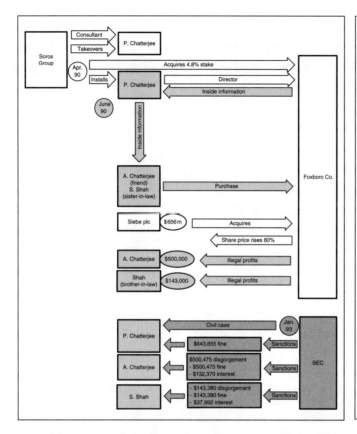

Fraud Facts

- Alleged Acts Date:
  June 1990
- Enforcement Date:
  January 13, 1993
- Main Defendants
  (hedge fund–related):
  Purnendu Chatterjee,
  Sukumar Shah, Anjan
  Chatterjee **(Soros
  Group)**
- Most Serious Charge:
  Insider trading
- Hedge Fund Role:
  Defendant was a hedge
  fund-appointed director
  in a target acquisition
- Damages $actual
  ($2005): $640,000
  ($1 million)
- No. of Investors: NA
- Highest Court: Civil
- Most Severe Sentence:
  Disgorgement and Civil
  monetary penalties

Sanctions:

- Purnendu Chatterjee: $643,855 civil monetary penalty, permanent injunction
- Sukumar Shah: $143,380 disgorgement, $37,992 interest, $143,380 fine
- Anjar Chatterjee: $500,475 disgorgement, $132,370 interest, $500,475 fine

Cases:

- *SEC v. Chatterjee* (93cv10070, civil, Dist. Mass.)

In this case, the defendant, a broker with a record of prior client complaints, attracted investors after winning a national investment contest and at some point began misappropriating investor money to pay personal expenses and to shore-up his brokerage company. Key points:

- An SEC case
- First hedge fund case in Texas
- Broker had a prior record of complaints
- Used questionable contest results to support performance claims
- Created both hedge fund and broker-dealer companies despite limited resources
- Continued to "prop trade" in parallel with fund investments and lost money
- Misappropriated fund assets to maintain regulatory capital (and for personal use)
- Failed to provide annual audits that would have discovered problems

Case Summary

Robert Doviak II had been employed as a stockbroker in Dallas, Texas, since 1987, first with Southwest Securities and then with Prudential Bache. During this time, Doviak had also been an active participant in the U.S. Trading Championship, a privately run, but widely followed, national contest based upon the performance of several different style-defined investment portfolios (for other contest-related cases see Case 37 PRISM/Prendergast, Case 48 HYANNIS/Hegarty, and Case 64 PRIME/Zadeh).

In December 1987, Doviak won the "stock division" of the contest with a result of 87.9 percent, all the more remarkable given the stock market crash a few months earlier. The contest served to raise Doviak's profile countrywide and to generate investor interest. Over the next few years, with continuing good contest results, Doviak capitalized on his notoriety by leaving his stockbroking job to establish a hedge fund and a securities company.

However, a closer inspection, with the benefit of hindsight, yields a less rosy picture of Doviak's prehedge fund background. First, the Dallas office of Pru-Bache at that time was somewhat akin to a "school for scandal." A New York Times article of May 24, 1993, outlined the cases of five other brokers employed at the branch at that time who incurred serious investor complaints, including churning, inappropriate investments, trading without authorization, and forging customer signatures. These violations were all the worse due to a lack of supervision and inadequate discipline at the branch. Doviak himself had five complaints made

against him while at Prudential and Southwest Securities. These complaints were settled for sums ranging from $11,000 to $75,000. One of Doviak's colleagues also claimed that Doviak had cheated in his investment contest results by selectively picking successful trades from different accounts. The contest itself was the subject of later SEC action and was closed down (see Case 64).

Around 1991, Doviak raised some $4 million for his newly launched hedge fund. By 1993, his brokerage and hedge fund were in deep trouble. Losses at the brokerage led to a shortfall in regulatory capital. Doviak borrowed and misappropriated money from the fund to bolster the broker. He also took money for his own needs. These declines were covered up by overvaluing holdings of small companies as well as by avoiding audits. All told, of the $4 million initially invested, about $1.3 million was misappropriated, including some $800,000 in the form of unsecured loans and advances to Doviak. Around $2 million was assessed as small company holdings and $350,000 remained in cash and securities.

In subsequent SEC civil and criminal actions, Doviak was sentenced to 27 months in prison, ordered to disgorge $844,000, fined $50,000, and served with a permanent injunction against future violations. The disgorgement was later waived due to Doviak's inability to pay. The court appointed a special master to oversee the liquidation of Doviak's remaining assets, including the winding up of his brokerage and fund companies.

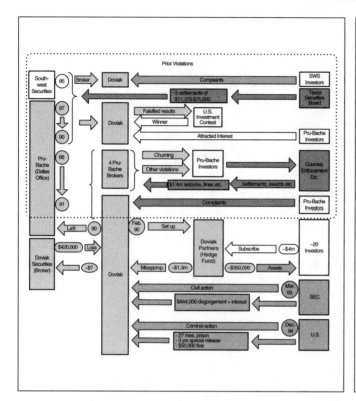

Fraud Facts

- Alleged Acts Date: February 1990
- Enforcement Date: March 4, 1993
- Main Defendants **(hedge fund–related): Robert Doviak II,** Doviak Securities Inc, **Doviak Partners Ltd.**
- Most Serious Charge: Misappropriation
- Hedge Fund Role: A named defendant where GP illegally withdrew and misused LP assets
- Damages $actual **($2005):** Approximately $1.3 million **($2.0 million)**
- No. of Investors: 20
- Highest Court: Criminal
- Most Severe Sentence: Prison

Sanctions:

- Robert Doviak II: 27 months' prison, 3 years' probation with conditions, $50,000 fine, $844,000 disgorgement (waived to $0), permanent. injunction

Cases:

- *SEC v. Doviak* (93cv00444, civil, N. Dist. Tx.)
- *U.S. v. Doviak* (94cr00423, criminal, N. Dist. Tx.)
- *U.S. v. Doviak* (04cv02286, civil, N. Dist. Tx.)

A financial consultant promoted several of his own unregistered commodity pool schemes and ran them as Ponzi scams. Key points:

- CFTC case
- Creating unregistered commodity pools while employed as a broker for Merrill Lynch
- Claimed investors would benefit from his being employed by Merrill Lynch
- Operated as a Ponzi scheme
- Receiver recovered around 60 percent of investor's assets
- Stiff jail sentence—44 months
- Merrill Lynch subject of separate investigation of Bell's activities

Case Summary

In November 1989, Richard Conroy Bell was hired as a financial consultant by the Tulsa, Oklahoma office of Merrill Lynch and, by summer 1990, he had become registered with the CFTC as an Associated Person of that firm. While employed there, Bell approached investors with a succession of trading strategies in which he sought to take advantage of his position including; receiving research, being aware of trades or avoiding some commissions or settlement constraints. According to case documents, Bell never intended and never did make any real trades for these "day trader" investors.

In early 1991, Bell was promoting an oil futures trading scheme and set up an unregistered commodity pool called Rick Bell Oil & Gas for this trading "sideline." In February 1992, he established Barrett Bell Investment Corp., based in Midland, Texas. All subsequent contracts with investors were arranged with this company.

In total, around $8 million had been raised from approximately 110 customers for these purported investments. While the scheme was in operation, Bell recirculated investor funds in a Ponzi-like fashion, while misappropriating much of the money for his own expenses, including a home and a twin-jet airplane. However, by soliciting so widely among his Merrill Lynch contacts word of his unorthodox extracurricular activities eventually reached the ears of Merrill's management who questioned Bell, but without result. Merrill Lynch was itself later subject to a CFTC investigation, which found some fault with management, but took no action apart from publishing its findings.

What finally got the attention of law enforcement was a report from a Texas bank to the FBI when Bell sought to arrange a substantial wire transfer to another bank in Tulsa. In October 1993, Bell was questioned by the FBI and confessed his fraudulent activities. The CFTC filed a six-count civil complaint against Bell and three of his business entities on November 16 and October 20, 1994. He was charged with one criminal count of fraud by wire in a separate action.

A receiver appointed in the civil case succeeded in recovering nearly $5 million of the $8 million invested, or about 63 percent. The criminal action resulted in a prison sentence of 44 months for Bell and a fine of $15,000. The CFTC investigation report on Merrill Lynch's culpability was published on March 19, 1997.

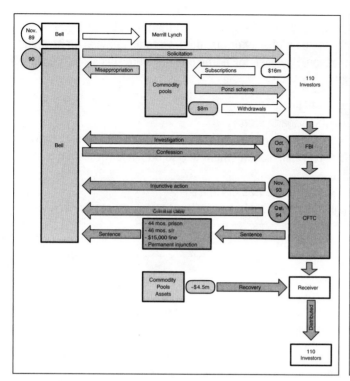

Fraud Facts

- Alleged Acts Date: 1990
- Enforcement Date: November 16, 1993
- **Main Defendants (hedge fund–related): Bell (Barrett Bell Investment Corp., Manticore Resources, ZIA Investments)**
- Most Serious Charge: Wire fraud
- Hedge Fund Role: Defendant
- Damages $actual ($2005): $7.8 million ($12 million)
- No. of Investors: 110
- Highest Court: Criminal
- Most Severe Sentence: 44 months' prison, $3.4 million restitution

Sanctions:

- Richard Conroy Bell: 44 months' prison, 36 months' probation, $3.4 million restitution, $15,000 fine, permanent injunction

Cases:

- *CFTC v. Bell* (93cv01022, civil, N Dist, Okla.)
- *U.S. v. Bell* (94cr00155, criminal, N Dist Okla.)
- *In the Matter of Merrill Lynch* (CFTC Investigation Report)

This is one of the earliest and largest blow-ups of a mortgage-related strategy hedge fund. While the manager made a number of errors, there were no grounds for anything beyond an administrative action. However, the prime brokers were successfully sued in private actions. Key points:

- Largest fund blow-up to that date
- Part of a wider failure of mortgage strategies
- Despite the size of the losses, the SEC response was modest—an administrative case resulting in a two-year bar, disgorgement of $50,000, and revocation of the manager's registration
- The main private class action case was dismissed
- Investors won substantial relief in a bankruptcy-related action against the brokers

Case Summary

Askin is included in even the shortest lists of hedge fund failures and is often the earliest case cited. The case also aired important issues such as the role of leverage, illiquid positions, "manager's marks," and prime broker liquidation of assets.

One-time head of bond research at Drexel's, David Askin left to join New Amsterdam Partners at the end of 1989 and then moved on to Whitehead/ Sterling Advisers, who aided his takeover of Granite Partners LP, Granite Corp. and Quartz hedge funds, with combined assets of around $180 million in early 1992. A fourth fund, concentrating on mortgages and mortgage derivates, was launched in January 1994 with $35 million. In the same month, rising inflation fears caused Treasury securities to decline sharply and, by early February, the Federal Reserve (Fed) raised rates for the first time in five years.

On March 25, Askin's investors were informed that "[d]ue to turbulent conditions . . . there has been a significant reduction in the valuations of securities in our portfolios." It was later disclosed that what Askin had claimed to be a 1.5 percent decline in February in the $170 million Granite Fund, had, in fact, been a 21.9 percent decline. He also referred to broker margin pressures as well as his need to use "manager's marks" because of difficulties in obtaining broker quotes in the more turbulent markets.

On March 28, Askin investors turned down a request for an extra $30 to 50 million to meet margin calls. One such demand from Bear Stearns left the fund $42 million short of cash. On March 30th the brokers liquidated the fund assets in a series of what articles at the time termed "fire sales." The funds filed for Chapter 11 protection in early April and the first lawsuit was filed on April 13. Apart from the trustee of the bankrupt funds, the bulk of the private suits were aggregated into a class action, while the SEC actions did not go beyond an administrative proceeding.

Although the class action charges were eventually dismissed, investors fared better in the bankruptcy court where the trustee reached meaningful settlements with the brokers; $30 million from DLJ, $39.5 million from Bear Stearns, and $19 million from Kidder Peabody. In 2003, after a judge reversed a ruling in favor of Merrill Lynch, they settled for $5.9 million.

David Askin himself got off lightly considering the gravity of the charges, the breadth of the legal efforts, and the scale of the losses incurred. In May 1995 he settled with the SEC, agreeing to a two-year industry bar, a cease-and-desist order against future violations, revocation of his asset management company, and a fine of $50,000 to be paid toward an investor compensation fund. The settlement with the SEC also allowed David Askin to neither admit nor deny his guilt.

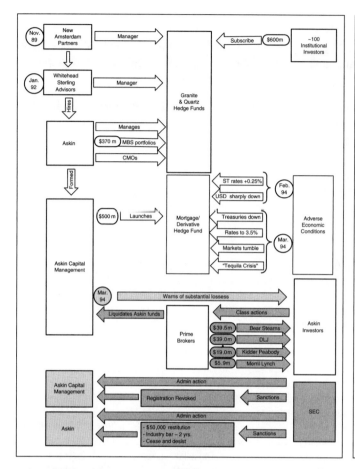

Fraud Facts

- Alleged Acts Date: February 1994
- Enforcement Date: April 12, 1994 (1st private action)
- Main Defendants **(hedge fund–related): David Askin, Geoffrey Bradshaw-Mack, Askin Capital Mgmt., Granite Partners, Granite Corp., Quartz Hedge Fund**
- Most Serious Charge: Fraud
- Hedge Fund Role: Defendant
- Damages $actual **($2005): $600 million ($790 million)**
- No. of Investors: Approximately 100 institutions
- Highest Court: SEC Administrative
- Most Severe Sentence: fine, bar, registration revoked

Sanctions:

- David Askin: $50,000 restitution, 2-year industry bar, cease and desist
- Askin Capital Management, LP: registration revoked
- Bear Stearns & Co., Inc.: $39.5 million settlement
- Donaldson, Lufkin, Jenrette, Sec. Corp.: $39.0 million settlement
- Kidder Peabody: $19.0 million settlement
- Merrill Lynch: $5.9 million settlement

Cases:

- *In the matter of David Askin* (SEC, administrative, Inv Adv Act Rel no 1492, May 23, 1995)
- *Granite Prtnrs v. Bear Stearns* (96cv7874, civil, S. Dist. N.Y.)
- *Primavera Famili v. Askin* (95cv08905, civil, S. Dist. N.Y.)
- *AIG Mgd Mkt v. Askin* (98cv07494, civil, S. Dist. N.Y.)

Two ex-penny-stock brokers started an unregistered commodity pool after their former employer had been raided by law enforcement and subsequently went bankrupt. They went on to misappropriate most of the money they raised from investors. Key points:

- CFTC/State of Ohio case
- Defendant's former employer was a large, scandal-ridden penny-stock broker
- Unregistered commodity pool
- Misrepresentations to promote pool
- False reporting used to maintain investor interest
- Misappropriated most of money
- Criminal case only against commodity pool

Case Summary

On October 22, 1992, the U.S. Attorney and local sheriff's office raided the offices of Dublin Securities, a large penny-stock broker-dealer based in Worthington, Ohio, a suburb of Columbus. Dublin had become the subject of an investigation and lawsuit relating to the illegal and fraudulent sale of shares of an Ohio start-up company. The company and its officers were named in a 327-count indictment and the subject of two multimillion dollar lawsuits brought by investors. On August 18, 1993, Dublin Securities and two of its sister companies filed for Chapter 11 bankruptcy.

In February 1993, as the final curtain was falling on Dublin Securities, two of its former brokers, Robert Bobo (who was about 23 years old at the time) and Jeffrey Smith, were busy soliciting for the Allied Financial Group, an unregistered commodity pool. Making use of false representations, the pair managed to raise around $844,000 from 49 of their fellow Ohioans, including the local Presbyterian church. A proportion of this money may have been invested in commodity futures. The majority of it was almost certainly simply misappropriated by the partners. The investors were further deceived with falsified monthly statements.

On October 11, 1994, a civil complaint was filed by both the CFTC and the Ohio Division of Securities. In November 1997, Bobo reached a consent judgment in which he and Allied Financial were jointly and severally responsible for restitution of $844,093 plus interest, though likely due to his financial condition, $693,757 of this amount was waived, leaving $150,336 to be paid to the investors. In June 1998, Jeffrey Smith agreed to make a lump sum payment of $19,000 to settle his case. The following year a criminal prosecution was brought against Allied Financial Group on one count of fraud.

Around the middle of 1997, Bobo had moved to San Francisco and established what became an award-winning film special effects studio. In 2000, he was ordered to pay a further $720,580 in restitution that had been waived in the earlier case.

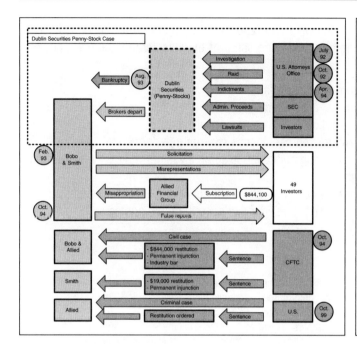

Fraud Facts

- Alleged Acts Date: February 1993
- Enforcement Date: October 11, 1994
- Defendants **(hedge funds): Bobo, Smith (Allied Financial Group, Inc.)**
- Most Serious Charge: Fraud
- Hedge Fund Role: Defendant
- Damages $actual **($2005): $844,093 ($1.14 million)**
- No. of Investors: 49
- Highest Court: Civil
- Most Severe Sentence: $844,000 restitution

Sanctions:

- Robert G. Bobo: $844,093 restitution (joint and severally with Allied), industry bar
- Jeffrey A. Smith: $19,000 disgorgement, permanent injunction
- Allied Financial Group Inc.: industry bar

Cases:

- *CFTC v. Allied* (94cv00981, civil, S. Dist. Oh.)
- *U.S. v. Allied* (99cr00146, criminal, S. Dist. Oh.)

The SEC, pursuing a hedge fund in a civil case for selling unregistered securities, found the defendant reoffending by transferring some of the investors to another fund. Key points:

- An SEC case with some CFTC overlap
- Defendant had published a newsletter
- Sold unregistered securities in an investment vehicle
- Made false claims and misrepresentations regarding performance
- Defrauded the SEC by paying restitution to some investors while secretly moving others to a new fund
- Made a plea deal that the government did not honor due to the reoffending
- Defendant appealed, receiving a stiffer sentence than that agreed in the plea

Case Summary

Beginning in 1992, Sanjay Saxena, a former computer science graduate and programmer, published the *Weekly Wealth Letter*, a financial newsletter with some 1,200 subscribers paying $200 per year. About a year later, he solicited this subscriber base for investment in an unregistered hedge fund, Infinity Investments. Promising returns of 50 percent per annum along with an offer to reimburse 25 percent of all losses, Saxena stood to gain a 25 percent fee on any profits made. He raised about $2.2 million from 165 investors in these efforts. Part of his strategic repertoire was an alleged proprietary computer-based trading system to market-time funds and sectors. However, while illustrating trading gains over a five-year period, he had only ever traded $5,000 to test his fund trading ideas prior to August 1992.

It appears that much of the money raised was utilized in investments; but a high proportion of these lost money. Between January and August 1993, there was an aggregate loss of roughly $360,000, which was covered up with false reports showing positive results.

Sometime in 1994, the SEC began investigating Infinity Investments. Saxena agreed to close down the fund and repay the investors and had done so to some extent, when the SEC filed a civil action in December 1994, charging him with selling unregistered securities and barring him as an investment adviser with a permanent injunction against future violations. In 1996, the CFTC revoked Saxena's registration.

At this point the Saxena story diverted from most other such frauds in the elaborate measures he took to circumvent the SEC industry bar and injunctions. His first deception was to comply with the SEC's restitution order, but in respect to only 120 of the 165 investors. The assets of the remaining 45 were secretly transferred to other funds (Phoenix, Index Timing Fund, LP, and Saxena Growth Fund) managed by another investment adviser (Saxena Capital Management, Inc.), which was managed by Saxena's wife, Mumtaz, and unwittingly aided by a consulting contract Saxena had with a legitimate broker.

The reoffending behavior triggered another civil suit and a criminal suit in 1998, along with several appeals. The civil action included Saxena and his wife and ordered them to pay further restitution of around $300,000 and a fine of $100,000. In the criminal action, he was sentenced to 33 months' prison, with 36 months of supervised release, a civil fine of $100,000, and ordered to pay the remaining restitution of $13,616. This was a harsher sentence than that negotiated in an earlier plea agreement prior to his reoffending becoming known. Saxena filed several appeals contesting the government's right to renege on the earlier plea. The appeals failed.

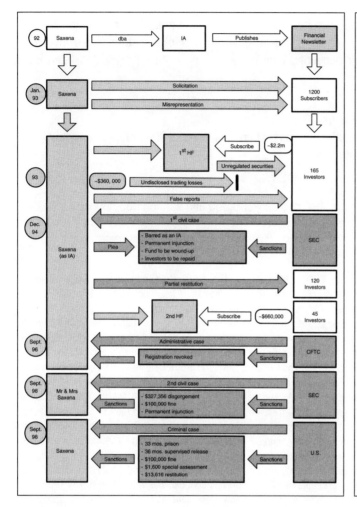

Fraud Facts

- Alleged Acts Date:
  November 1993
- Enforcement Date:
  December 8, 1994
- Main Defendants
  (hedge fund–related):
  M. Saxena, S. Saxena
  (Infinity Investment,
  Phoenix Group, Select
  Sector), Index Timing
  Fund, Saxena Cap.
  Mgmt., Saxena Growth
  Fund
- Most Serious Charge:
  Sale of unregistered
  securities
- Hedge Fund Role:
  Defendant
- Damages $actual
  ($2005): $703,000
  ($950,000)
- No. of Investors: 165
- Highest Court: Criminal
- Most Severe Sentence:
  33 months' prison,
  $100,000 fine, $703,000
  disgorgement

Sanctions:

- Mumtaz Saxena: Approximately $330,000 disgorgement (joint and several), $50,000 fine
- Sanjay Saxena: 33 months' prison, 3 years' supervised release, ~$700,000 restitution, $100,000 civil
  fine, $1,600 special assessment, CFTC registration revoked, investment industry bar, newsletter bar

Cases:

- *SEC v. Saxena* (94cv12419, civil, Dist. Mass.)
- *CFTC v. Saxena* (administrative action)
- *SEC v. Saxena* (98cv11918 civil, Dist. Mass.)
- *U.S. v. Saxena* (98cr10298, criminal Dist. Mass.)
- *U.S. v. Saxena* (99–1842, USCOA 1st C)
- *U.S. v. Saxena* (00–2360, USCOA 1st C)

Via an unregistered commodity pool and pool operator, the defendant largely misappropriated money solicited from a small number of investors. When investors sought to liquidate their accounts, they were told all of their money had been lost. Key points:

- CFTC civil case
- An unregistered CP and CPO
- Possibly targeted females, soliciting approximately $62,000 from four individuals
- Made no investments
- Misappropriated much of the money
- Claimed all money was lost
- Paid restitution and civil fine of over $200,000 and banned from industry

Case Summary

Though not registered with the CFTC, Zebedee McLaurin held himself out as a trader of commodity futures. Beginning around October 1992, he secured investments totaling around $62,000 from four individuals (all of whom happened to be women) for his ZMV Capital. These "investors" were instructed to deposit their money into accounts McLaurin had with futures commission merchants. The investors had no ownership rights over these accounts and McLaurin made numerous withdrawals without authorization or notification, most if not all of this to pay personal expenses. It is not clear that any commodity futures investments were made. The investors were given false reports of their trading performance and, when they requested liquidation of their accounts with ZMV Capital, they were given bad checks or told that all of the money had been lost.

The CFTC filed a civil complaint charging two counts of fraud on January 17, 1995, and a summary judgment ordered McLaurin to pay restitution plus interest totaling $61,608.50 and a civil fine of $146,292.57. The CFTC also imposed a permanent injunction and an industry b/an.

NFA records for the immediate period preceding these violations may have foreshadowed his later troubles. In March 1991, McLaurin was listed as a pending Associated Person of Goldman Sachs, with the Associated Person status withdrawn just one year later in March 1992. And, in April 1992, McLaurin was listed as a pending Associated Person of Prudential Equity Group. This designation, too, was withdrawn in May 1992. The first fraudulent incident commenced about six months later.

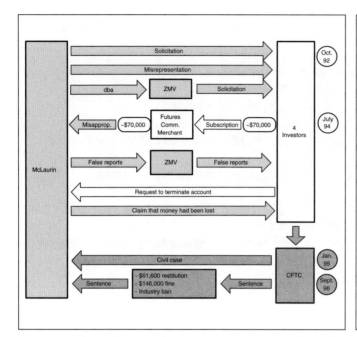

Fraud Facts
- Alleged Acts Date: 1992
- Enforcement Date:
  June 15, 1994
- Main Defendants
  (hedge fund–related):
  McLaurin (ZMV Capital)
- Most Serious Charge:
  Fraud, misappropriation
- Hedge Fund Role:
  Defendant
- Damages $actual
  ($2005): $62,000
  ($81,000)
- No. of Investors: 4
- Highest Court: Civil
- Most Severe Sentence:
  $62,000 disgorgement,
  $146,000 civil fine

Sanctions:
- Zebedee V. McLaurin: $62,000 restitution, $146,000 civil fine, industry bar

Cases:
- *CFTC v. McLaurin* (95cv00285, civil, N. Dist. Ill.)

The defendant, a hedge fund investment adviser, is an early example of the so-called "rogue trader." Key points:

- First hedge fund "rogue trader" case
- Covered-up losses for at least three years
- The Common Fund sustained losses of $137.5 million
- Investment adviser and its four partners guilty of failure to supervise
- Calculation and accounting procedures allowed Ahrens to hide losses within "open trades"
- The Common Fund unsuccessfully sued accountants KPMG for breach of contract and negligence
- Princeton University had dropped First Capital Strategists three years earlier due to a lack of internal controls
- The trader was imprisoned and the investment adviser fined and its registration revoked

Case Summary

Note: While FCS did not refer to itself as a "hedge fund," it has been included here because it exhibited all of the key attributes of a hedge fund such as the receipt of performance-related fees, engagement in index and fixed income arbitrage, and its obligation to hedge all positions.

Kent Ahrens, billed as a "rogue trader," was employed by First Capital Strategists (FCS) of York, Pennsylvania, an SEC-registered investment adviser and a CFTC-registered commodities trading adviser. Primarily known as a "securities agent," arranging stock loan services for its clients, FCS also maintained a profitable related arbitrage business. In 1981, it became the exclusive securities lending agent for the Common Fund, a large asset aggregator and allocator of university endowment funds. The following year the Common Fund authorized FCS to carry out fully hedged equity index arbitrage in order to enhance its stock loan revenues. Kent Ahrens joined FCS in 1983 and in 1989 was put in charge of the trading for the equity index arbitrage strategies.

Typical of frauds that are not criminal enterprises from the outset, this case began with a small loss-making error. Unable to complete one side of a hedged position, Ahrens incurred a loss of $250,000. Instead of reporting the loss to the partners of FCS, and in contravention of the trading guidelines agreed between his employer and their client, he sought to recoup the loss with some directional trades.

The growing losses that resulted were actively concealed for three years when they had reached $137.6 million. Ahrens's deceptions included failure to report, reporting falsely, and avoiding recognition of losses by keeping positions open. His improper conduct was aided by the FCS computer system, which could not calculate mark-to-market prices for Ahrens' trades.

Above and beyond Ahrens's violations, the four partners of FCS were held culpable by the SEC and accused of improper supervision and for not disclosing an earlier violation where another FCS trader cost the firm's two clients a loss of $1.5 million. On that occasion, the partners reimbursed both clients for their losses, but only disclosed the error to one. The SEC also faulted the FCS partners for not having an accounting system that could calculate mark-to-market values for open trades.

Ahrens faced criminal and civil prosecutions and administrative proceedings. He pled guilty to one count of wire fraud and was sent to prison for 34 months, in the criminal case, received a permanent injunction and disgorgement demand of $455,465, waived to $182,000 in the civil suit, and barred from the industry in the administrative case. FCS's four partners were collectively ordered to disgorge $2.6 million, the company's registration was revoked and the partners were all suspended from the industry for 12 months and barred from any supervisory positions for five years.

The final chapter in the FCS/Ahrens case was the Common Fund bringing a suit against their auditors, KPMG, Peat Marwick for professional malpractice. This suit was dismissed. It was appealed in 2003 and was again denied.

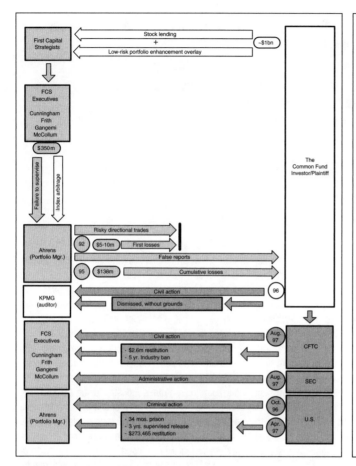

Fraud Facts

- Alleged Acts Date: 1992
- Enforcement Date: July 3, 1995
- Main Defendants **(hedge fund–related): Kent Ahrens, First Capital Strategists**
- Most Serious Charge: Wire fraud
- Hedge Fund Role: Defendant—Failure to supervise "rogue trader"
- Damages $actual **($2005): $137.6 million ($176 million)**
- No. of Investors: 1,421
- Highest Court: Criminal
- Most Severe Sentence: 34 months' prison

Sanctions:

- Kent Ahrens: 34 months' prison, 3 years' supervised release, $273,465 restitution
- Kent Ahrens: $455,465 disgorgement (waived to $182,000), industry bar
- First Capital Strategists: $2.6 million disgorgement, investment adviser registration revoked
- Robert Frith: 1-year suspension, barred from supervision
- Keith Cunningham: 1-year suspension, barred from supervision
- Paul Gangemi: 1-year suspension, barred from supervision
- John McCollum: 1-year suspension, barred from supervision

Cases:

- *U.S. v. Ahrens* (96cr00257, criminal, M. Dist. Pa.)
- *SEC v. Ahrens* (96cv01854, civil, M. Dist. Pa.)
- *In the Matter of Ahrens* (SEC Admin. Proc. 3–9249)
- *CFTC v. Ahrens*
- *Common Fund v. KPMG* (96cv00255, civil, S. Dist. N.Y.)

An unregistered commodities trading adviser commingled investor money and misappropriated much of it. Key points:

- An unregistered CTA
- Misrepresentation in soliciting to individuals in Indiana and Illinois
- Misappropriation and commingling of most of the monies received
- Misappropriated monies channeled to personal expenses via two trusts
- U.S. government prosecuted and won a $5 million tax judgment against Mr. and Mrs. Anderson
- In a civil case the CFTC won restitution and barred Anderson for life

Case Summary

On September 22, 1995, the CFTC filed a civil complaint against Gary Bruce Anderson of Syracuse, Indiana (about 100 miles east of Chicago). Anderson had been charged with operating an unregistered commodity trading adviser, and of commingling and misappropriating money he solicited from about 30 investors, while misrepresenting the true circumstances to these same investors both prior to and following their transfer of cash to him. Misrepresentations included the claim that the money was invested in S&P 500 futures contracts and overstating the price of those contracts. In reality, much of the cash was commingled with personal monies and misappropriated to meet personal expenses, including mortgage and school fees.

Shortly after filing its complaint, the court ordered a preliminary injunction against further violations, a freeze on assets, and an order not to destroy books and records. A receiver was also appointed. Separately, the U.S. government brought another suit against Anderson, his wife and two related trusts, for tax violations.

In the CFTC case, a consent settlement was reached in which Anderson was ordered to pay $460,899 restitution and was barred for life from the commodity futures industry. In the tax case the Andersons (husband and wife) and their trusts, were ordered to pay $5 million to cover, outstanding state, county, and federal taxes. Liens were placed on the Andersons real estate property and the related costs for selling this asset was also covered by the settlement.

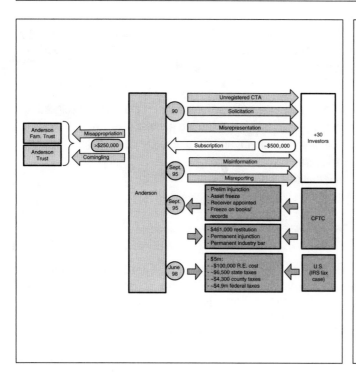

Fraud Facts

- Alleged Acts Date: 1990
- Enforcement Date: October 22, 1995
- Main Defendants **(hedge fund–related)**: **Anderson** (unregistered commodity trading adviser)
- Most Serious Charge: Misappropriation, tax evasion
- Hedge Fund Role: Defendant
- Damages $actual **($2005)**: $461,000 **($590,000)**
- No. of Investors: 30
- Highest Court: Civil
- Most Severe Sentence: $461,000 restitution, industry ban

Sanctions:

- Gary B. Anderson: $461,000 restitution, permanent industry ban, permanent injunction
- Gary B. Anderson (tax case): $5 million plus interest, liens on real estate
- Gail L. Anderson (tax case): $5 million plus interest, liens on real estate

Cases:

- *CFTC v. Anderson* (95cv05422, civil, N. Dist. Ill.)
- *U.S. v. Anderson* (98cv00317, civil, N. Dist. In.)

A former commodities broker, with a prior history of violations, set up a new commodity pool, lost a substantial portion of the invested capital, and then issued false reports to cover up the losses. Key points:

- CFTC case
- Defendant had a significantly blemished prior record that remained undisclosed
- Investor money was never placed into client trading accounts
- Misappropriation was substantial, direct, and from an early date
- Redemption refusals triggered investor action
- CFTC civil and federal criminal actions followed
- 41-month prison term and restitution in excess of $2 million ordered

Case Summary

Prior to establishing New Forest Capital Management, Inc., a CFTC-registered commodity pool, in 1994, Robert Besner had had at least one significant regulatory problem that was unknown to his new investors. In 1987, he had been fined $40,000 by the CME for "prearranged trading" and an "act of bad faith" involving a customer. He left the exchange in 1989.

In 1995, a year or less after raising as much as $4 million from his unsuspecting investors Besner was expelled from the National Futures Association, a fact also not disclosed. At the same time, he had been trading his investor's money under his own name and, according to reports, sustained sizeable losses in doing so. Instead of disclosing these losses, he sent the investors false reports claiming returns of as much as 40 percent. Perhaps compounding his sense of financial stress, Besner had earlier fought off a foreclosure action on his $600,000 house.

For the investors, the alarm bells did not start ringing until one or more of them requested redemptions and were refused on the grounds that the money was tied up in offshore accounts. This led to the initiation of private lawsuits, which were ultimately combined into a single involuntary bankruptcy case.

Around December 8, 1995, after meeting with an irate client, Besner, his wife, and two children locked up their house and fled. On December 27, a Cook County Circuit judge issued a freeze order on Besner's and New Forest's assets.

The CFTC filed a civil suit in January 1996, and a federal criminal action was filed in October 1997. The case brought to light the fact that as much as $2 million of investor money had been directly misappropriated to meet personal expenses. Besner pled guilty to one count of fraud in the latter action and was sentenced to 41 months' prison and ordered to pay $2.8 million restitution.

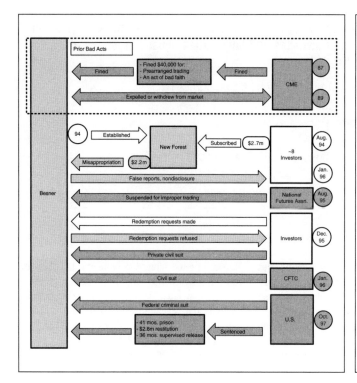

Fraud Facts

- Alleged Acts Date: August 1994
- Enforcement Date: January 4, 1996
- Main Defendants **(hedge fund–related): Besner (New Forest Capital Mgmt.)**
- Most Serious Charge: Criminal fraud
- Hedge Fund Role: Defendant
- Damages $actual **($2005)**: Approximately $4 million **(approximately $5 million)**
- No. of Investors: Approximately 8
- Highest Court: Criminal
- Most Severe Sentence: $2.8 million restitution, 41 months' prison

Sanctions:

- Robert A. Besner: $2.8 million restitution, 41 months' prison, 36 months' probation

Cases:

- *CFTC v. Besner* (96cv00076, civil, N. Dist. Ill.)
- *U.S. v. Besner* (97cr00731, criminal, N. Dist. Ill.)

A registered commodity trading adviser commenced a Ponzi scheme after generating steady losses for a group of investors and later turned himself in when redemptions outpaced subscriptions. Key points:

- Civil case against a CTA brought by both SEC and CFTC
- Lost 14 percent in January 1993
- Fictitious "paper trading"
- Ponzi scheme
- Unable to meet redemptions, the defendant turned himself in
- 60-month prison term
- Around 18 percent of assets recovered by receiver

Case Summary

In 1989, Michael Tropiano traded commodities futures for himself and some business associates. Over the next few years, he increased the number of investors and the amount he managed. One investor, Robert Tatarowicz, invested $123,000 and later became associated with Tropiano and his company, Ardmore Financial Services, in the soliciting of other investors. Anecdotal reports suggest that the trading at this time was factual and successful.

However, in January 1993, the funds under management are thought to have declined in value by around 14 percent. At this point, the commodities pools began operating as a Ponzi scheme, with "paper trading" results presented in fictitious reports sent to the investors. By January 1996, the recycling of subscription monies became unsustainable, making redemptions impossible, circumstances that alarmed some of the investors.

Tropiano turned himself over to the U.S. District Attorney in Cherry Hill, New Jersey. Shortly thereafter, a legal civil action was commenced jointly by the SEC and the CFTC. A criminal action was filed in October 1996. Tropiano pled guilty to 70 counts including: mail fraud, securities fraud, commodities fraud, and tax evasion. He was sentenced to 60 months in prison and had assets seized by the receiver. Tatarowicz, who had been involved in the sale of Ardmore's unregistered securities, was subject of an SEC administrative action, in which a settlement was reached resulting in the issuance of a cease-and-desist order against him. The receiver's efforts netted around $960,000, less costs and fees, including personal assets worth approximately $500,000, plus $350,000 remaining in the fund and the recovery of over $100,000 from a number of third-party defendants, after obtaining favorable judgments against them.

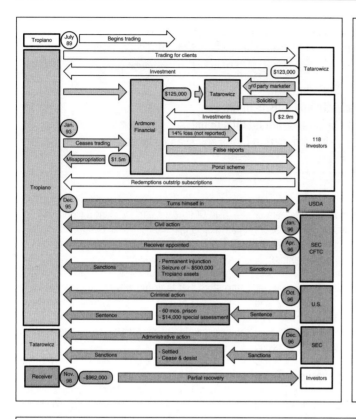

Fraud Facts

- Alleged Acts Date: 1989
- Enforcement Date:
  January 11, 1996
- Main Defendants
  **(hedge fund–related):
  Tropiano, Tatarowicz
  (Ardmore Financial
  Services)**
- Most Serious Charge:
  Criminal fraud
- Hedge Fund Role:
  Defendant
- Damages $actual
  ($2005): $2.9 million
  ($3.6 million)
- No. of Investors: 118
- Highest Court: Criminal
- Most Severe Sentence:
  60 months' prison

Sanctions:

- Patrick McGrath: $6,700 restitution
- Amy Sim: $1,700 restitution
- Robert Sim: $1,700 restitution
- James R. Smith: $101,700 restitution
- Robert Tatarowicz: cease & desist order
- Michael Tropiano: 60 months' prison, $3,500 special assessment, personal assets seized

Cases:

- *SEC v. Tropiano* (96cv00228, civil, Dist. N.J.)
- *U.S. v. Tropiano* (96cr00614, criminal, Dist. N.J.)

In this case, a registered commodity broker launched an investment partnership and then improperly borrowed money from the partnership that was never repaid. Key points:

- Case involved CFTC, SEC, and NASD
- Defendants included wife and a local bank
- Money embezzled to help fund defendant's house construction
- Defendant first tried using embezzled funds solely as collateral for a loan

Case Summary

In December 1994, Mark Shaner was president of CFTC-registered commodity broker Shaner & Co. At that time, he started selling limited partnership interests in Shaner Fund LP and, by October 1995, had raised an estimated $2.65 million. In April 1995, in the midst of the fund-raising period, Shaner improperly removed some $675,000 from the fund in order to purchase a certificate of deposit to be used as collateral for a personal $475,000 housing construction–related loan from Iowa State Bank and Trust. However, by October 1995, the Shaners had apparently defaulted on the loan after using around $100,000 of that money to pay personal expenses. In consequence, the Iowa State Bank accepted payment of $521,000 of the loan collateral.

Several lawsuits arose in the wake of these actions, including civil suits brought by the CFTC and the SEC, a federal criminal action, and an administrative proceeding by NASD. The Iowa State Bank was itself a defendant in the CFTC case for unjustly enriching itself by calling in the CD collateral. Shaner's wife, Jane, was also named as a defendant.

The CFTC case against Mark Shaner was one of misappropriation. The SEC case mentioned Shaner's misrepresentation and omission of material facts in using a substantial portion of the fund's assets to purchase a CD, while advising investors that their funds would be used to trade commodity futures, with one portion of the money allocated to futures margining and another portion held separately by the fund's clearing agent held in 90-day T-bills.

The result of these legal actions was a two-year prison term, with two years of supervised release, for pleading guilty to one count of embezzlement and converting a commodity fund's property in the criminal case. Other penalties included permanent injunction orders from the CFTC and SEC, a revocation of registration, an industry bar $621,805 restitution and a $100,000 fine from the NASD. The Iowa State Bank and Trust settled with the CFTC and agreed to repay $565,000, including the $521,804.85 it received from the CD plus around $44,000 interest.

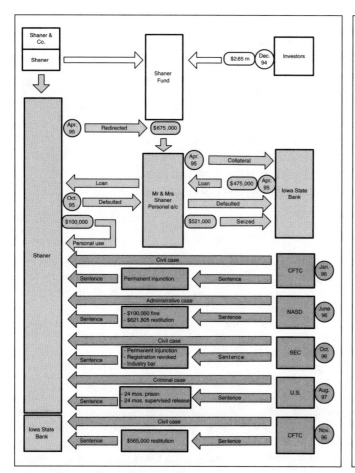

Fraud Facts

- Alleged Acts Date: December 1994
- Enforcement Date: January 4, 1996
- Main Defendants **(hedge fund–related): M. Shaner**, J. Shaner, Iowa State Bank & Trust **(Shaner & Company, Inc., Shaner Fund)**
- Most Serious Charge: Embezzlement
- Hedge Fund Role: Defendant
- Damages $actual **($2005): $622,000 ($770,000)**
- No. of Investors: NA
- Highest Court: Criminal
- Most Severe Sentence: 24 months' prison, $621,000 restitution, $100,000 fine

Sanctions:

- Mark Shaner: 24 months' prison, 24 months' supervised release, $621,803 restitution, $100,000 fine, permanent injunction, industry bar, revocation of registration
- Iowa State Bank and Trust: $565,000 restitution
- Shaner & Company: Permanent injunction, registration revoked

Cases:

- *CFTC v. Shaner* (96cv7005, civil, S. Dist. Ia.)
- *SEC v. Shaner* (96cv70767, civil, S. Dist. Ia.)
- *NASD Discp. Actns.*, June 96
- *U.S. v. Shaner* (97cr00124, criminal, S. Dist. Ia.)
- *U.S. v. Shaner* (98–2016, appeal, 8thC COA)

The defendant, sole executive of a broker-dealer, a hedge fund, and a hedge fund adviser, sent investors false reports after incurring substantial losses on directional short positions. Key points:

- SEC and CTFC civil and administrative cases filed
- Severe lack of checks and balances due to overconcentration of authority and limited staffing
- Fund subjected to risky directional short positions
- Defendant claimed misrepresentations due to innocent errors
- Lack of independent auditor kept problems from being known
- Appeal filed, including charges against some SEC staff—unsuccessful

Case Summary

Brett Brubaker established a broker-dealer, Abraham & Sons, in 1985 and procured his NASD registration the following year after accumulating 11 years of practical experience as an analyst. He appears to have been well thought of in the professional community. His views were often quoted in the financial press, and this exposure helped to secure institutional clients for Abraham & Sons.

Six years after establishing the broker-dealer Brubaker launched a hedge fund (Abraham & Sons, LP) and an SEC-registered Investment Adviser (Abraham & Sons Capital, Inc). At some point the operations moved from a New York home to a Chicago office. Brubaker was the sole principal of these businesses. The only other staff members were his wife, who acted as bookkeeper for the broker-dealer and a young trading assistant named Timothy Christiansen. At its peak in July 1995, the hedge fund had approximately 50 limited partners and assets of about $12.8 million.

As sole executive, Brubaker was the compliance officer in the broker-dealer, hedge fund, and hedge fund adviser. Brubaker and his investment advisory company (ASCI) were the only general partners of the hedge fund (ASLP). The concentration of authority and limitations on human resources, experience, and skills resulted in implicit conflicts of interest and vulnerabilities to change.

For Brubaker the sequence of events that brought him down, involved:

- A wrong bet on market direction, which led to a losing short position
- An unfortunately timed Christmas break, when prices moved against him unobserved

- A computer-based accounting system that either did not properly represent or was not properly utilized so that it could represent the short positions
- A misunderstood stock split in a shorted stock that led to an incorrect valuation of the fund's NAV
- A concentration of authority that limited the resources available for checking and reviewing of position accounts

The SEC instituted administrative proceedings in October 1997, charging Brubaker with defrauding his 50 limited partners by substantially overstating the value of the fund's assets over a six-month period, a time when the fund experienced a loss of around 50 percent of its NAV. In March 1998, the CFTC also filed a six-count complaint against Brubaker and ASCI for operating an unregistered commodity pool and defrauding its customers. Brubaker reached an agreement with the CFTC calling for:

- Cease and desist from future violations
- A permanent bar against future registration and/ or any activities requiring registration
- $3.5 million restitution

The SEC had similar sanctions but was only seeking civil penalties of $100,000 (from Brubaker and his investment advisory company). However, subsequent documents suggest that the SEC was not able to collect its fines. As late as 2005, it was still trying to collect this money via the courts. Brett Brubaker filed for bankruptcy under Chapter 7 in February 2003.

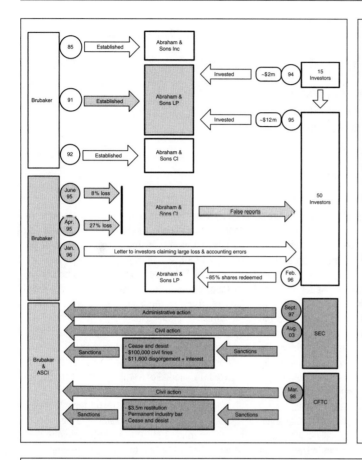

Fraud Facts

- Alleged Acts Date: 1992
- Enforcement Date: October 1997
- Main Defendants **(hedge fund–related): Brett Brubaker, Abraham & Sons Capital, Abraham & Sons LP**
- Most Serious Charge: Wire fraud
- Hedge Fund Role: Defendant investment adviser defrauded captive hedge fund
- Damages $actual **($2005)**: $3.5 million **($4.5 million)**
- No. of Investors: 50
- Highest Court: Civil
- Most Severe Sentence: $3.5 million restitution, $100,000 civil penalties

---

Sanctions:

- Brett Brubaker: $11,600 plus interest, disgorgement, $50,000 civil penalty
- Brett Brubaker: 6 months' suspension, cease & desist,
- $3.5 million restitution, industry bar
- Abraham & Sons Cap.: $50,000 civil penalties, cease & desist

---

Cases:

- *In the matter of Brubaker* (SEC Admin. Proc. No. 3–9448)
- *CFTC v. Brubaker* (CFTC Docket no. 98–7, administrative)
- *SEC v. Brubaker* (03cv01637, civil, Dist. Colorado.)
- *Brubaker—Chap 7 Bankruptcy* (03–08988, Ill. Bankruptcy Court)

Two individuals used false claims to lure several people into an unregistered commodity pool. Key points:

- CFTC case
- Unregistered commodity pool and pool operators
- Solicited among local residents
- Made claims that money could not be lost
- Investor funds were commingled with defendants

Case Summary

This is a thinly documented case centering on two Florida residents, Robert Hoffman and Michael Indihar, and the two local companies they owned or controlled: Computer Warehouse, Inc., and Automated Trading Systems Inc., both based in the upscale town of Jupiter in Palm Beach County, Florida. In a seven-count civil suit filed on April 1, 1996, the CFTC charged the two men and two companies, variously, as being unregistered commodity pools and acting as unregistered commodity pool operators, soliciting as such, making false claims as to their experience, performance, and strategies, and acting as futures commission merchants in executing trades.

The sparse facts available suggest that at some point in time one or both of the individuals had or purported to have developed a computerized system for trading commodity futures and that as early as July 1995, they had approached at least three other residents of their community with a proposal to invest some $17,000 with them. As the charges stated, Hoffman and Indihar told their prospective customers that they were "making lots of money" with the trading system and that it was "foolproof." It appears that the investor's money may have been invested in commodities—as there were no charges of misappropriation or embezzlement and no criminal case, but that substantially all of the money was subsequently lost in trading.

On April 3, Indihar's offices were searched by investigators and he was taken into custody and later released. As the legal matters went forward, the progress of the cases against Hoffman and Indihar took diverging paths. It appears that Indihar and the two companies were cooperative with the authorities and, by November 1996, had their case referred to mediation, while Hoffman remained uncooperative or unavailable.

Indihar's case was wound up on June 25, 1999, with a consent judgment including a permanent injunction and $24,309 restitution jointly and severally with the two companies, plus interest. This sum and intended civil fines were waived to zero based on financial statements supplied to the court showing the defendant's inability to pay. The case against Hoffman was brought to a close on September 29, 1999, with a default judgment comprising a permanent injunction and restitution of $55,940 including $12,189 interest.

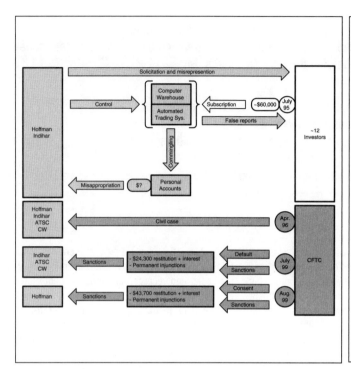

Fraud Facts

- Alleged Acts Date: July 1995
- Enforcement Date: April 1, 1996
- Main Defendants (**hedge fund–related**): Hoffman, Indihar (**Automated Trading Systems**), Computer Warehouse
- Most Serious Charge: Fraud
- Hedge Fund Role: Defendant
- Damages $actual (**$2005**): $68,000 (**$86,000**)
- No. of Investors: 12
- Highest Court: Civil
- Most Severe Sentence: $68,000 restitution, permanent injunction

Sanctions:

- Robert P. Hoffman: $55,940 restitution, including interest, permanent injunction
- Michael Indihar: $24,309 restitution, plus interest, permanent injunction
- Automated Trading Systems, Inc.: $24,309 restitution, plus interest, permanent injunction
- Computer Warehouse: $24,309 restitution, plus interest, permanent injunction

Cases:

- *CFTC v. Indihar* (96cv08202, civil, S. Dist. Fl.)

An unregistered commodity pool operator (CPO) victimized members of his church to invest in his unregistered commodity pool (CP), after which he lost some of the money in poor trading and embezzled the rest. Key points:

- Unregistered CPO
- Pastor and a "missionary" enlisted as aiders and abettors
- Victimized other church member investors
- 26 percent of money traded, 18 percent paid to aiders and abettors, approximately 60 percent embezzled
- Main perpetrator reoffended in a similar scheme in another state 10 years later

Case Summary

In 1992, Keith Dominick, a resident of Kissimmee, Florida, began soliciting investors in several states on behalf of Main Street Investment Group, his unregistered CP, and misrepresenting his investment strategy while doing so. Dominick was aided in raising money from members of the Heartland Worship Center by its pastor, Rev. Smith, and a "missionary," Blevins. These three, with several others, succeeded in gathering around $6 million from some 70 believing investors. Approximately $1.6 million of the money collected was used to trade commodity futures, generally unsuccessfully, though investors only received falsified reports indicating positive gains.

The involvement of the clergyman and missionary give this case an "affinity crime" aspect. Smith had received $378,000 for his solicitation of $1.5 million from 38 investors and, Blevins received commissions of $305,000 for his raising of $2.5 million from at least eight investors. In addition to these commissions, Dominick also made a $500,000 donation to the Heartland church as well as a $19,000 contribution to a charity Blevins was affiliated with. It was later found that Dominick also directed large payments to several other individuals (Moat, Swart, and Tanzillo, who were also investors).

On May 12, 1994, Dominick received a letter from the CFTC requesting an examination of his books and records, and about a month later, the CFTC filed a civil complaint together with a temporary restraining order, an asset freeze, and the appointment of a temporary receiver. The investigation found that Dominick had deployed around $1.6 million in commodities futures trading, and recycled some cash back to investors to meet redemptions. The majority of the investor capital, however, went to meet Dominick's personal expenses, as well as paying "commissions" and "donations" to Rev. Smith and Blevins.

A criminal suit was filed against Dominick on June 13, 1997. He pled guilty to two counts of embezzlement and received a 37-month prison sentence and a restitution order of $4.5 million. Smith, Blevins, and several other local church-related individuals were also ordered to pay restitution.

As a footnote, Dominick was found guilty in 2005 of perpetrating a very similar scheme in Ohio. In a criminal action there, he was sentenced to one count of securities fraud and sentenced to 51 months in prison, three years' supervised release, and ordered to pay $912,300 restitution.

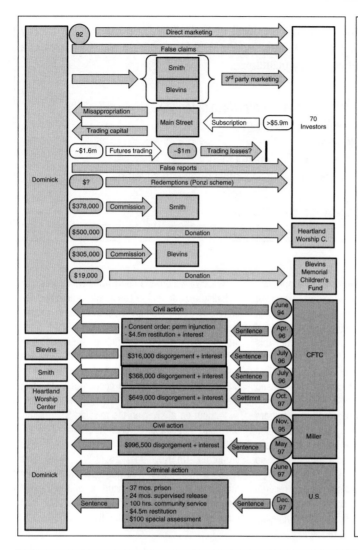

Fraud Facts

- Alleged Acts Date: 1992
- Enforcement Date: June 15, 1994
- Main Defendants (**hedge fund–related**): Blevins, **Dominick**, Smith, Heartland Worship Center, **Main Street Investment Group**
- Most Serious Charge: Embezzlement
- Hedge Fund Role: Defendant
- Damages $actual (**$2005**): $6.2 million (**$7.7 million**)
- No. of Investors: 70
- Highest Court: Criminal
- Most Severe Sentence: 37 months' prison

Sanctions:

- Ray Bartolo: $375 disgorgement
- Jay Blevins: $377,616 disgorgement (plus interest)
- Keith Dominick: 37 months' prison, 24 months' supervised release, 100 hours community service, $4,528,237 restitution
- David Piercefield: $1,400 disgorgement
- David Moats: $26,300 disgorgement
- Wayne Richard: $100,500 plus interest restitution
- Gary Smith: $441,487 disgorgement (plus interest)
- Andrew Tanzillo: $39,000 disgorgement
- Heartland Worship Center: $648,779.03 plus interest restitution

Cases:

- *CFTC v. Dominick* (94cv00661, civil, M. Dist. Fl.)
- *Miller v. Dominick* (95cv01135, civil, M. Dist. Fl.)
- *U.S. v. Dominick* (97cr00111, criminal, M. Dist. Fl.)

An unregistered CPO raised money to invest in a strategy based upon "complexity theory." A subsequent investor complaint and refusal to cooperate with CFTC led to a civil suit and a contempt order. Key points:

- Unregistered CPO
- Working from a rustic cabin in a remote Washington valley
- Got 274 investors to subscribe $17.5 million
- No fund/pool vehicle named
- Claimed to be using esoteric "complexity theory"
- Refused to tell CFTC about missing $12 million—jailed seven months for contempt
- At least $5.5 million recovered by court receiver

Case Summary

In the early 1990s, Ken Willey lived in a primitive wood cabin in a remote valley on the eastern edge of the enormous area comprising the North Cascades, Okanogan, and Wenatchee National Forests, which is about 70 miles inland from Seattle. From this cabin, he managed roughly $17.5 million of assets in an unregistered commodity pool on behalf of 274 investors by a method he claimed to be based upon "complexity theory."

While the investors were receiving reports from Willey indicating that they were earning reasonable returns on their capital, the accountant of one investor became concerned about the numbers he saw and contacted the CFTC, which resulted in a request for Willey to produce his books and records for inspection. From the CFTC perspective, Willey was already violating the Commodity Code by managing a commodity pool without being registered.

In a civil action, the court froze Willey's assets, including a $380,000 account with a commodities broker. No other money was discovered related to commodities trading. All told, the CFTC located around $5.5 million, including a number of Willey's other accounts. That left some $12 million unaccounted for. Willey was cited for contempt on May 8, 1996, for failing to cooperate in locating these other assets and was placed in jail.

Without an answer on the missing $12 million, the court appointed a receiver on the July 26, 1996, and a distribution of remaining assets was organized. On November 26, 1997, Willey was released from custody, having spent about seven months in jail, and the court issued a default judgment including a permanent injunction and further discovery on November 5.

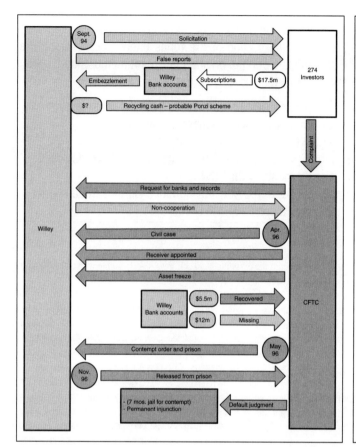

Fraud Facts

- Alleged Acts Date: January 1991
- Enforcement Date: April 9, 1996
- Main Defendants **(hedge fund–related): Ken Willey**
- Most Serious Charge: Wire Fraud
- Hedge Fund Role: Unregistered commodity pool
- Damages $actual **($2005): $17.5 million ($21.7 million)**
- No. of Investors: 274
- Highest Court: Civil
- Most Severe Sentence: 7 months' jail for contempt

Sanctions:

- Ken Willey: 7 months' jail for contempt, permanent injunction, $5 million recovered by receiver

Cases:

- *CFTC v. Willey* (96cv00200, civil, E. Dist. Wa.)

Defendant managed an unregistered and undisclosed commodity pool while employed as a broker. After losing a substantial portion of the funds under management, the defendant abandoned the strategy laid out in a private placement memorandum (PPM) without notifying the investors of this change. Key points:

- Like Doviak (see Case 22), Prendergast utilized results from the same investment championship contest to attract investors and promote performance
- Enforcement action initiated by CFTC and pursued by NASD
- An unregistered hedge fund managed by a broker employee and not disclosed
- Use of funds contrary to statements in the PPM
- A recidivist, Prendergast was convicted of a subsequent securities fraud shortly after this enforcement action (Falcon Financial Group)

Case Summary

In September 1991, Prendergast placed among the top 30 in the "conservative growth" category of a national investment championship contest run by Norm Zadeh's Money Manager Verified Rating Service. The results were widely followed at the time and enabled unknown money managers to attract investors. Several of the contestants, as well as the contest organizer, Norman Zadeh, ended up in subsequent enforcement actions. (See Case 17, Doviak, and Case 64, Zadeh.)

On January 6, 1994, Prendergast's Prism Financial Corporation distributed a PPM offering document, the summary of which stated that the company had been created six months earlier to "promote investment concepts and products based upon proprietary computerized trading programs developed by . . . Brian Prendergast." At that time, Prendergast was a Registered Representative employed by AmeriNational Financial Services, Inc.

About $920,000 was raised from some 34 investors. It was claimed that the funds would be invested, 60 percent in a "hedge fund," which the PPM described as: "elements of traditional products" combined with a "proprietary S&P 500 stock index trading program." The remaining 40 percent of funds was to be allocated to market timing of mutual funds. It was implied that the mutual fund investment was a hedge for the stock index trading, and would act as a form of "principal protection."

A number of S&P 500 transactions were made in March 1994. These realized a loss of $71,960.70 out of $262,000 (–27.5 percent) at the end of the first month. This pattern continued for a further eight months, along with a steady drift away from S&P 500 futures to government fixed income securities and ultimately to foreign currencies. By November, the $543,500 in the trading account had diminished to $64,000, a cumulative loss of over 88 percent.

On September 9, a trading account was opened with Rocky Mountain Securities & Investments. Earlier trades had been executed by Prendergast's employer AmeriNational, though without disclosing the existence of the Prism fund as required. Prendergast also failed to notify his employer of the new account with Rocky Mountain.

Enforcement action commenced on February 20, 1996, with the filing of a complaint and preliminary injunction by the CFTC against Brian Prendergast, Joel de Angelis, Prism Financial Corp. and AmeriNational, and also authorized the NASD to take custody of books and records and investigate Prism. NASD filed a complaint on August 2, 1996, charging Prendergast with (1) not having a broker/dealer registration; (2) investing in a manner inconsistent with the private placement memorandum; (3) material misrepresentations in the PPM; (4) communications with purchasers did not conform to standards; (5) failure to notify employer of an account with another member and vice versa; and (6) failure to provide information requested by NASD.

Prendergast was censured and barred from associating with any member firm in any capacity. The SEC reviewed the findings on appeal in 2001 and upheld the NASD sanctions. The court also granted an order of permanent injunction against Joel De Angelis, another principal of Prism Financial, on January 10, 1997, and against Brian Prendergast on the January 27. The following day the court issued a default judgment against Prism Financial. AmeriNational was ordered to disgorge $2496.16 to the benefit of Prism customers, and Prism to disgorge $946,148 to the Commission (CFTC) for the Prism investors. Prendergast filed for voluntary personal bankruptcy in 1997 and started another fraudulent scheme the same year.

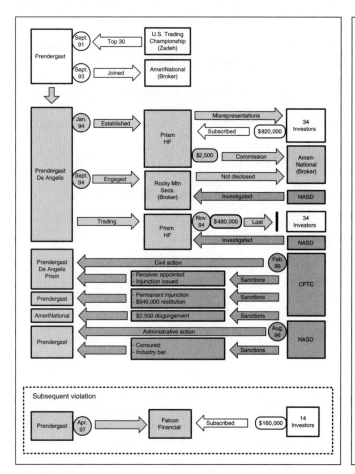

Fraud Facts

- Alleged Acts Date: January 1994
- Enforcement Date: February 1996
- Defendants **(hedge funds): Joel de Angelis, Brian Prendergast**, AmeriNational Financial Services, **Prism Financial**
- Most Serious Charge: Fraud
- Hedge Fund Role: Defendant in fraud action
- Damages $actual **($2005)**: Approximately $920,000 **($1.1 million)**
- No. of Investors: 34
- Highest Court: Civil
- Most Severe Sentence: $946,000 restitution

Sanctions:

- Brian Prendergast: Permanent injunction (CFTC), censured and barred (NASD)
- Joel Deangelis: Permanent injunction (CFTC)
- AmeriNational Financial Services: $2,496 disgorgement
- Prism Financial Corp.: $946,148 restitution

Cases:

- *CFTC v. Prism* (96cv00389, civil, Dist. Co.)
- *In the matter of Prendergast* (NASD No. C3A960033)
- *Prendergast*, 97–17759 (bankruptcy, Dist. Co.)

When an unregistered commodity pool suffered disastrous losses in trading, its unregistered pool operator resorted to deception to hide the true facts from the investors as well as from other principals of the pool operator. Key points:

- Unregistered CP and CPO partly defrauded another unregistered CP and CPO and 12 of their investors
- Main defendant claimed to be a commodity futures trader and to have developed a trading system
- Trading soon incurred losses that wiped out most of the investors' money
- Trader then sought to hide the losses via deception
- When, apparently not able to resort to a Ponzi scheme, the main defendant confessed to associates

Case Summary

Sometime around January 1993, Christopher Schafer, a resident of Alpharetta, Georgia, sole proprietor of an unregistered entity called A.R.S. Financial Services, was soliciting for commodity futures investors. Among other things, Schafer mentioned good returns and claimed to have developed a trading system. Documents suggest that he succeeded in attracting some investors by these means and that by March 1995 most of these investors were directed to place their money into the Genesis Limited Partnership, an unregistered commodity pool.

Shafer had also formed a commercial association with the Alchemy Financial Group, Inc., a Texas corporation, and its two principals, Peter Urbani and William Eldridge. None of these entities had ever been registered with the CFTC. Eldridge and Urbani had also been soliciting for Genesis pool investors from their base in Cypress, Texas. In concert, these parties raised between $107,000 to $253,000 from some 12 to 15 individuals. Within this commercial collaboration, Schafer was the trader, and was entitled to receive 25 percent of the Genesis profits, while Urbani and Eldridge were to receive 12.5 percent each. There were some indications that Schafer was misappropriating and commingling funds from Alchemy for his own personal trading and was also redistributing gains to cover losses among the accounts.

By January 1996, Schafer's trading resulted in a catastrophic loss of investor capital, and he decided to pursue a course of further deception rather than admitting fault. Urbani and Eldridge later claimed that they too had been deceived along with the investors. In March 1996, at a time when the Genesis NAV was nearly zero, Schafer stated that the Genesis pool had assets worth $161,000, implying profits of more than $90,000.

On April 17, 1996, the CFTC filed a civil complaint, naming Schafer, ARS, Alchemy, Eldridge, and Urbani as defendants. The CFTC filed a separate civil action in Georgia solely against Schafer in June 1998 on a related case (for which he was ordered to pay restitution of $249,785). In the Texas trial, Schafer was ordered to pay restitution of $109,300 and was banned from the industry. With Alchemy, he was ordered to jointly and severally pay restitution of $70,832.

In May 1999, 1 of the 15 original Genesis investors had recovered $3,793 in a separate small claims court case; another had redeemed before the case; and a third was excluded for reasons that are not clear. The remaining 12 had received $14,134 in partial restitution, leaving an unpaid balance of $70,832.

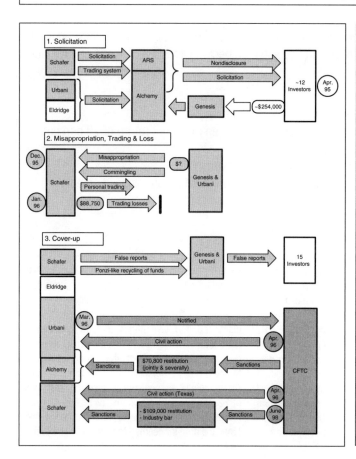

Fraud Facts

- Alleged Acts Date: March 1995
- Enforcement Date: April 17, 1996
- Main Defendants **(hedge fund–related): Eldridge, Schafer, Urbani (Alchemy, ARS, Genesis LP)**
- Most Serious Charge: Felony fraud
- Hedge Fund Role: Defrauded by its CPO
- Damages $actual **($2005)**: Approximately $107,000 **($140,000)**
- No. of Investors: 15
- Highest Court: Civil
- Most Severe Sentence: $109,000 civil penalty, industry bar

Sanctions:

- Christopher Schafer: $109,000 restitution, industry bar
- Peter Urbani: $71,000 restitution (w/ Alchemy)
- Alchemy Financial Group: $71,000 restitution (w/ Alchemy)

Cases:

- *CFTC v. Schafer* (96cv01213, civil, S. Dist. Tx.)
- *CFTC v. Schafer* (98cv01594, civil, N. Dist. Ga.)
- *Matz v. Urbani* (no. 30574, Sm. Clms. Ct. Pct. 5, Pl. 1 Harris Co., Tx.)

Investors were defrauded by the operator of an unregistered commodity pool who embezzled the majority of the money and then became a fugitive to avoid enforcement. Key points:

- CFTC case
- Apparently no trading of fund, pure embezzlement
- Claimed to use a promissory note to guarantee minimum return of 23 percent
- Defendant became a fugitive
- Defendant committed suicide while a fugitive
- Restitution and stiff civil penalty of three times restitution imposed on estate

Case Summary

Commencing in 1991, Donald Chancey of Valdosta, Georgia, started soliciting for investors in an unregistered CP, Southeastern Venture Partners Group, and was able to raise about $3 million from at least 19 investors. One inducement offered to these investors was an alleged promissory note guaranteeing a return of 23 percent per annum.

It is not clear whether any of the money was invested in commodities as indicated, but most, if not all, was embezzled by Chancey for personal use. In July 1996, the CFTC filed a civil complaint and the FBI sought to question him. Sensing that his time as a practicing fraudster was drawing short,

Chancey became a fugitive of the law. A warrant for his arrest was issued however, when the marshals caught up with him in Louisiana, Chancey was dead of a gunshot wound, an apparent suicide.

After his death, the criminal charges were dismissed, but civil litigation continued against his estate. On May 13, 1999, the court issued a default judgment against the estate of Donald Chancey and Southeastern Venture Partners Group, jointly and severally, ordering restitution of $2,948,831 and a civil fine of $8,846,494 plus interest, the latter sum being a punitive fine of three times the amount deemed to have been embezzled.

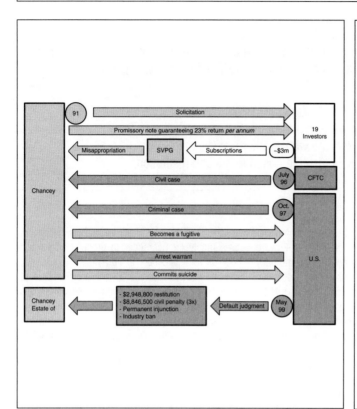

Fraud Facts

- Alleged Acts Date: 1991
- Enforcement Date: July 1, 1996
- Main Defendants **(hedge fund–related): Chancey**, Chancey Estate **(Southeastern Venture PartnersGroup)**
- Most Serious Charge: Mail fraud
- Hedge Fund Role: Defendant in fraud action
- Damages $actual **($2005)**: Approximately $3.0 million **($4.5 million)**
- No. of Investors: 19
- Highest Court: Criminal (dismissed due to death of defendant)
- Most Severe Sentence: $2.9 million restitution, $8.8 million civil fine

Sanctions:

- Estate of D. Chancey: $2.9 million restitution, $8.8 million civil fine, industry bar, permanent injunction
- Southeastern V. P. Group.: (joint and several)

Cases:

- *CFTC v. Chancey* (96cv00061, civil, USDC M. Dist. Ga.)
- *U.S. v. Chancey* (97cr00044, criminal, USDC, M. Dist. Ga.)

After losing more than a third of his investors' capital in trading, the operator of an unregistered CPO resorted to numerous frauds to maintain operations, including an arrangement with another unregistered CPO to launder money. Key points:

- CFTC case
- Unregistered CP and CPO
- Substantial trading losses led to fraud
- Money laundering scheme with another unregistered CPO
- Civil and criminal suits result in prison terms and restitution

Case Summary

Beginning around June 1990, Edward Schroeder began soliciting for investors in the Edward Schroder Living Trust, an unregistered commodity pool based in Los Angeles. He ultimately succeeded in attracting around 40 investors and $3 million. In trading and managing this pool, Schroeder was assisted by Andre Fite. Schroeder and his Trust were accused of converting customer money for personal use, and any trading they did resulted in an accumulated loss of over $1 million. However, investors were provided false reports to hide the reality of these losses. Some investors were told that that the pool had a record of 62 months of consecutive positive returns and that annual returns of 18 to 36 percent were guaranteed.

At some point, Schroeder formulated an additional scheme with Carl Hermans and his unregistered business entity, California Traders Group, to launder the Living Trust money in what seemed to be a further effort to falsify the trading results. Hermans had also raised some $100,000 for investors in his entity.

There is evidence that the CFTC first started pursuing Schroeder in February 1996 in a civil action to enforce an administrative subpoena, presumably for Schroeder to produce books and records for inspection. In July of the same year, the Commission followed up with a civil securities fraud suit, which included a restraining order and asset freeze. In July 1997, Andre Fite consented to the imposition of a permanent injunction and this appears to be the only enforcement action taken against him.

In August 1997, Schroeder was ordered to pay restitution of over $2.6 million and disgorgement of $45,722. A receiver was appointed and plans were drawn up to distribute assets to the investors. In July 1999, Schroeder and Hermans were indicted in a criminal action, probably when the separate money laundering scheme came to light as a result of the earlier investigations. Both men received 15-month prison terms. Schroeder and Hermans were convicted of mail fraud and aiding and abetting. Hermans was also ordered to pay restitution of $387,600 at the rate of $300 per month. In November 2002, Schroeder was found guilty of violating his supervised release and received an additional six months of prison time.

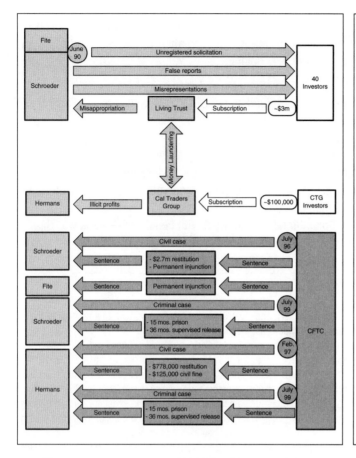

Fraud Facts

- Alleged Acts Date: June 1990
- Enforcement Date: July 1, 1996
- Main Defendants **(hedge fund–related):** Fite, Hermans, **Schroeder (California Traders Assn, Schroeder Living Trust)**
- Most Serious Charge: Money laundering
- Hedge Fund Role: Defendant in fraud action
- Damages $actual **($2005):** Approximately $3.0 million **($3.7 million)**
- No. of Investors: 40
- Highest Court: Criminal
- Most Severe Sentence: 15 months' prison, $2.7 million restitution

Sanctions:

- Andre Fite: Permanent injunction
- Carl Hermans: 15 months' prison, 3 years' supervised release, $778,200 restitution, $125,000 civil fine, permanent injunction
- Edward Schroeder: 15 months' prison, 3 years' supervised release, $2.69 million restitution, including $45,700 disgorgement, permanent injunction, 2-year bar

Cases:

- *CFTC v. Schroeder* (96cv01023, civil, C. Dist. Ca.)
- *CFTC v. Schroeder* (96cv04563, civil, C. Dist. Ca.)
- *CFTC v. Hermans* (97cv00777, civil, C. Dist. Ca.)
- *U.S. v. Schroeder* (99cr00742, criminal, C. Dist. Ca.)
- *U.S. v. Hermans* (99cr00742, criminal, C. Dist. Ca.)

The defendant, a hedge fund manager, was sued for breach of contract by an investor after the defendant was charged with market manipulation by the SEC and CFTC for cornering the U.S. Treasury market. Key points:

- Fenchurch cornered the U.S. Treasury note market
- Investigations and civil suits were filed by the CFTC, CBT, SEC, and the Federal Reserve Bank of New York (N.Y. Fed)
- $600,000 civil fine was imposed
- Fenchurch hedge fund investor sued the company for breach of contract
- Investor claimed damages for manager's failure to disclose investigations
- Investor also claimed failure to observe capital preservation measures set forth in the private placement memorandum
- Defendant argued that plaintiff had no contract with Fenchurch—case was ultimately dismissed with prejudice

Case Summary

This is a complex case comprising: (1) the defendant Fenchurch Capital's serious violations as a proprietary trader in cornering the U.S. Treasury markets; and (2), allegations that Fenchurch, as a hedge fund manager for the Gamma Fund, failed to disclose the investigation of the Treasury market violations by the SEC and CFTC, and in its apparent failure to implement capital preservation policies set out in the fund's PPM.

The sequence of events started around September 1992, when Galaxy Investments, Inc., having received a PPM for the Fenchurch Gamma Fund, subscribed to nearly $2 million of shares and subscribed a further $.5 million in February 1993. In June 1993 and possibly at other times, Fenchurch Capital, acting on its own behalf, engineered a series of complex trades in the U.S. Treasury note market and in its related "repo" market, including the purchase of these securities at auction by itself and related companies and the arranging of collateral for them. The effect of these actions was to create a corner in a particular note that was, at that time, the "cheapest to deliver" by short-sellers, forcing them to purchase the more expensive next-cheapest-to-deliver Treasury note, thereby generating a profit

for Fenchurch, who had tied up a number of these more expensive notes as well.

Galaxy's case was based on its breach of contract claims that it would have redeemed all of its Gamma Fund shares at an earlier date, prior to a precipitous decline in the latter part of 1995, had Fenchurch disclosed the regulatory investigations (SEC and CFTC) and by the apparent fact of having not been in compliance with SEC codes, as well as implicitly having been at variance with Fenchurch's own management policies stated in its PPM. This private placement memorandum, among other provisions, called for selling assets that declined by more than 10 percent. Galaxy had redeemed its shares in November 1995, realizing some $2.75 million (as against the roughly $2.5 million it subscribed), when it could have redeemed as much as $4.3 million at an earlier date had it been properly informed.

In its SEC–CFTC Treasury market case (filed in July 1996), Fenchurch was ultimately ordered to pay a fine of $600,000. However, the case brought by Galaxy, while judged to be a valid claim by an appeal court, was, nevertheless, dismissed with prejudice.

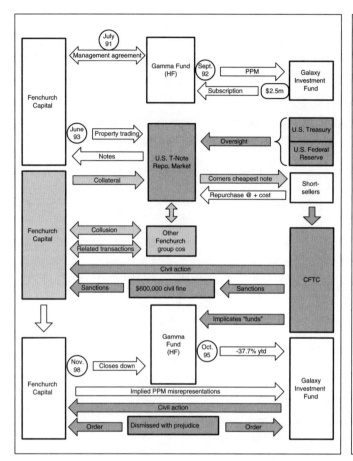

Fraud Facts

- Alleged Acts Date: June 1993
- Enforcement Date: July 10, 1996
- Main Defendants **(hedge fund–related): Fenchurch Capital Mgmt, Fenchurch Gamma Fund**
- Most Serious Charge: Market manipulation
- Hedge Fund Role: Allegedly defrauded by investment adviser
- Damages $actual **($2005)**: Sought in Galaxy case: $1.6 million **($2.2 million)**: SEC Treasury case: $750,000 **($1.0 million)**
- No. of Investors: 1
- Highest Court: Civil
- Most Severe Sentence: $600,000 civil penalty (Galaxy case dismissed)

Sanctions:

- **Fenchurch Capital Mgmt:** $600,000 civil penalty, cease-and-desist order, reporting requirements

Cases:

- *SEC v. Fenchurch Capital* (96cv04162, civil, N. Dist. Ill.)
- *Galaxy Inv. Fund v. Fenchurch* (96cv8098, civil, N. Dist. Ill.)

The defendant acted as an unregistered commodity pool operator who commingled investor money and provided investors with false reports after losses were incurred. Key points:

- CFTC case
- Unregistered CPO and CP
- CPO commenced trading, but resorted to fraud when money was lost
- CFTC brought a civil case, which defendant settled and agreed to make restitution
- Receiver appointed and made a distribution of remaining assets

Case Summary

From January 1996 or earlier, Everett Hobbs, an unregistered CPO based in Anderson, California, solicited prospective investors by telephone and mail for his unregistered commodity pool, Commodity Futures Investment. He raised around $375,000 from some 25 investors. When Hobbs' trading started registering losses, he falsified reports to the investors in at least one case, claiming to have earned 12 percent or more per month. Hobbs' illegal actions were added to by his failure to operate the commodity pool as a separate legal entity and his commingling of investors funds with his own.

The CFTC filed a civil complaint on August 13, 1996, and followed with a temporary restraining order a few days later. Over the next several months the CFTC successively imposed a preliminary injunction and appointed a permanent receiver while discovery continued apace.

In December 1997, plans to go to trial were averted when Hobbs agreed to settle the case and a final order and judgment were issued in 1999 on March 25 and 30, respectively. In addition to the imposition of a permanent injunction, Hobbs was ordered to pay restitution of $327,241 plus interest. On July 9, 1999, the receiver produced a final distribution plan for the funds and terminating his appointment.

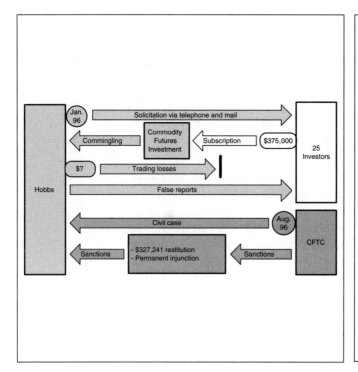

Fraud Facts
- Alleged Acts Date: January 1996
- Enforcement Date: August 13, 1996
- Main Defendants **(hedge fund–related): Hobbs (Commodity Futures Investment)**
- Charge: Fraud, Unregistered CP, commingling,
- Hedge Fund Role: Defendant in fraud action
- Damages $actual **($2005)**: Approximately $327,000 **($405,000)**
- No. of Investors: 25
- Highest Court: Civil
- Most Severe Sentence: $327,000 restitution

Sanctions:
- Everett Hobbs: $327,241 restitution plus interest, permanent injunction

Cases:
- *CFTC v. Hobbs* (96cv05946, civil, E. Dist.E. Dist. Ca.)

The principal defendant and several accomplices engineered two scams targeting elderly individuals. One of the scams attracted investors into two unregistered commodity pools billed as "investment clubs" from which most of the money was misappropriated. Key points:

- SEC and CFTC case
- Subject of administrative, civil, and criminal actions
- Two different scams: fake certificates of deposit, and misappropriation from unregistered commodity pools
- CD scam employed the ruse of a fictitious international bank
- Other scam made use of purported "investment clubs"
- Targeted elderly individuals
- Principal defendant was assisted in scams by tax preparer and others
- Most money was misappropriated, little if anything recovered

Case Summary

The defendants in this case were implicated in two separate scams, only one of which involved fraudulent activities relating to commodity pools or hedge funds. This aspect of the case was pursued by the CFTC and concerned actions dating from October 1992. The other aspect of the case, which was subject to SEC enforcement, involved a fraudulent CD investment scam which victimized some 120 investors, mainly elderly retired individuals in Michigan, and $3 million of their money.

In the CFTC case, some 57 elderly individuals in Michigan invested a total of about $1 million in two unregistered commodity pools that Berus had established (Profit Masters, and Meca International), both of which were presented as "investment clubs." Thirty-seven of the number subscribed $700,000 with Profit Masters and 20 subscribed $300,000 in Meca International. Prospects were told that the investments bore little risk and were expected to generate an annual return of 12 to 24 percent. A doctored track record was also presented. A proportion of the investors to these "clubs" were knowingly lured in by Patricia Gale, a tax preparer/

financial adviser who worked with Berus and who received commission for doing so.

About $600,000 of the funds invested were misappropriated by Berus, most of it to pay his personal expenses. Some of this money was "recycled" in a Ponzi fashion to pay fictitious dividends and redemptions. Around $400,000 was invested in commodity futures and options. Of this sum, $177,000 (44 percent) was apparently lost in trading.

In September 1996, both the SEC and CFTC filed civil complaints against Berus and Gale and also named Meca International (in the CFTC case) and three other individuals (in the SEC case) as defendants. In July 1999, Berus was also the subject of a criminal suit, in which he did a deal involving a guilty plea on one count of mail fraud and was sentenced to 15 months in prison, 36 months of supervised release, and $450,000 restitution, though this was waived based on his ability to pay.

In the civil suits, Berus and Gale received permanent injunctions against future violations and Berus and Meca were banned from the industry. Gale was also ordered to disgorge $10,000 of ill-gotten gains received as commissions.

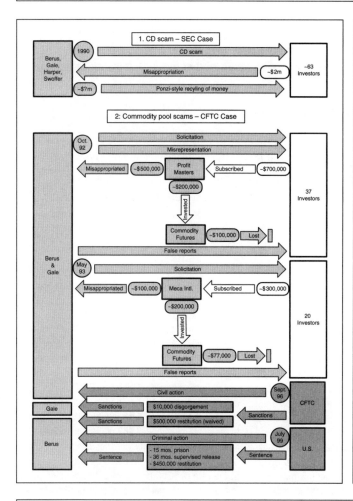

Fraud Facts

- Alleged Acts Date: October 1992
- Enforcement Date: September 30, 1996
- Main Defendants **(hedge fund–related): Berus**, Gale, M. Harper, R. Harper, Swoffer **(Profit Masters, Meca Intl.)**
- Most Serious Charge: Mail fraud
- Hedge Fund Role: Defendant
- Damages $actual **($2005)**: $3 million, of which $1 million in commodity pool scams **($1.38 million)**
- No. of Investors: 120
- Highest Court: Criminal
- Most Severe Sentence: 15 months' prison, $450,000 restitution, waived

---

Sanctions:

- Gary Berus: 15 months' prison, 36 months' supervised release, $450,000 restitution (waived), permanent injunction, industry bar
- Patricia Gale: $10,000 disgorgement
- Ronald Harper: Permanent injunction, industry bar
- Meca Intl: Permanent injunction, industry bar

Cases:

- *SEC v. Berus* (96cv74524, civil, E. Dist.E. Dist. Mich.)
- *CFTC v. Berus* (96cv74525, civil, E. Dist.E. Dist. Mich.)
- *In the matter of Berus* (SEC Admin. Proc. 3–9365)
- *U.S. v. Berus* (99cr80742, criminal, E. Dist.E. Dist. Mich.)

In this case, the defendant acted as an unregistered commodity trading adviser in soliciting investor money to trade commodity options and futures. Most of the money raised was lost over the next four to five years and some was misappropriated. Key points:

- Registered CTA until 1984
- Criminal securities case in 1987
- Massage therapist and business broker in the 1990s
- Held himself out as CTA in 1990s while not registered
- Solicited approximately $100,000 from six investors
- Misappropriated and/or lost approximately two-thirds of the investors' money
- Case settled with agreement to pay restitution and banned from industry

Case Summary

When questioned by the CFTC on January 23, 1997, in Richardson, Texas, Eugene Walter claimed that his income in the early 1990s had been solely derived from his work as a massage therapist and that in the last two years he had also been working as a "business broker." This latter employment was for a company called "I Need A Business, Inc.," which purported to find small businesses for people that wanted to buy them. This business was a scam run by Ronald Digiorno, himself subject to a criminal action several years later. However, the CFTC's central interest at that time was the fact that Walter had held himself out as a commodity trading adviser when he was not registered to do so. Under this guise and employing various misrepresentations he solicited close to $95,000 from six investors for the intended purpose of trading commodity futures and options.

From July 1992, Walter started receiving money from his investors. The monies were deposited in Walter's trading account, Vision Limited Partnership. Over the next four to five years, $62,000 of this money was lost and almost $10,000 was later shown to have been misappropriated for Walter's personal use.

On September 30, 1996, the CFTC filed a civil complaint against Walter and a settlement was reached the following June in which Walter agreed to repay his investors all $62,000 of the money they lost. However, since he had established with the CFTC that he had no net assets, he would only pay at the rate of $200 per quarter (implying 77 years to reach his goal, not including any interest). He also agreed to a permanent injunction and a permanent industry ban.

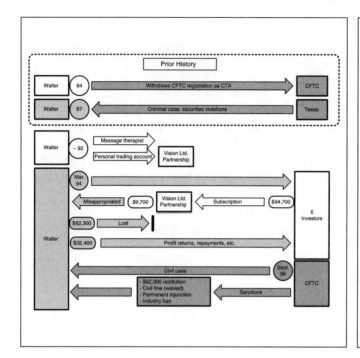

Fraud Facts

- Alleged Acts Date: July 31, 1992
- Enforcement Date: September 30, 1996
- Main Defendants (hedge fund–related): **Walter, Vision Ltd. Partnership**
- Most Serious Charge: Fraud
- Hedge Fund Role: Defendant acted as an unregistered CTA
- Damages $actual **($2005): $62,000 ($86,000)**
- No. of Investors: 6
- Highest Court: Civil
- Most Severe Sentence: $62,000 restitution, industry ban

Sanctions:

- Eugene Walter: $62,300 restitution, permanent injunction, industry bar

Cases:

- *CFTC v. Walter* (96cv02734, civil, N. Dist. Tx.)

Two criminal associates employed multiple deceits to raise money and hold onto the money while their fund rapidly lost most of its value in reckless trades and misappropriations. Key points:

- Defendants launched a hedge fund with a prospectus containing gross misrepresentations
- Over $13 million was raised and the fund was recommended by at least one prominent consultancy (Van Hedge Fund Advisors)
- Van Hedge Fund also invested $850,000 via its fund-of-funds, Bernoulli Fund, LP
- Only 26 percent of the assets remained after less than a year of reckless trading and misappropriation
- Civil, criminal, and class action suits were filed
- Both perpetrators were imprisoned and ordered to pay substantial restitution

Case Summary

The case began with two perpetrators, two hedge funds, and substantial misrepresentation and ended with substantial loss and criminal sentences. Beginning in September 1995, defendants Bell and Rubel raised $13.3 million from about 32 investors for their Theta Group hedge fund, a broker-dealer member of the Chicago Board Options Exchange. Theta's PPM and its executives/promoters, made a number of fraudulent claims; that the fund generated profits in excess of 30 percent in both 1993 and 1994, years when Theta did not exist, that Rubel was a premed/biochemistry graduate of Loyola University, that Theta was a "market neutral" fund and later that Bell had received a nondisclosed $1.9 million consulting fee, substantially in excess of the maximum allowable for such expenses in the PPM.

From the time Theta was launched in January 1996, the principals continued to misinform investors about the fund's performance, basing much their bogus pricing on their own "theoretical" prices, when it was actually incurring double-digit losses on a long-short strategy in related securities. By the summer of 1996, investors stopped receiving monthly faxes. According to an unaudited account, Theta was down around $3 million at that time. It was also around this time that Bell allegedly removed $1.9 million from the fund account as a consulting fee.

Van Hedge Fund Advisors, who recommended Theta and included it in its hedge funds database, had numerous clients invested, including its own Bernoulli Fund, fund-of-funds, persuaded Bell and Rubel to set the record straight regarding rumors of losses. On October 18, a number of investors voted to redeem all their remaining assets, despite the stricture of a one-year lock-up. Exhibit A of the criminal case indicated that three of the investors did receive 100 percent of their initial investment sums from Theta and a fourth got around 45 percent. All told, $2,313,836 was returned in this way. On December 5, 1996, the SEC asked the court to issue a temporary restraining order against Theta, Shadowstone (a second fund set up to trade options on the Philadelphia Exchange), Bell, and Rubel. Civil, class action, and criminal suits followed.

The SEC had the funds shut down before the end of 1996, froze remaining assets of $3.7 million, and returned about one-third of the assets to investors. Bell and Rubel received prison terms of 36 and 27 months, respectively, and disgorgement orders totaling more than $14 million. Theta had its membership revoked. The class action, filed on January 27, 1997, was settled on July 7, 2000, including substantial restitution orders.

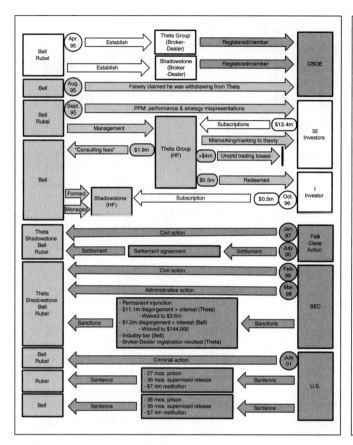

Fraud Facts

- Alleged Acts Date: September 1995
- Enforcement Date: October 23, 1996
- Main Defendants **(hedge fund–related): Scott Bell, R. Scot Rubel, Theta Group, Shadowstone Partners I**
- Most Serious Charge: Fraud
- Hedge Fund Role: Defendant
- Damages $actual **($2005): $13.4 million ($17.6 million)**
- No. of Investors: 32
- Highest Court: Criminal
- Most Severe Sentence: 36 months prison, $14.6 million restitution

Sanctions:

- Theta Group: $11.1 million disgorgement, waived to $3.6 million
- Theta Group: Permanent injunction, registration revoked, freeze funds
- Shadowstone Partners I: Permanent injunction, freeze funds
- Scott Bell: 36 months' prison, 36 months' supervised release, industry bar
- Scott Bell: $1.2 million disgorgement, waived to $144,000, permanent injunction
- Scott Bell: $7,423,182 restitution
- R. Scot Rubel: 27 months' prison, 36 months' supervised release, industry bar
- R. Scot Rubel: $7,423,182 restitution

Cases:

- *U.S. v. Bell & Rubel* (01cr669, criminal, N. Dist. Ill.)
- *SEC v. Theta* (96cv07987, civil, N. Dist. Ill.)
- *Falk v. Theta* (97cv00565, civil/class act, N. Dist. Ill.)
- *In the matter of Bell . . .* (SEC admin. proc. 3–9559)

An unregistered CPO gathered around $600,000 from four individual acquaintances to trade commodity futures in managed accounts. The defendant used multiple accounts to misappropriate most of this money and lost the balance in risky trading, using false reports to cover his tracks. Key points:

- CFTC and State of Florida
- Unregistered CPO
- Solicited from local acquaintances
- Used multiple FCM (futures commission merchant) and CPO accounts to facilitate misappropriation
- Tried more risky trading to replace lost money, which backfired
- Deception ended when customers sought redemptions
- Civil and criminal prosecution resulted in a prison term and restitution

Case Summary

Up until about 1986, James Dowler had been registered with the CFTC, but not afterward. In 1990, there were some signs that Dowler may have been experiencing some financial stress in the form of a civil action to enforce an IRS summons in April 1990 and the filing of a voluntary Chapter 7 bankruptcy petition in November 1990. Dowler & Beekman, Inc., a commercial entity controlled by Dowler was listed as a creditor in the bankruptcy proceedings. In July 1987, Dowler had also established Dowler & Beekman Trading Company, Ltd. (DBTC), whose stated purpose was to trade commodity futures, even though it was never registered with the CFTC.

In the early 1990s, Dowler started to approach acquaintances to invest in commodity futures via managed accounts. Between January 1992 and January 1995, he succeeded in getting at least four of them to invest $608,400 with him. This money was pooled and was first placed in an account Dowler had under the name of Dowler & Beekman (D&B) with a futures commission merchant (FCM). He then moved the money to another FCM under the name of Dowler & Beekman Trading Company (D&BTC). He moved it to a third FCM still pooled under the DBTC name. These account shifts and the similarity of D&B and D&BTC names may have been important in enabling the redirection of customer money to Dowler's personal accounts. In total, Dowler misappropriated about $400,000 from the investor's accounts.

Between June and November 1994, Dowler's commodities trading appears to have been profitable, realizing a gain of $302,189 on a capital base of $269,895. However, during this period, he misappropriated around $285,800 from the accounts, including the trading gains. Dowler's trading strategy became increasingly risky as he sought to replace the funds he was siphoning off, but this only served to increase the losses. In December 1994, losses amounted to $124,929 and a further $143,750 in February 1995, by which time, the accounts had been completely emptied.

By January 1996, while he covered up the misappropriations and later losses with false reports to the investors, Dowler came under increasing pressure to meet redemptions and in March 1996 wrote letters to the investors telling them that their money was "gone," and admitted that he had done a "terrible thing," adding, "I failed you . . . I can offer no excuses. The funds ran out." In November 1996, the CFTC and the State of Florida Department of Banking and Finance jointly filed a civil suit, with a criminal suit following in October 1998. Dowler was sentenced to one year and one day in prison and 36 months of supervised release in the criminal case and a consent agreement calling for $977,000 in restitution and permanent injunction in the civil case.

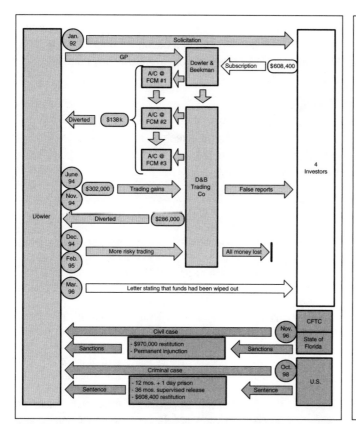

Fraud Facts

- Alleged Acts Date:
  January 18, 1992
- Enforcement Date:
  November 4, 1996
- Main Defendants **(hedge fund–related): Dowler, Dowler & Beekman Trading Co.**
- Most Serious Charge:
  Fraud
- Hedge Fund Role:
  Dofondant
- Damages $actual **($2005): $977,000 ($1.2 million)**
- No. of Investors: 4
- Highest Court: Criminal
- Most Severe Sentence:
  12 months' prison,
  $977,000 restitution

Sanctions:

- James Dowler: 12 months' prison, 36 months' supervised release, $977,000, permanent injunction, industry bar
- Dowler & Beekman: permanent injunction

Cases:

- *CFTC v. Dowler*, (96cv14284, civil, S. Dist. Fl.)
- *U.S. v. Dowler*, (98cr14050, criminal, S. Dist. Fl.)

A registered commodity pool operator and an Associated Person/commodity trading adviser quickly lost all of their capital trading, leading to a deception using false reports and the peculiar ruse of obtaining personal loans from the investors. Key points:

- Registered CPO and CTA
- Rapidly lost all assets in trading
- Resorted to false reporting to cover up losses
- Sought and received personal loans from some investors, in part linked to CP
- One investor alerted the NFA of the loan scheme
- Administrative, civil, and criminal actions followed

Case Summary

Daniel O'Shaughnessey, a resident of Midland, Michigan, was registered with the CFTC as a CTA and as an AP and principal and president of the Glory Fund, Inc., a registered CPO, since July 1996. As early as April 1996 (i.e., prior to registration), he began soliciting individuals for a commodity futures investment in the Glory Fund LLC. As of September 1996, he had raised around $200,000 from some 12 individuals.

After establishing registered entities and standings for himself, his CP, and CPO, O'Shaughnessey apparently quickly proceeded to engage in violative conduct that ultimately destroyed his enterprise and landed him in prison.

O'Shaughnessey did his trading via a futures commission merchant (FCM), where he maintained at least three separate accounts; a personal one for himself, and corporate accounts for his CPO and CP. These were paralleled with three bank accounts. The trading started to lose money at an early stage and continued to do so for a number of successive months, ultimately wiping out most if not all of the investor capital as well as a $100,000 or more of his money.

The commodity pool account, which had net deposits of $141,000 on September 20, was down to $34,923 by the following November 12, indicating a loss of around $106,000 during that two-month period. O'Shaughnessey had also accumulated a personal trading loss of around $65,000 during a 12-month period from October

1995. The CPO's corporate account had also lost all of the $125,000 balance that it had in June 1996. In total, the aggregated losses were almost $300,000. Added to initial set-up costs, it may have dealt a mortal blow to the start-up.

Instead of notifying investors of the losses, O'Shaughnessey took the fraudster's low road of issuing false reports indicating that all was well. In another, slightly odd course of action, he also sought to convert new subscription interests to personal loans, on which he proposed to pay the greater of 20 percent per annum or the returns of the Glory Fund. The subscription and loan income, and the commingling of various personal and corporate trading and banking accounts, facilitated the movement of money from the customers to O'Shaughnessey.

It was one of the loan agreement proposal letters forwarded to the NFA that started the wheels of enforcement moving against O'Shaughnessey and Glory. He was ultimately subject to administrative, civil, and criminal actions that resulted in his imprisonment for 18 months with supervised release for 36 months, an order for restitution of over $470,000, permanent injunction, and being barred from the industry. Sadly, O'Shaughnessey committed suicide on October 23, 2003. (Case 39 had a similar suicide ending, though the defendant in that case had been on the run.) He was 48. A month before his death, he had been appealing his garnishment sentence. His appeal was denied.

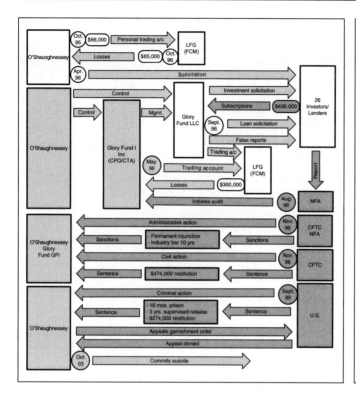

Fraud Facts

- Alleged Acts Date: April 1996
- Enforcement Date: November 20, 1996
- Main Defendants **(hedge fund–related): O'Shaughnessey, Glory Fund LLC, Glory Fund I Inc.**
- Most Serious Charge: Fraud
- Hedge Fund Role: Defendant
- Damages $actual **($2005): $436,000 ($606,000)**
- No. of Investors: 26
- Highest Court: Criminal
- Most Severe Sentence: 18 months' prison, $474,000 restitution

Sanctions:

- Daniel M. O'Shaughnessey: 18 months' prison, 36 months' supervised release, approximately $475,000 restitution, permanent injunction, industry bar
- Glory Fund I, Inc.: Permanent injunction, industry bar
- Glory Fund, LLC: Permanent injunction, industry bar

Cases:

- *NFA v. O'Shaughnessey* (96-ARA-003)
- *NFA v. Glory Fund* (96-MRA-006)
- *CFTC v. O'Shaughnessey* (96cv10421, civil, E. Dist. Mich.)
- *U.S. v. O'Shaughnessey* (99cr20062, criminal, E. Dist. Mich.)

Rapid growth in clients in a one-man investment adviser caused risk control failures that led to a fund blow-up. Management of the adviser was also compromised by the conflicted interests of the principal's brother who ran an unrelated broker-dealer while assisting in the management of the adviser. Key points:

- First place in the "U.S. Investing Championship" attracted initial investors (see Cases 22, Doviak and 37 Prendergast)
- Defendant's brother operated an unrelated broker-dealer that executed trades for most of the Hyannis investors
- Defendant's brother also assisted in the operations of the investment adviser
- Rapid growth in the number of investors caused a serious failure in internal account risk controls that led to catastrophic losses
- The Hyannis fund blew up within one year
- The Hegarty brothers were subject to moderate fines, disgorgement and five-year bans

Case Summary

Jeremiah Hegarty fits the profile common to other cases of talent gone bad. A self-taught observer of market behavior, Hegarty used his insights to build several options models. The confidence gained in doing so probably encouraged him to enter Norm Zadeh's popular U.S. Investing Championships with $2,000 (see Cases 22 Doviak and 37 Prendergast). At the end of December 1990, Hegarty ranked first in the options division with an annual return of 180 percent. This, together with a fourth place result the following year, enabled Hegarty to attract some initial investors.

In 1991, Hyannis Trading was set up as a registered investment adviser and Hegarty's brother, Michael Hegarty, was enlisted to assist with marketing, client relations, and book and position keeping. Michael, who had an MBA from Northeastern University, first became a broker and set up a branch office of Financial Services Network in West Bridgewater, Massachusetts. Most of Hyannis's investment transactions and its client's broking business was directed to Michael Hegarty's branch brokerage.

While not employed by Hyannis, Michael continued to directly assisted Jeremiah in many administrative capacities. However, as the number of clients and AUM grew, Michael's client accounting system became increasingly overwhelmed, leading

to Jeremiah's reliance on "eyeballing" values. As account clarity diminished, Jeremiah also started using a higher-risk strategy without notifying investors. These conditions were sufficient to cause a subsequent catastrophic loss of $5.7 million of the $6.5 million AUM (87.7 percent).

The SEC brought civil and administrative actions charging the following instances of misconduct: (1) distributing misleading promotional materials; (2) failure to disclose an absence of client account information; (3) change of investment strategy, without notification, from that originally disclosed; (4) unsuitable investments for some clients; (5) illegally charging performance fees; and (6) records-keeping violations.

The brothers were both barred from the industry for five years and Michael was ordered to pay disgorgement of $92,998 and Jeremiah $125,000 penalties. One somewhat puzzling aspect is the long delay between the timing of the violations in 1992, the date of the first enforcement action in November 1996 and the final pronouncements in the SEC administrative proceedings in March 20, 2002, 10-years after the violations. Another unclear aspect is the lack of an order for restitution, given the size of the losses.

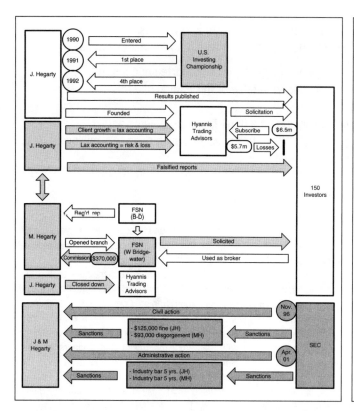

Fraud Facts

- Alleged Acts Date: October–December 1992
- Enforcement Date: November 25, 1996
- Main Defendants **(hedge fund–related)**: Jeremiah Hegarty, Michael Hegarty, **Hyannis Trading Corp.**
- Most Serious Charge: Fraud
- Hedge Fund Role: Would have been a defendant if not wound up voluntarily
- Damages $actual **($2005)**: $5.7 million **($8.1 million)**
- No. of Investors: 150
- Highest Court: Civil
- Most Severe Sentence: $125,000 penalty, $93,000 disgorgement

Sanctions:

- Jeremiah Hegarty: $125,000 penalties, barred 5 years
- Michael Hegarty: $92,998 disgorgement, barred 5 years

Cases:

- *SEC v. Hegarty* (96cv12367, civil, Dist. Mass.)
- *In the matter of Hegarty* (SEC admin. action, 3–10455)

The defendant was a serial fraudster whose fourth known fraud was the creation of a wholly fictitious hedge fund for the purpose of misappropriation. Key points:

- First documented case of a wholly fictitious or purported hedge fund
- Issued promotional information with false or misleading statements
- Made no investments
- Had four other convictions including a bank fraud three years earlier
- Launched another fake fund ("Wizards") in 2000, which raised $1 million
- Received 78-month prison sentence in 2000

Case Summary

A citizen of Sri Lanka, Channa Wick, also known by the alias Wickremeratne, was an outright fraudster and multiple offender. He was linked to at least five incidents between 1988 and 2000 in which disciplinary and legal action had been taken against him. The fourth such incident involved the solicitation of subscriptions for a fictitious hedge fund called the Options Trading Group Corp.

In 1988, "Wick," then 22 years old, was convicted of a misdemeanor in an Illinois state court for stealing $13,800 from his employer, a collection agency for the *Chicago Sun-Times*. In 1991, then a clerk in the credit department of a Sumitomo Bank subsidiary, Wick posed as a treasurer of the bank and obtained a $1 million line of credit from Chemical Bank.

The scheme was exposed by a chance meeting between executives from the two banks. He was fired by Sumitomo and went to live in Chicago where, having failed to disclose the reason for leaving the previous post, he got a job as an assistant dealer in the money market division at Harris Bank. There he filed false accounts to cover losses in his trading, which reached $98,000. In 1994, Wick pled guilty

to both crimes and received a one-year prison sentence and five years' probation and was ordered to undergo psychological counseling.

The fourth encounter mentioned earlier, resulted from his marketing of a fictitious hedge fund called Options Group Trading Corp. in April 1996, from which he raised approximately $354,000 from some six investors. Wick made no investments with the proceeds raised and appears to have simply pocketed the money and used it for his own purposes. The SEC obtained a temporary restraining order against Wick and Options Trading Group on May 14, 1997. Wick pled guilty to one count of fraud and was sentenced to 27 months' prison for that as well as parole violations from his earlier sentences.

At the age of 34 in 2000, and down but not yet out Wick was arraigned for his fifth white collar crime—defrauding six investors of more than $1 million from another bogus fund called "Wizards of OZ Park Investment Club." Having served a two-year prison term for his 1997 crimes, he was now sentenced to 78 months in prison, three years' probation, and restitution of $742,000.

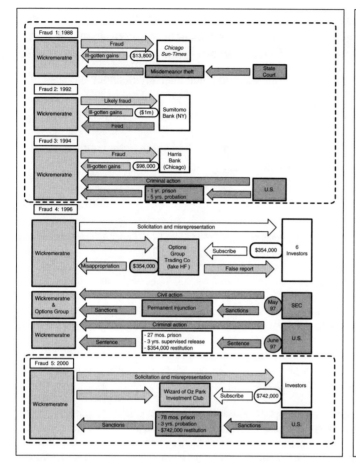

Fraud Facts

- Alleged Acts Date: March 1996
- Enforcement Date: May 14, 1997
- Main Defendants (hedge fund–related): **Channa Wick** (a.k.a. Wickremeratne), **Options Group Trading Co.**
- Most Serious Charge: Fraud
- Hedge Fund Role: Defendant
- Damages $actual. **($2005):** $354,000 **($440,000)**
- No. of Investors: Approximately 6
- Highest Court: Criminal
- Most Severe Sentence: 10 months' prison (followed by 2 years' prison for probation violations, then six years for a later offense)

Sanctions:

- Channa Wick (1997): 27 months' prison, 3 years' probation, $354,000 restitution
- Channa Wick (2000): 78 months' prison, 3 years' probation, $742,000 restitution

Cases:

- *USA v. Wickremeratne* (97cr418–1, criminal, N. Dist. Ill.)
- *SEC v. Wick* (97cv3558, civil, N. Dist. Ill.)
- *U.S. v. Wick* (1:00cr00339–1, criminal, N. Dist. Ill.)

The defendant in this case created an unregistered CPO, including an advisory entity and a hedge fund. Having raised money based on numerous misrepresentations, within a year nearly half of the money had been lost or misappropriated. Key points:

- Split between outright misappropriation and failed investments not clear
- Fund blew-up within one year
- Hedge fund name may have been misleading including both "Berkshire" and "hedge fund" in the name
- Guaranteed 5 to 15 percent a month returns and lied about actual returns
- Around $2 million (approximately 50 percent) was recovered by the receiver

Case Summary

In January 1997, Michael Myatt started marketing Berkshire Hedge Fund LP II, an unregistered commodity pool. In doing so, he made some unfounded representations to prospective investors, including a promise of returns between 5 percent and 15 percent per month. Myatt was able to raise $3,931,524 from 168 investors. However, contrary to the performance guaranteed, the fund soon started losing money, ultimately accumulating $1.5 million in losses. Despite this, Myatt wrote to investors to reassure them that the fund was "solvent and highly profitable."

On June 4, the CFTC filed a three-count complaint in the U.S. District Court and ordered a preliminary restraining order and a freeze over approximately $1.9 million that was still in the fund. While the main focus of enforcement was the Berkshire Hedge Fund II, since it still held substantial assets, the CFTC action also included PragmaCapital Corp., the general partner of Berkshire, and Michael Myatt, the president and chief operations officer (COO) of PragmaCapital. At the end of August 1997, a private civil suit was filed by 12 Berkshire investors seeking the return of $263,379.

A criminal case against Myatt was filed on December 29, 1998, and took precedence over the civil actions pending. The criminal court issued a consent order of permanent injunction and found that: (1) defendants committed fraud in the operation of an unregistered commodity pool (unregistered with the CFTC or with the state of Oregon); (2) issuing false reports of profits; and (3) commingling of investor assets with Myatt's personal accounts. Myatt pled guilty to two counts—mail fraud, and issuing false statements—and on August 18, 2000, was sentenced to two concurrent 15-month prison terms, three years of supervised release, and a demand for restitution of $1,707,240.

Myatt was cooperative with the restitution order, and the court-appointed receiver was able to distribute nearly $2 million to the investors: about 50 percent of the amount invested at subscription. Myatt was also ordered to continue to repay investor losses for a further five years.

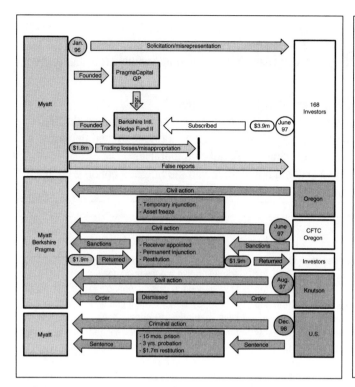

Fraud Facts

- Alleged Acts Date:
  January 1996
- Enforcement Date:
  June 4, 1997
- Main Defendants **(hedge
  fund–related): Michael
  Myatt, Pragma Capital
  Corp., Berkshire Intl.
  Hedge Fund LP II**
- Most Serious Charge:
  Mail fraud
- Hedge Fund Role:
  Defendant
- Damages $actual
  ($2005): $3.9 million
  ($5.0 million)
- No. of Investors: 168
- Highest Court: Criminal
- Most Severe Sentence:
  15 months' prison,
  3 years' probation,
  $1.7 million restitution

Sanctions:

- Michael Myatt: 15 months' prison, 3 years' probation, $1,707,240 restitution

Cases:

- *CFTC v. Berkshire* (3:97cv00838-KI, civil, Dist. Ore.)
- *Knutson v. Berkshire* (3:97cv01266-KI, civil, Dist. Ore.)
- *U.S. v. Myatt* (3:98cr00576-HA-1, criminal, Dist. Ore.)

This is a precedent-setting case in which the SEC brought administrative proceedings against an offshore hedge fund that engaged in an arbitrage strategy involving the sale of previously restricted "Reg S" shares back into U.S. markets without registering them. Key points:

- Helped to define the SEC's extraterritorial legal authority
- Regulation S was problematic in application from the time it was enacted in 1990
- Regulation abused by arbitraging offshore discount during restricted period
- SEC implementing a policy of reining in Regulation S abuses
- Defendant entered into a consent agreement with the SEC and got off with just a cease-and-desist order

Case Summary

In April 1990, the U.S. Securities and Exchange Commission added Regulation S (Reg. S) to the Securities Act of 1933 in an effort to open foreign capital markets to U.S. companies, both to tap additional sources of capital and reduce issuing costs. However, it soon became apparent that, as originally constructed, the act was subject to abuse by cash-starved small companies, penny-stock promoters, and arbitrageurs who sought to use a loophole in the regulation to resell discounted foreign restricted stock back into the United States. These abuses led to a rash of enforcement actions and a tightening of the regulation in 1998.

GFL Ultra Fund Ltd., a Netherlands Antilles company founded in 1994, was involved in two sets of related Reg. S cases. The first was a group of private suits and countersuits in 1996, including one in which a principal of investment manager, Genesee Service Corp., sued an employee and his wife for receiving kickbacks for finding investments for Genesee's offshore hedge fund, GFL Ultra Ltd., during the period 1991–1995. The suit charged that in exchange for Ultra's investment of $2.4 million in Reg. S debt and equity issues in Synagro Technologies, defendant Christopher Secreto's company, Mercury Capital, received $62,500. Synagro also sued Genesee for violating Reg. S by having a U.S. citizen investing in GFL Ultra.

In 1997, the SEC pursued precedent-setting administrative proceedings against GFL Ultra Fund Ltd., seeking to close a loophole in the then Reg. S statute, by which foreign companies such as GFL sold restricted securities back into the United States after expiry of the required 40-day waiting period. This practice enabled companies such as GFL to execute a near-perfect arbitrage by buying discounted Reg. S stock overseas and, at the same time, executing an equivalent short position in the United States, thereby locking in the value of the discount. The trade would be unwound at the end of the 40-day waiting period and the profit realized. According to SEC documents, GFL had participated in some 62 such arbitrage deals.

The SEC charged GFL with violations of Section 5 of the Securities Act, which prohibits the sale of unregistered securities across state lines without qualifying for exemption. Largely due to its distribution activities, GFL was held to be a "statutory underwriter" as defined by Section 2(11) of the Securities Act. As such, GFL did not qualify for exemption under Reg. S, which would have allowed for resale in the United States at the end of the 40-day wait period. After agreeing a settlement with GFL, the SEC issued GFL with a cease-and-desist order not to violate this statute in the future.

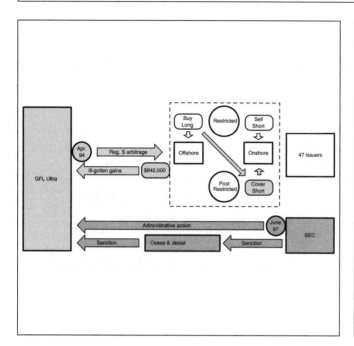

Fraud Facts

- Alleged Acts Date: April 1994
- Enforcement Date: June 18, 1997
- Main Defendants (**hedge fund–related): GFL Ultra Fund Ltd.**
- Most Serious Charge: Reg. S violation
- Hedge Fund Role: Defendant
- Damages $actual **($2005): >$840,000 ($1.1 million)**
- No. of Investors: NA
- Highest Court: Administrative
- Most Severe Sentence: Cease-and-desist order

Sanctions:

- GFL Ultra Fund Corp.: Cease-and-desist order

Cases:

- *In the matter of GFL Ultra Fund* (SEC Admin. Proc., Release No. 3–9333)

Precedents:

- SEC's rights to pursue a foreign company trading in the United States

The defendant, a registered commodity pool operator, diverted client funds to meet his personal expenses, while providing false reports to his limited partners and evading their redemption requests. Key points:

- CFTC case
- Registered CPO
- Six years of operations prior to fraud
- Money diverted from CPO account
- Criminal case dismissed without prejudice on government motion
- Receiver distributed $100,000 from funds frozen by court
- CFTC contested defendant's bankruptcy action to retain access to debt

Case Summary

Oscar Klitin was a registered commodity pool operator based in Great Neck, New York. He established the Klitin Associates II commodity pool in 1989. From that time, Klitin sold some $200,000 of partnership units to about 40 limited partners. In 1996, Klitin moved partnership funds to his own personal bank account. These funds were used for a variety of personal uses including mortgage payments, transfers to his mother-in-law, and personal loans to himself.

Quarterly reports to investors repeatedly failed to mention any of these transfers. Investors had also not received accounting statements or annual reports since November 1996; and Klitin did not respond to the requests from 11 of his pool participants to redeem their holdings.

On August 25, 1997, the CFTC filed a civil complaint charging him with three counts of CPO Fraud, Embezzlement of Client Funds, and Failure to Report. On January 4, 1999, Klitin and his wife sought bankruptcy protection in a Chapter 7 filing. Criminal fraud charges were filed on January 20, 1999, but this case was dismissed without prejudice. Then, in August of the same year, the CFTC filed an adversarial action in the Klitin bankruptcy case. This resulted in a consent order. In the bankruptcy proceedings, the Klitins' house was sold for more than $1 million.

In the civil action, Klitin's consent order stipulated a permanent injunction against future violations, disgorgement of $115,772.86 (including prejudgment interest), and an industry bar. Civil financial fines were waived on the basis of financial statements submitted to the court by Klitin. The court-appointed receiver also distributed $100,000 of partnership funds, which had been frozen by the court, to the limited partners.

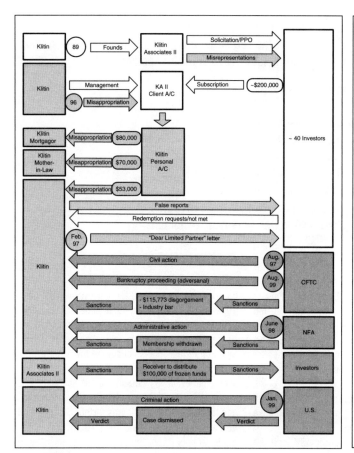

Fraud Facts

- Alleged Acts Date: January 1996
- Enforcement Date: August 25, 1997
- Main Defendants **(hedge fund–related): Oscar Klitin, Klitin Associates II, Inc.**
- Most Serious Charge: Commodity pool operator fraud, embezzlement
- Hedge Fund Role: Defendant
- Damages $actual **($2005): ~$200,000 ($250,000)**
- No. of Investors: 40
- Highest Court: Criminal (dismissed)
- Most Severe Sentence: $100,000 disgorgement, $116,000 restitution, permanent bar

Sanctions:

- Oscar Klitin: $115,773 disgorgement, barred for life; $100,000 distributed by the Receiver

Cases:

- *CFTC v. Klitin* (97cv4973, civil, E. Dist. N.Y.)
- *U.S. v. Klitin* (99mj00068, criminal, E. Dist. N.Y.)
- *CFTC v. Klitin* (99–08350, bankruptcy, E. Dist. N.Y.)
- *NFA Disciplinary Action* (97MRA00002)

In this case, an SEC applicant began acting as an investment adviser prior to finalizing registration. He then failed to amend the registration and committed other violations. The SEC and CFTC both pursued administrative actions. Key points:

- SEC and CFTC administrative cases
- Registration violations
- Acted as an IA before registration became effective
- Failed to disclose a cease-and-desist order from the Michigan State Securities Bureau
- Invested less than 10 percent of funds
- Misused and commingled majority of money
- Most of fund cash returned to investors in consent agreement
- Most of restitution was waived due to financial condition

Case Summary

Although Kerzinger applied for registration as an investment adviser with the SEC, he violated securities regulations by commencing IA activities prior to his registration becoming effective. This error was compounded by misinforming his 22 investors and by failing to revise his Form ADV (SEC registration application). From that point, Kerzinger's infractions continued to mount and included commingling of client money, issuing false reports, and misappropriation.

The defendant had filed a Form ADV with the SEC on June 30, 1989, and his registration as an investment adviser was to become effective from August 14. However, on August 18, a cease-and-desist order was entered against him by the Michigan State Department of Commerce, Corporations and Securities Bureau for selling exempt securities and engaging in exempt transactions prior to his registration with the SEC. According to the SEC, this information should have been included as an amendment to his Form ADV. The SEC also charged Kerzinger with a number of other violations related to his registration, including failure to file Forms ADV-S (annual updating of ADV for disclosure to investors—later revised) for fiscal years 1990, and 1992–1995, and failure to provide his investors with a copy of Part Two of his ADV as required. He had also held himself out as a licensed CTA and made other false claims about the investments.

The SEC found that Kerzinger had deposited client money in his personal bank accounts and commingled it with money from his other personal and business activities. It was further charged that he had only invested less than 10 percent of the funds he was given, the rest of it was invested in real estate, used to pay for services and equipment, and misappropriated to pay for personal expenses and investors' dividends.

Both the SEC and CFTC pursued administrative actions against Kerzinger on September 4, 1997. A settlement was reached in both cases. Kersinger was ordered to pay restitution of $168,461.67, largely the difference between the estimated $798,700 he received from investors and some $630,000 he returned to them in cash and in kind. All but $15,000 of the restitution was waived due to his financial condition. He was also banned from the securities and commodities industry.

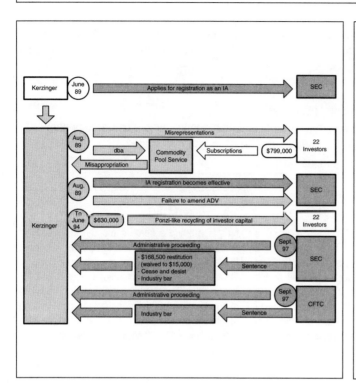

Fraud Facts

- Alleged Acts Date:
  August 1989
- Enforcement Date:
  September 4, 1997
- Main Defendants
  (hedge fund–related):
  Kerzinger, Commodity
  Pool Service
- Most Serious Charge:
  Misappropriation
- Hedge Fund Role:
  Defendant
- Damages $actual
  ($2005): $168,000
  ($267,000)
- No. of Investors: 22
- Highest Court:
  Administrative
- Most Severe Sentence:
  $168,460 disgorgement
  (waived to $15,000),
  industry ban

Sanctions:

- Willy Kerzinger: $168,500 restitution (waived to $15,000), industry bar, cease-and-desist order

Cases:

- *In the Matter of Kerzinger* (SEC Admin. Proc. 3–9390)
- *re Kerzinger* (CFTC Docket No. 97–15)

The defendant was prosecuted for two financial crimes, one of which involved raising money for an unregistered commodity pool. The majority of this money was converted for personal use. Key points:

- CFTC case
- Unregistered commodity pool operator
- Prosecuted for two separate frauds, of which one involved a commodity pool
- Also perpetrated a hoax trade on the Chicago Board of Trade
- Converted funds for personal use

Case Summary

Anthony Ramirez, a resident of Blue Island, Illinois, a suburb of Chicago, perpetrated two related crimes. One involved a CFTC commodity pool action and the other was a criminal hoax prosecuted by the U.S. Attorney's Office. On September 16, 1997, the CFTC filed a civil complaint against Ramirez and Abacus Investment Group, Inc., charging him with five counts of defrauding investors. The CFTC complaint stated that Ramirez had raised around $507,000 from a range of individuals, including his own grandmother and a member of his church (who was confined to a wheelchair), and that he had converted some $385,000 of this money for his personal use.

On the September 23, a week after his civil case was filed, Ramirez agreed to a consent order of permanent injunction "and other equitable relief."

On the same day that the civil complaint was filed (September 16), the U.S. Attorney's Office filed a criminal complaint charging Ramirez with one count of Frauds and Swindles (U.S. Code 18:1341)

for perpetrating a hoax at the Chicago Board of Trade on November 15, 1993. Ramirez, a former Prudential Securities floor runner and clerk at the CBOT grain room, impersonating a Prudential trader, called in an order to sell 14 million bushels of soybeans and 5 million bushels of corn, aiming to benefit by depressing the market short term while selling a $1,500 options position that he held. Prudential executed the order and lost $561,000 by the time it discovered the false trade. However, Ramirez was not quick enough to benefit from his deception.

On February 19, 1998, Ramirez was sentenced to 46 months of prison, 36 months of supervised release, and restitution of $1,090,952. It appears that the restitution included the sum of ill-gotten gains from both of his crimes.

As of August 2002, Ramirez worked for a mattress company. Forty dollars is garnered from each one of his paychecks toward restitution.

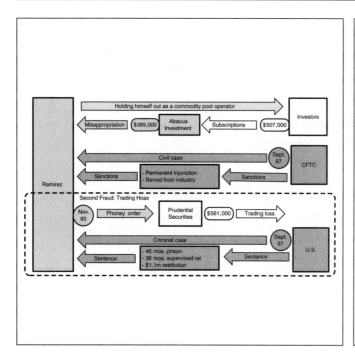

Fraud Facts

- Alleged Acts Date: November 1993
- Enforcement Date: September 16, 1997
- Main Defendants **(hedge fund–related): Ramirez, Abacus Investment Group**
- Most Serious Charge: Fraud (criminal)
- Hedge Fund Role: Defendant
- Damages $actual **($2005): $385,000 ($477,000)**
- No. of Investors: NA
- Highest Court: Criminal
- Most Severe Sentence: 46 months' prison, $1 million restitution

Sanctions:

- Anthony Ramirez (criminal): 46 months' prison, 36 months' supervised release, $1.1 million restitution
- Anthony Ramirez (civil): Permanent injunction, industry bar
- Abacus Investment Group, Inc.: Permanent injunction, industry bar

Cases:

- *CFTC v. Ramirez* (97cv06528, civil, N. Dist. Ill.)
- *U.S. v. Ramirez* (97cr00652, criminal, N. Dist. Ill.)

This multi-entity, multilevel crime involved two individual defendants and another group of three or more defendants. Each created several unregistered commodity pools and solicited to different groups of investors, losing or misappropriating most of the money. Key points:

- CFTC case
- Revolved around unnamed "Trader A," his "multilevel business plan," and "Profit 22" black box computer trading system
- Resembled a pyramid marketing scheme in its structure and operation
- Focused on recruiting promoters and general partners for limited partnerships that were unregistered commodity pools

Case Summary

In reconstructing this complex case, the apparent sequence of events commenced in November 1995 when two individuals, Terry Wigton and Randall Williams, jointly or separately agreed to pursue a "business plan" involving a "multilevel marketing operation" with another individual identified only as "Trader A," who claimed to have developed a proprietary trading system called "Profit 22." Trader A was to be paid 30 percent of all profits, while Wigton and Williams would earn a smaller percentage for enlisting others to become general or limited partners in a series of commodity pools. Together they created some nine pools and raised nearly $2 million from more than 100 investors.

In June 1996, three additional individuals, Foreman, Munn, and Stevens—apparently recruited by Williams and acting as the general partners of one of William's pools (FTI Financial Group)—had participated in the solicitation of some 20 investors in five of the pools and had received approximately $200,000 for fees and costs.

In October 1996, the FTI general partners sought to replace Trader A with a new, "Trader B" (neither Trader A nor B were registered with the CFTC), in an effort to reduce the impact of Trader A's 30 percent fee haircut. However, by June 1997, when the pool closed down, it had losses of over $700,000.

In Wigton's pools, apart from numerous serious misrepresentations and false reports, there was also evidence of Ponzi-like recycling of one investor's money to another to disguise actual performance. For his part, William's false reports included accounts to investors showing realized gains while omitting unrealized losses.

Things came to a head in October 1997 when the CFTC filed a civil complaint naming eight defendants, including one company (FTI Financial Group) and nine individuals, of whom one had the case dismissed without prejudice due to death. This group did not include Trader A or Trader B, both of whom appear not to have been charged in this or any related case.

The defendants generally opted for consent agreements with the CFTC, which included provisions for restitution, permanent injunctions, and industry bars.

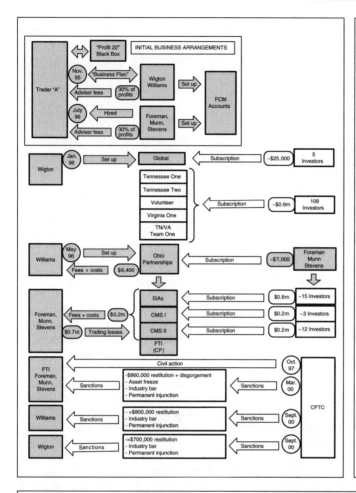

Fraud Facts

- Alleged Acts Date: December 1995
- Enforcement Date: October 9, 1997
- Main Defendants **(hedge fund–related):** Crawford, Foreman, Holt, Munn, Stevens, Wigton, Williams, **FTI Financial Group, CMS I&II, II, Tennessee One & Two, Volunteer Investors, Virginia One, Global Fin.**
- Most Serious Charge: Unregistered commodity pool, misrepresentation
- Hedge Fund Role: Defendant
- Damages $act. **($2005)**: Approximately $2 million **($2.4 million)**
- No. of Investors: Approximately 120
- Highest Court: Civil
- Most Severe Sentence: Approximately $2 million restitution, permanent injunction, industry bar

---

Sanctions:

- James Crawford: dismissed without prejudice
- Anthony Holt: $50,000 civil fine
- Samuel Foreman, Carolyn Munn, Mark Stevens: $860,445 restitution, permanent bar, permanent injunction
- Terry Wigton: $703,755 restitution, permanent bar, permanent injunction
- Randall Williams: $860,445 restitution, permanent bar, permanent injunction

---

Cases:

- *CFTC v. FTI Financial* (97cv7061, civil, N. Dist. Ill.)

A lone Ponzi-scheme operator managed to keep the deception described in this case going for 13 years. Key points:

- CFTC case
- Criminal activity allegedly began in 1984, 13 years prior to discovery or legal action
- One-man Ponzi scheme operator
- Succeeded by continuously refreshing the client pool, recycling a substantial portion of assets (approximately 70 percent) back to investors, and providing investors with detailed monthly reports
- Like other cases, only a small portion of money traded and sustained substantial losses

Case Summary

In August 1984, James Zoller began soliciting individuals with false reports and misrepresentations in an effort to raise money for commodity investments in his Tech-Comm Limited Partnerships, a group of unregistered commodity pools. He ultimately succeeded in convincing at least 219 people, most residing in Minnesota, to invest as much as $13 million in 29 of these limited partnerships.

Zoller kept this deception going for 13 years. During this period, he recycled $9.2 million back to his investors to provide evidence of profits on the investments. He also allegedly embezzled around $3.6 million for personal expenses, including: a home, car, and insurance policies, as well as setting up his office and paying himself commissions. Around 10 percent of the money (approximately $1.3 million) was invested in futures, although these investments apparently lost some $232,000 (approximately 18 percent).

On November 21, 1997, the CFTC filed a civil complaint against Zoller and 29 of his limited partnerships. This was followed by a criminal action in March 1998, to which he pled guilty to four counts of mail fraud and one count of embezzlement in a plea agreement. For this, he was sentenced to 41 months in prison and ordered to pay a restitution of $4.9 million. A receiver, appointed by the court, was instructed to sell Zoller's house, office property, and life insurance policies.

Zoller was 57 when he started his scam. At the time of his criminal trial, he was already 70 years old. Zoller died in 2005, at the age of 78, which absolved him of paying any restitution remaining. Documents suggest little if any had been paid by that time.

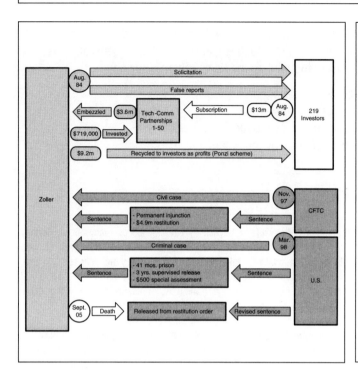

Fraud Facts

- Alleged Acts Date: August 1984
- Enforcement Date: November 21, 1997
- Main Defendants **(hedge fund–related): Zoller, Tech-Comm 1–50**
- Most Serious Charge: Mail fraud, embezzlement
- Hedge Fund Role: Defendant
- Damages $actual **($2005)**: Approximately $4.9 million **($8.1 million)**
- No. of Investors: 219
- Highest Court: Criminal
- Most Severe Sentence: Approximately 41 months' prison

Sanctions:

- James M. Zoller: 41 months' prison, 36 months' supervised release, $4,907,383 restitution, permanent injunction, industry bar
- Tech-Comm (1–50): permanent injunction, industry bar

Cases:

- *CFTC v. Zoller* (97cv02585, civil, Dist. Minn.)
- *U.S. v. Zoller* (98cr00018, criminal, Dist. Minn.)
- *Zoller v. U.S.* (99cv00800, appellate, Dist. Minn.)

An unregistered commodity pool operator employed misrepresentations to raise money, about half of which was traded and lost, and the other half went to personal and business expenses and funds necessary to maintain the Ponzi scheme. Key points:

- CFTC and state of Wisconsin case
- Unregistered commodity pool operator
- No CP entity used in scam—money direct to operator
- Kept Ponzi scheme going for nearly four years
- Civil case

Case Summary

Beginning in September 1993, James Bonney of Plover, Wisconsin, solicited some 13 individuals to invest with him in commodity futures. He made false representations in doing so, including guaranteeing an annual return of 10 to 25 percent, to be paid monthly. He included the innovative device of providing his investors with a personal check for the full amount they invested, with the proviso that they notify him before cashing them. However, there never was any cash balance to support these checks.

According to the reports, Bonney received around $540,000 over the period from September 1993 to June 1997. The money was deposited in Bonney's personal bank accounts and from there he transferred $281,000 into trading accounts under his name. Of this sum, he ultimately lost $264,000 (94 percent) in unsuccessful trading. A portion of the money was likely used to circulate some capital back to investors in the guise of returns.

When the trading losses materialized, Bonney altered statements and issued the investors with false reports as late as May and July 1997. In later statements, he represented that he had $950,000 in the trading accounts, at a time when these accounts held less than $100.

On June 29, 1998, the CFTC filed a five-count civil complaint against Bonney and on February 2 of the following year, he reached an agreement with the CFTC resulting in a consent order of permanent injunction. In a supplemental order in October, the court set his restitution at $315,000, to be paid over a five-year period and to be distributed to 13 of his investors. He was also barred from registration with the CFTC and from participation in commodity futures trading. The state of Wisconsin, in an administrative action, had also barred him in similar terms on September 10, 1998.

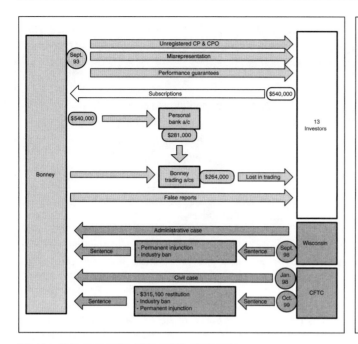

Fraud Facts

- Alleged Acts Date: September 1993
- Enforcement Date: January 29, 1998
- Main Defendants **(hedge fund–related): Bonney**
- Most Serious Charge: Unregistered commodity pool
- Hedge Fund Role: Defendant
- Damages $actual **($2005)**: Approximately $540,000 **($640,000)**
- No. of Investors: 13
- Highest Court: Civil
- Most Severe Sentence: $315,100 restitution, industry bar

Sanctions:

- James F. Bonney: $315,100 restitution, permanent injunction, industry bar

Cases:

- *CFTC v. Bonney* (98cv0087, civil, W. Dist. Wis.)
- *Wisconsin v. Bonney* (admin. proc., Wis.)

The defendant created and operated an unregistered commodity pool in this case. With the money he raised, he sustained trading losses in six out of eight years and converted his operation to a Ponzi scheme. Key points:

- CFTC case
- Unregistered commodity pool and commodity pool adviser
- Investors including family, friends, retirees, and a prostate cancer support group
- Carried on trading for eight years and lost money in six of them
- Turned into a Ponzi scheme before becoming unsustainable
- Received a 15-month prison sentence and a $2.8 million restitution order

Case Summary

Starting in March 1989, Thomas Lamar, a resident of Waterford, Michigan, began soliciting prospective investors for an unregistered commodity pool amongst friends, relatives, and, in at least one instance, members of a prostate cancer support group he attended. By October 1996, as much as $5 million had been raised from around 85 investors, including retirement assets from, many of the older individuals that had invested.

The cash flow for his trading was funneled through 16 investment accounts in his name or that of his commodity pool (LIG) as well as seven bank accounts under these two names. From 1989 to 1996 the trading records for these accounts showed losses in six of eight years, cumulatively amounting to nearly $1.4 million. $560,000 of the invested capital was also converted for personal use.

The continuing trading losses drove Lamar to create fictitious Ponzi-like cash flows back to the investors along with false reports to sustain an appearance of normalcy. However, maintaining the Ponzi scheme required a steady supply of new investors to fund the older ones. When this supply eventually diminished the scheme became unsustainable and a voluntary Chapter 13 bankruptcy filing was made on October 4, 1996. The claims register for that case includes as many as 99 names, claiming a total of over $5 million.

Bankruptcy was granted on July 28, 1997, seven months before the CFTC complaint was filed on February 13, 1998. A criminal case had been filed a day earlier after a federal grand jury indicted him on eight counts including; mail fraud, wire fraud, embezzlement, and money laundering. Lamar was found guilty on two criminal charges: mail fraud, and, fraud, false reporting and deception in commodity futures trading. He was sentenced to 15 months' incarceration (in a halfway house) followed by 15 months of home confinement and ordered to pay $2.84 million restitution. The civil action added a permanent injunction against future violations and a permanent ban against future work in the commodities industry.

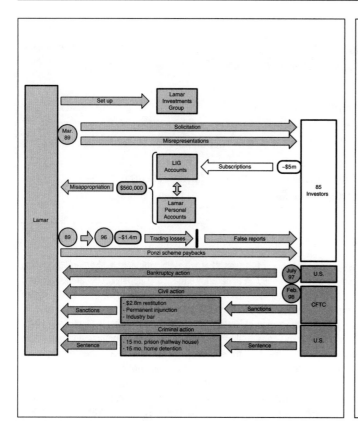

Fraud Facts
- Alleged Acts Date: March 1989
- Enforcement Date: February 12, 1998
- Main Defendants **(hedge fund–related): Thomas Lamar, Lamar Investments Group**
- Most Serious Charge: Mail fraud, wire fraud, money laundering
- Hedge Fund Role: Defendant
- Damages $actual **($2005)**: Approximately $2 million **($2.4 million)**
- No. of Investors: Approximately 85
- Highest Court: Criminal
- Most Severe Sentence: 15 months' incarceration, 15 months' probation, $2.8 million restitution, industry bar

Sanctions:
- Thomas Lamar: 15 months' prison, 15 months' probation, permanent bar, permanent injunction

Cases:
- *Lamar Chap 13 Bankruptcy* (96–53266, E. Dist. Mich.)
- *CFTC v. Lamar* (98cv70619, civil, USDC E. Dist. Mich.)
- *U.S. v. Lamar* (98cr80173, criminal, USDC E. Dist. Mich.)

A soft-dollar broker undergoing reorganization made payments on some fraudulent invoice items to a hedge fund counter-party. The hedge fund also failed to disclose these arrangements to its investors. Key points:

- SEC case
- Fraud in the use of soft dollars
- Result of a 1996–1997 investigation of broker-adviser soft-dollar arrangements
- Corporate reorganization at broker largely responsible for violations not being spotted
- Adviser created fictitious invoices and invoices for nonresearch costs
- Adviser did not disclose soft-dollar arrangement to its investors

Case Summary

At least three sets of charges were filed, one of which involved a hedge fund adviser, Sweeney Capital Management (SCM), and one of its soft-dollar brokers, Republic New York, and senior executives of both firms: Timothy Sweeney and James Sweeney, respectively, who are unrelated. This case also highlighted the risks that come from lapses in diligence during a corporate reorganization.

In April 1994, San Francisco-based adviser SCM concluded a soft-dollar agreement with Republic New York based on a ratio of one soft dollar per $1.75 of broking commission. Republic was active in the soft-dollar business at that time, having about 15 employees and 80 accounts.

In May 1994, acting on the advice of a consultant, James Sweeney of Republic closed its soft-dollar department and laid off its staff, but did not terminate its existing accounts. Republic continued to process some of SCM's invoices, but it no longer had dedicated staff to perform due diligence on the invoices. Instead, the invoices were handled by James Sweeney, the former consultant who had become COO and president of Republic.

The SEC charges allege that between May 1994, when the soft-dollar department was closed, and April 1995, SCM was paid some $84,000 in "soft dollar" rebates by Republic. SCM's violations involved, among other things, not disclosing the arrangement to the investors, allocating the soft dollars to nonallowable expenses, and falsifying related expense accounts. Republic, by its actions,

was charged with aiding and abetting. SCM also apparently engaged in illegal soft dollar transactions with other brokers worth about $25,000, bringing its total ill-gotten gains to $109,000.

The SEC filed a civil case on March 10, 1998, that resulted in permanent injunctions against the three defendants as well as a disgorgement order for $158,629 against Timothy Sweeney and SCM. However, payment of the disgorgement was waived on the basis of financial statements submitted to the court by Sweeney, demonstrating his inability to pay. Civil penalties were also not ordered for the same reason.

On February 10, 1999, the SEC instituted administrative proceedings against Republic New York and James Sweeney for aiding and abetting SCM, which resulted in censures, cease-and-desist orders, and civil fines of $50,000 and $25,000, respectively.

On September 29, 2000, the SEC instituted administrative proceedings against Timothy Sweeney and one of his staff, Susan Gorski, and having received and accepted Offers of Settlement from each, ordered that both be barred from association with investment advisers. SCM and Sweeney were ordered to disgorge $158,600, though payment of this sum was waived based on the defendants demonstrated inability to pay. The defendants neither admitted nor denied any guilt, but consented to the SEC's issuance of these orders.

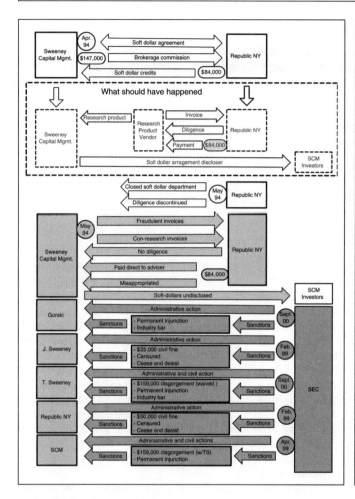

Fraud Facts

- Alleged Acts Date: April 1994
- Enforcement Date: March 10, 1998
- Main Defendants **(hedge fund–related): Timothy Sweeney, Susan Gorski, Sweeney Capital Management Inc.**
- Most Serious Charge: Misappropriation of "soft dollar" rebates
- Hedge Fund Role: Defendant
- Damages $actual **($2005)**: Approximately $109,000 **($136,000)**
- No. of Investors: NA
- Highest Court: Civil
- Most Severe Sentence: Waived $158,629 disgorgement, permanent injunction

Sanctions:

- Susan Gorski: Permanent injunction, barred as an investment adviser
- James Sweeney (unrelated): Civil penalty $25,000, censure, cease-and-desist order
- Timothy Sweeney: $158,600 disgorgement (waived), permanent injunction, barred as investment adviser
- Sweeney Capital Mgmt. Inc.: Waived disgorgement (w/T. Sweeney), registration withdrawn
- Republic N.Y. Sec. Corp.: Civil penalty $50,000, censure, cease-and-desist order

Cases:

- *SEC v. Sweeney* (98cv00937, civil, N. Dist. Ca.)
- *In the matter of T. Sweeney* (SEC Admin. Proc. 3–10329)
- *In the matter of S. Gorski* (SEC Admin. Proc. 3–10330)
- *In the matter of Republic N.Y.* (SEC Admin. Proc. 3–9823)

In this case, two related CFTC cases involving unregistered commodity pools and commodity pool operators in which investors lost the majority of their investments due to poor trading, misrepresentation, false reporting, misappropriation, and fraud. Key points:

- CFTC case
- Two interrelated frauds
- Unregistered CPs and CPOs
- Defendants based in Utah
- Pools lost money in most months they traded
- Substantial restitution was achieved in a civil action

Case Summary

John Larry Schenk was at the center of two related commodity pool frauds prosecuted by the CFTC in 1998. A resident of Salt Lake City, Utah, Schenk was registered as a commodity trading adviser and commodity pool operator with the CFTC from October 1990. He was also a principal of Linz Gruppe, a registered introducing broker, and Fidelity Traders, which acted as CPO of the Wasatch Fund, a commodity pool, and as one of the CPOs for a group of three other pools under the umbrella of the Capital Advantage Group II.

In the case of the Wasatch Fund, Schenk Sam Gray, an unregistered Fidelity Traders associate, solicited and raised some $402,000 from 16 individuals, based on false representations regarding past performance, fees, and investment methodology. The Wasatch Fund commenced commodities trading in September 1993 and lost money in almost every month through December 1997, resulting in a cumulative loss of $234,434 (58 percent of NAV). Gray and Schenk continued to issue false reports to investors until January 1998, despite the fact that the fund had ceased trading in July 1996. The pair also misappropriated $68,000 from the fund.

In the related case, three unregistered CPOs, Douglas Foster, Robert Moncur, and Brian Tobler, hired Schenk to provide services as a CPO for three commodity pools they had established: Augusta Fund, LLC, Brighton Fund, LLC, and the Capital Advantage Fund II, LLC. Foster, Moncur, and Tobler had been under the misguided impression that by forming three small pools from what had been one, in which 23 investors had placed roughly $325,000, they had avoided the requirement to be registered.

In addition to misrepresentations Foster, Moncur, and Tobler made regarding Schenk, there were numerous violations in the way the pools were managed and ultimately most of the money was lost.

The CFTC started a civil action against Schenk, Foster, Moncur, Tobler (and others, including two family relations of Schenk's, John S. and Mark Schenk) on March 27, 1998, and over the following two years reached consent agreements with the defendants resulting in substantial restitution of monies lost, as well as permanent injunctions against future violations and permanent or 10-year bars on professional practice.

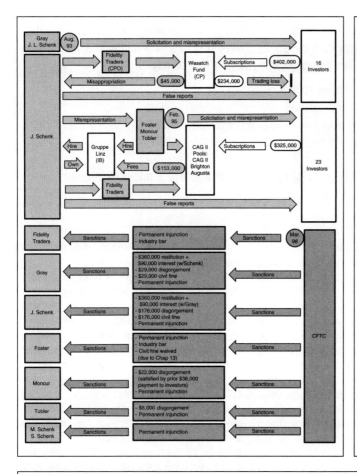

Fraud Facts

- Alleged Acts Date: September 23, 1992
- Enforcement Date: March 27, 1998
- Main Defendants **(hedge fund–related): John L Schenk, Sam Gray, Mark Schenk, John S Schenk, Douglas Foster, Robert Moncur, Brian Tobler, Fidelity Traders Group, Wasatch Fund, CMG II Fund, Augusta Fund, Brighton Fund, CAG II LLC**
- Most Serious Charge: Misappropriation
- Damages $actual **($2005)**: Approximately $850,000 **($1.1 million)**
- No. of Investors: 39
- Highest Court: Civil
- Most Severe Sentence: $450,000 restitution, industry bar

Sanctions:

- Douglas Foster: Permanent injunction, industry bar, civil fine waived
- Sam Gray: $30,000 disgorgement, $30,000 civil fine
- John L. Schenk: $176,000 disgorgement, $176,000 civil fine
- Mark Schenk: $16,000 disgorgement, 10-year industry bar
- John S. Schenk: $16,000 disgorgement, 10-year industry bar
- Robert Moncur: $22,000, disgorgement, permanent injunction, industry bar
- Brian Tobler: $6,000 disgorgement, permanent injunction, industry bar
- Fidelity Traders: Permanent injunction, industry bar

Cases:

- *CFTC v. Schenk* (98cv00216, civil, Utah)

The defendant, a well-known hedge fund manager with a mortgage-backed securities strategy got caught mispricing assets to cover-up losses and received a long prison sentence and a substantial demand for restitution. Key points:

- Former Wharton business school professor
- Former Goldman Sachs partner
- Recruited by a large aggressive S&L that was later seized and shut down
- Prior disciplinary action for mispricing
- Class-action
- Smirlock was sentenced to four years' prison and $12.6 million restitution

Case Summary

Michael Smirlock had earned a Ph.D. from Washington University (St. Louis) and was teaching finance at the Wharton School of Business by the age of 25. At 31, he was a tenured professor and was lured from academia by Franklin Savings Association in Kansas, as part of a new mortgage bond team, where he was responsible for asset acquisitions within the overall hedging operations. After some badly timed acquisitions Franklin suffered some losses and was later seized by the bank's regulator, an action that proved contentious.

Smirlock departed Franklin for Goldman Sachs Asset Management where he was chief investment officer (CIO) for fixed income investment. He was made a partner, at the age of 35 in October 1992, but just five months later was suspended for "irregularities" in the allocation of trades to client accounts. The matter was referred to the SEC and in December 1993, Smirlock was fined $50,000, suspended, and ordered to cease and desist for recordkeeping violations involving transfers of some $5 million of client securities.

Neither admitting nor denying guilt Smirlock was next picked up in early 1994 by Appaloosa Partners, a hedge fund founded a year earlier by David Tepper, also an ex-Goldman executive and staffed by several other former Goldman personnel.

Smirlock was hired to develop and trade mortgage-related products.

Over the next three years, he was given portfolio management responsibility for all of Appaloosa's mortgage funds and, in August 1997, this was formalized with the establishment of Laser Advisers, 78 percent owned by Smirlock and 22 percent owned by Appaloosa. About eight months later, conditions in the interest rate market became unstable and losses appeared in Laser's funds. Court documents alleged that Smirlock had started mispricing assets from December 1997 and did so on occasions from then through May 1988. This practice resulted in April and May 1998 published NAVs for the Shetland Fund of 0.31 percent and 0.7 percent, while actual returns for the two months was −14 percent. The total mispricing value was $71 million.

Smirlock disclosed the true situation to the fund boards in June 1998, and they informed the investors. In July, Smirlock gave up control and then resigned from Laser. Administrative, civil class action, and criminal lawsuits followed, the last of which ordered him to be incarcerated for four years and to pay restitution of $12.6 million. The class action was settled in 2005 and agreed a distribution amongst the plaintiff parties.

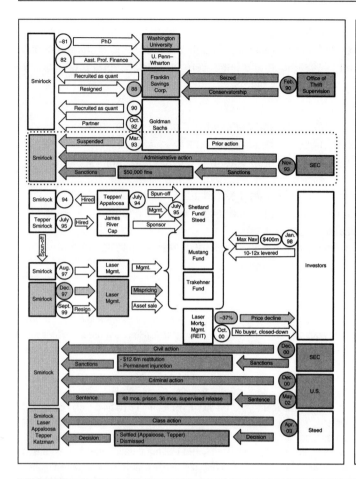

Fraud Facts

- Alleged Acts Date: December 1997
- Enforcement Date: December 21, 2000 (prior enforcement action, November 1993)
- Main Defendants **(hedge fund–related): Michael Smirlock, Laser Advisors, Mustang Fund, Shetland Fund, Steed Finance, Trakehner Fund**
- Most Serious Charge: Fraud
- Damages $actual **($2005): $71 million ($85 million)**
- No. of Investors: NA
- Highest Court: Criminal
- Most Severe Sentence: 48 months' prison, $12.6 million restitution

Sanctions:

- Michael Smirlock: 48 months' prison, 3 years' probation, $12.6 million restitution, permanent injunction
- Laser Advisors, Inc.: Permanent injunction
- David Tepper: Settled
- Appaloosa Management: Settled
- Class Action "Class": 54.04 percent of settlement
- "Steed" plaintiff: 38.24 percent of settlement
- "Republic" plaintiffs: 7.72 percent of settlement

Cases:

- *Steed Finance v. Smirlock* (99cv04222, civil, S. Dist. N.Y.)
- *U.S. v. Smirlock* (1:00cr01292, criminal, S. Dist. N.Y.)
- *SEC v. Smirlock* (1:00cv09680, civil, S. Dist. N.Y.)

U.S. expats in Panama defrauded a group of individuals, mostly chiropractors. The CFTC filed civil charges of selling unregistered securities. Private and criminal actions followed. Over $45 million of restitution and fines were ordered. Several probationary prison terms were also handed out. Key points:

- CFTC case
- Commodity pool, CPO companies and management based in Panama
- Victims all U.S. citizens, most residents of Alabama
- Chief perpetrator (Busch) was a chiropractor and linked to an earlier insurance fraud
- Defendant Busch became a fugitive until extradited
- One of main defendants (Amos) had experience in criminal operations in Panama (Marc Harris Organization, Agora Press)
- Prison sentences surprisingly light given the seriousness and scale of crime

Case Summary

This complex case involves an unregistered commodity pool, a group of chiropractors, and a Panama backdrop, and it is set against a darker prior history involving solicitation to commit murder. The central character was Dr. Richard E. Busch, a chiropractor, formerly of Fort Wayne, Indiana, who fled to Panama in 1993 after law enforcement began investigating a chiropractic malpractice insurance company of which he was president, and which also published a chiropractic professional journal. His senior partner (and possibly alter ego) in these ventures, William Rose, also a chiropractor, had been sentenced to 20 years in prison in 1986 for attempting to contract four murders. (He was paroled in 1993.)

In Panama, Busch reestablished his journal, *American Chiropractor*, and became associated with other individuals who were knowledgeable in the ways of offshore finance. One of these, William Amos, a lawyer and former insurance consultant, had been employed with the Marc Harris Organization in Panama and had ghostwritten for Agora Press on offshore financial techniques including tax avoidance under the penname Adam Starchild.

Busch and Amos created the Millennium Fund, an unregistered commodity pool. Some 14 investors, mainly Alabama chiropractors, were solicited with many misrepresentations including a profit guarantee from a nonexistent insurance company, and subsequently subscribed around $11 million. These investors were told that the only way they could invest in the Panama-based fund was via two other entities, ChateauForte Consortium and WorldEx, Inc., which was also the pool's manager. A second and third tier of incentive-based marketers (Hanks, Bowden, Burgdorf) were enlisted.

On July 7, 1998, the CFTC filed a civil complaint against all of the Millennium-related entities for selling unregistered securities and followed this in March 1999 with a default order against Busch for $10.8 million. This was followed by a criminal conspiracy action, the extradition of Busch from Panama, and his sentencing to five months' prison, $5.6 million restitution, and a maximum civil fine of over $32 million. Amos and another associate, Hanks, received probationary sentences along with joint-and-several restitution. There were also at least two major private actions against these same defendants (*Smith v. Busch*, *Osceola v. Busch*), both of which won several million in further financial damages against the same defendants.

As a footnote, there is a Dr. Richard E. Busch III practicing chiropractics in Fort Wayne, Indiana, who was featured on the cover of the March 2007 issue of *American Chiropractor*. His profile in the article states, under the heading of "Vacations," "Very spontaneous, short weekends with the family, frequently to Panama and Florida to see the family."

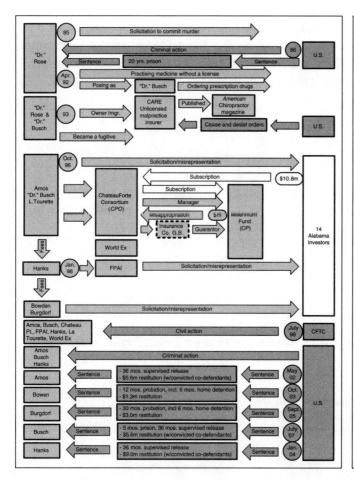

Fraud Facts

- Alleged Acts Date: October 1996
- Enforcement Date: July 31, 1998
- Main Defendants **(hedge fund–related): Amos, J Busch, R Busch, Hanks, Latourette, ChateauForte, Millennium Fund. WorldEx**
- Most Serious Charge: Conspiracy against the U.S., fraud
- Damages $actual **($2005): $10.8 million ($13.4 million)**
- No. of Investors: 14
- Highest Court: Criminal
- Most Severe Sentence: 15 months' prison, $45 million restitution and fines

Sanctions:

- William Earl Amos Jr.: 3 years' probation, $5.6 million restitution (joint and several with Busch)
- R. Stephen Bowden: 1 year probation, 6 months' home detention, $1.3 million restitution
- Brian Burgdorf: 30 months' probation, $3.0 million restitution
- Dr. Richard E. Busch: 5 months' prison, 5 months' home detention, permanent injunction
- Dr. Richard E. Busch: $13.1 million restitution (joint and several), $32.5 million civil fine
- James Michael Hanks: 36 months' probation, $8.95 million restitution, joint and several
- ChateauForte Consortium, Inc.: $2.43 million judgment, joint and several

Cases:

- *CFTC v. ChateauForte*
- *Osceola v. Busch* (98cv03110, civil, W. Dist. Tenn.)
- *Smith v. Busch* (99cv00024, civil, N. Dist. Ala.)
- *U.S. v. Amos* (01cr00504, criminal, N. Dist. Ala.)
- *U.S. v. Hanks* (03cr00055, criminal, N. Dist. Ala.)
- *U.S. v. Busch* (03cr00055, criminal, N. Dist. Ala.)
- *Busch v. CFTC* (U.S. Supreme Court 01–363)

The defendant, a hedge fund general partner closed down after suffering nearly a 50 percent decline in NAV over a number of months. The defendant declared bankruptcy and was sued, along with the prime broker and fund accountants, by investors in a civil class action for overvaluing private equity holdings. The case was settled in compulsory arbitration. Key points:

- Private (class) action at the county level
- No enforcement agency actions
- Prime broker and accountants named as defendants
- Hollywood names included among investors
- Class action alleged NAV distorted by improper valuations on private equities
- Case settled in compulsory arbitration, reportedly paying 1 to 2 percent back to investors

Case Summary

In 1991, Robert Pryt, a former Bear Stearns broker, created the BKP Partners hedge fund group. Over the next six to seven years, BKP attracted as much as $270 million from an investor group that contained several prominent Hollywood personalities, including singer-actress Barbara Streisand and her one-time partner, producer Jon Peters.

In the stock market turbulence of 1997, the fund lost 40 percent of its NAV, and then, in 1998, it suffered a further 27 percent decline through May. A number of investor legal actions followed, which were consolidated into a single class action—Crescent Porter Hale Foundation et. al. v. Bob K. Pryt et. al. filed in San Francisco County Superior Court, on October 19. The investor suit also named Bear Stearns and Deloitte, Touche, BKP's prime broker and auditor, respectively.

According to the Class Action Reporter of February 24, 1999, the investor suit stated the following grounds for their action:

- Committed common law fraud
- Negligent misrepresentation and civil conspiracy
- Breached a fiduciary duty
- Breached a covenant of good faith and fair dealing
- Aiding and abetting of the above allegations

Investors believed that Pryt "went beyond the scope that his investors had approved," in particular, that he had "tried to turn a hedge fund into a venture capital fund." Related to this comment were concerns that Pryt had used private placements as a means of overvaluing the fund, its performance and, as a consequence, overvaluing Pryt's performance fees.

The courts upheld the plaintiff's request for compulsory arbitration and a settlement was ultimately reached, which, according to newspaper reports, paid out around 1 to 2 percent of the value of the assets invested.

BKP Partners filed for bankruptcy in mid-to-late 1999.

There appeared to have been no actions taken by regulators or other law enforcement agencies.

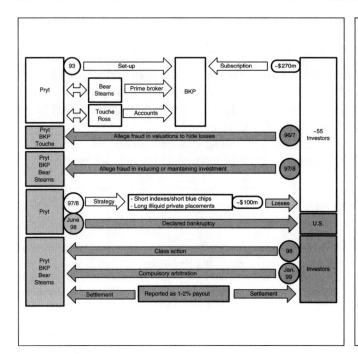

Fraud Facts

- Alleged Acts Date: 1997
- Enforcement Date: October 19, 1998
- Main Defendants **(hedge fund–related): Pryt, BKP Partners,** Bear Stearns, Deloitte Touche
- Most Serious Charge: Misrepresentation, breach of fiduciary duty
- Damages $actual **($2005): $100 million ($123 million)**
- No. of Investors: Approximately 55
- Highest Court: Class action, state court
- Most Severe Sentence: NA (compulsory arbitration)

Sanctions:

- Bob Pryt: None (arbitration)
- BKP Partners, LP: none (arbitration)
- BKP Capital Mgmt, LLC: None (arbitration)
- Bear Stearns & Co.: None (arbitration)
- Bear Stearns Securities Corp.: None (arbitration)
- Deloitte Touche: None (arbitration)

Cases:

- *Crescent PHF v. Pryt* (CGC-98–998637, civil class action, Superior Court San Francisco, Ca.Ca.)
- *Harbor Finance v. Pryt* (Contra Costa Co.)

The defendant improperly data-mined an extensive newsletter and contest mailing list to prospect for investors in six unregistered hedge funds. Key points:

- Defendant's U.S. Investment Championships provided a unique showcase for promoting unknown traders and hedge fund managers. The championships and related enterprises yielded a large mailing list, which the defendants utilized to seek investors for a group of hedge funds
- No damages—the defendants paid fines rather than restitution
- Championship was also subject to abuse by dishonest traders (see Cases: 6, 22, 37, 48)

Case Summary

Norman Zadeh was one of the more colorful characters to have been the subject of an SEC hedge fund action. His father, Lotfi Zadeh, a gifted scientist and professor from Azerbaijan, was a founder of that branch of mathematics known as fuzzy logic. "Norm," the son, was a math Ph.D., publisher of scholarly papers and a book on poker-playing strategies. But, he was perhaps best known as the creator of the U.S. Investment Championship contests. Launched in 1983, the "Championship" was widely followed by the investment community during the 12 years of its existence. It was also partly responsible for establishing the careers and reputations of many traders and investment managers. Zadeh himself was implicated in a case of conduct that became the basis of an SEC administrative proceeding, *In the matter of Prime Advisors, . . . Zadeh . . . Goodstein*, 3–9664, 31 July 1998.

In that action, the SEC charged that Zadeh and his partner, Jeffrey Goodstein, improperly solicited for hedge fund investors from an 11,000-name mailing list derived from his contests and a newsletter. Zadeh and Goodstein had raised about $159 million for Prime Advisors Inc. (PAI) from about 400 investors. Zadeh was also charged with not keeping proper ledgers as required by the Advisers Act (Rule 204–2(a)(2).

The three defendants were censured and the subjects of cease-and-desist orders and had to pay civil fines of $165,000 (Zadeh), $137,500 (PAI), $27,500 (Goodstein).

Some of the famous and infamous names that appeared among the Championship winners over the years included Guarente (see Case 6), Doviak (see Case 22), Prendergast (see Case 37), Hegarty (see Case 48), Zadeh (see Case 64), and Moses (SEC Administrative Proceeding, File No. 3–10807, 06/20/02). The famous included: Paul Tudor Jones, Marty Schwartz ("Market Wizards"), and Gil Blake ("Market Wizards"). In several cases, the Championship record was instrumental for a new manager to attract investors and, in at least one or two cases, these records or the traders themselves were using it as a prop to promote a fraud.

In a footnote to the case, Goodstein soon sought suit against Zadeh charging that his (Zadeh's) recent activities in publishing a new pornographic magazine (*Perfect 10*, i.e. no silicone) had resulted in injury to the commercial interests of their jointly owned company, Prime Advisors, Inc. Zadeh filed an appeal. The case was dismissed.

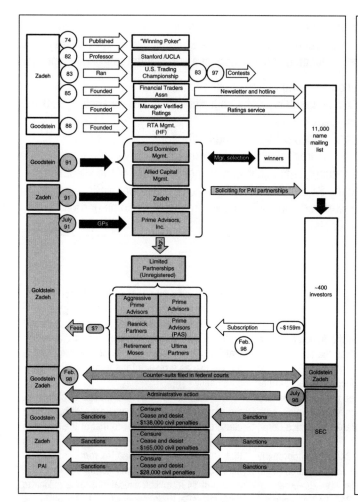

Fraud Facts

- Alleged Acts Date: 1991
- Enforcement Date: July 31, 1998
- Main Defendants **(hedge fund–related): Jeffrey Goodstein, Norman Zadeh, Prime Advisors, Inc., Aggressive Prime Advisors, Prime Advr. (PAS)**, Resnick Prtnrs., Retrmnt. Moses
- Most Serious Charge: Registration and recordkeeping violations
- Damages $actual **($2005)**: none
- No. of Investors: 400
- Highest Court: Administrative
- Most Severe Sentence: $300,000 civil penalties (total 3 defendants), cease-and-desist order, censure

Sanctions:

- Jeffrey Goodstein: Censured, cease-and-desist order, $27,500 civil penalties
- Norman Zadeh: Censured, cease-and-desist order, $165,000 civil penalties
- Prime Advisors, Inc.: Censured, cease-and-desist order, $137,500 civil penalties

Cases:

- *SEC v. Prime* (Admin. Proc. 3–9664, administrative)
- *Goodstein v. Zadeh* (98cv01348, civil, C. Dist. Ca.)
- *Zadeh v. Goodstein* (98–56119, 9th Cir.)

The defendants were subject of a class action based on inadequate disclosure and incorrect accounting of transactions accompanying a strategic tie-up with a struggling hedge fund, This adversely impacted shareholders in a subsequent merger. Key points:

- Successful class action resulting in a major settlement
- SEC administrative action resulting in the imposition of sanctions against Bank of America Corporation (BAC)
- SEC found instances of "incorrect accounting treatment"
- Actions concerned disclosures related to a bank merger
- Hedge fund not a defendant, although it was an indirect cause of the allegations
- BAC had injected nearly $1.4 billion into DE Shaw and later took a $372 million write-off after Shaw suffered substantial losses in its fixed income portfolio in the wake of the Russian Crisis

Case Summary

In March 1998, Bank of America Corp. extended and formalized what had been a productive relationship with D.E. Shaw & Co., a hedge fund created in 1988 by David E. Shaw, with the structuring of a broad financial "alliance." It was the terms of this alliance, and their disclosure to the SEC and to the shareholders of subsequent merger partner NationsBank Corp., that formed the basis of an SEC administrative action and a civil class action, both of which the merged entity, Bank of America Corp., settled.

The SEC charged that BAC had improperly accounted a $100 million subordinated loan agreement and a credit facility agreement it concluded with D.E. Shaw. BAC had categorized as a "loan," what should have been claimed as an investment and reported as noninterest income. The SEC argued that the terms of these agreements in combination paid BAC over 50 percent of the net profits of D.E. Shaw Securities. The SEC also held that BAC did not adequately disclose its exposure to market risk as a result of the terms of the alliance agreement.

The class action had two groups of claimants, the shareholders of NationsBank Corp., whose cause of action was similar to that of the SEC, and the shareholders of BankAmerica Corp. claiming that NationsBank Corp. had, in retrospect, made misleading statements prior to the merger. The payout of $490 million allocated $333.2 million to the NationsBank claimants and $156.8 million to BAC claimants.

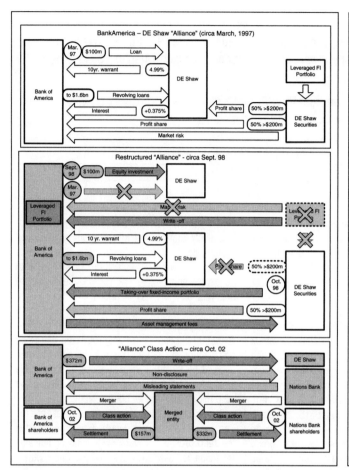

Fraud Facts

- Alleged Acts Date: March 1997
- Enforcement Date: October 2, 2002
- Main Defendants **(hedge fund–related):** Bank of America Corp., **D.E. Shaw & Co.**
- Most Serious Charge: Reporting and disclosure
- Damages $actual **($2005): $333.2 million ($405 million)**
- No. of Investors:100,000+
- Highest Court: Civil (class action)
- Most Severe Sentence: cease-and-desist order (SEC), $490 million restitution (class action)

Sanctions:

- Bank of America Corp.: cease-and-desist order (SEC)
- Bank of America Corp.: $490 million restitution (class action)

Cases:

- *In the matter of BankAmerica Corp.* (SECAdmin. Proc. 3–10541)
- *Re BankAmerica Corp.* (4:99md01264, civil, Eastern District, Mo.)

The defendant in this case established a hedge fund and with false credentials raised money from personal acquaintances and leads provided by them. Losses and false reports appeared within two years and bankruptcy was filed when investors pressed for their money. Key points:

- No enforcement action from the SEC or CFTC or other regulatory agency
- Made false performance reports to investors
- Filed for Chapter 7 bankruptcy
- More than $1 million recovered by bankruptcy trustee

Case Summary

The enforcement documentation for this case includes a federal criminal action (*USA v. Roon*) and several bankruptcy actions, including Roon's voluntary Chapter 7 filing (98–55088). There are no related civil or administrative actions by the SEC or CFTC. This may be due to the fact that Roon filed for bankruptcy before any litigation was filed.

Richard Roon established Nidra Capital, Inc., a hedge fund, in 1996 after soliciting personal contacts, including his lawyer, and his dentist, and other prominent people recommended by them such as a top fashion model couple, a partner in a major law firm, and a former CEO of a large securities company. From about 15 of these direct and indirect relationships he raised around $2 million. Among the terms these investors agreed to was the unusual condition that Roon was to be guaranteed an income of $20,000 per month. This was in addition to a more modest performance fee of 15 percent.

Roon later claimed that at the outset he managed the fund responsibly. However, the evidence suggests that by 1998 he was issuing false performance reports to cover mounting losses. Before long, he would also have to dodge redemption requests when they were submitted.

Investors were shocked into action when they learned that Roon had filed for voluntary Chapter 7 bankruptcy for Nidra Capital in November 1998,

initiating private lawsuits and private investigations. It is likely that federal investigators got involved at that point, charging Roon with three counts of criminal fraud in March 2000. Roon agreed to cooperate and pled guilty. He was sentenced to one year and one day in prison and three years' supervised release.

Investigators found that Nidra Capital had lost $700,000 between 1996 and 1998 and that Roon had withdrawn $380,000 more for his services than allowed by the fund memorandum to support his lifestyle. By 1998, the fund had liabilities exceeding $2.6 million and was all but insolvent.

Investigators also found that most of the impressive education and work experience cited in the fund prospectus were misleading or fictional. He failed to mention a prior employment with a notorious penny-stock company, an indictment in the 1980s related to a failed business, and that he had only attended college for two years before dropping out. Roon also made reference in the document to his "Knowledge Advantage"—a special insight into companies that "the vast majority of analysts and investors were unable to ascertain."

A fortunate development was the recovery of nearly $1.4 million by the bankruptcy trustee, most of it going to the investors, equivalent to around 42 percent of their losses.

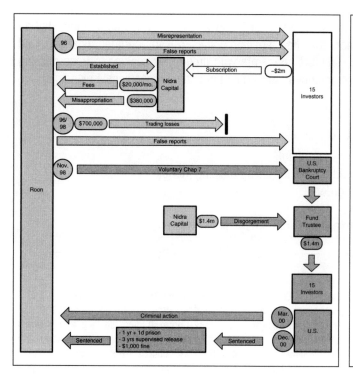

Fraud Facts

- Alleged Acts Date: Approximately 1996
- Enforcement Date: March 24, 2000
- Main Defendants **(hedge fund–related): Richard Roon, Nidra Capital**
- Most Serious Charge: Mail fraud
- Damages $actual **($2005)**: Approximately $2 million **($2.6 million)**
- No. of Investors: 15
- Highest Court: Criminal
- Most Severe Sentence: 12 months' plus 1 day prison, 3 years' supervised release, $1,000 fine

Sanctions:

- Richard Roon: 12 months' plus 1 day prison, 3 years' probation, $1,000 fine

Cases:

- *USA v. Roon* (00cr00176, criminal, N.J.)

The defendant created an unregistered CPO and solicited, by means that included an Internet site, funds of more than half a million dollars, misappropriated most of it, and lost some in trading. He failed to cooperate with authorities seeking to trace missing funds and was found in contempt in subsequent criminal proceedings. Key points:

- CFTC case
- Unregistered CPO
- Used an Internet site to solicit
- Cycled funds to an offshore bank
- Did not cooperate with courts in tracing missing money
- Received contempt order
- Became a fugitive
- Sentenced in a criminal case for perjury six years later

Case Summary

Michael Colton was not registered with the CFTC nor was his purported commodity pool operator, Future-Comm Trading, nor was it a proper legal entity. Despite this lack of status, Colton began soliciting for pool participants from January 1997 via an Internet site, brochures, and face-to-face meetings. Through these marketing channels, Colton made numerous false representations about himself and his commodity pool, including the claim that it was registered with the CFTC. He also later claimed spectacular past profits, exceeding 400 percent for 1997, using a proprietary trading system to trade S&P 500 futures when, in reality, he had lost money for that year.

Through these efforts, Colton raised around $524,000, which was deposited in various bank accounts, some business and some personal accounts, including under aliases and offshore (Dominica). Despite claims that his proprietary system achieved "low risk with a high probability of success," Colton lost money on trading in 1997 that included 77 "roundtrip" trades on the S&P 500, only 37 of which were profitable. In 1998, he lost more than $100,000.

On December 16, 1998, the CFTC filed a civil complaint against Michael Colton, doing business as Future-Comm Trading, seeking a permanent injunction, industry ban, financial restitution, and civil fines. The court froze the assets of the pool and appointed a receiver. Over the following four years, Colton resisted efforts to account for and repatriate the missing funds. This resistance brought about a citation for contempt, an arrest warrant, a period as a fugitive, and several stretches on remand and on probation. In 2004, he was also tried for perjury in criminal court and given three years' probation and six months of home detention.

While the receiver and the CFTC finally accounted for all but around $35,000 of the lost money, it is unclear how much if any was recovered and returned to the investors. Colton claimed that all but around $20,000 of the missing money was paid to investors, but no proof was ever offered to support this. In all likelihood, most had been spent on business and personal expenses.

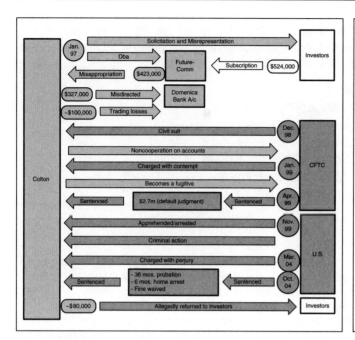

Fraud Facts

- Alleged Acts Date: January 1997
- Enforcement Date: December 1998
- Main Defendants **(hedge fund–related): Michael Colton, Future-Comm Trading**
- Most Serious Charge: Fraud
- Damages $actual **($2005):** Approximately $524,000 **($628,000)**
- No. of Investors: >15
- Highest Court: Criminal
- Most Severe Sentence: 36 months' probation, 6 months' house arrest

Sanctions:

- Michael Colton: 3 years' probation, 6 months' home arrest, fines waived

Cases:

- *CFTC v. Colton* (98cv02575, civil, M. Dist. Fl.)
- *USA v. Colton* (04cr00097, criminal, M. Dist. Fl.)

The commodity trader defendant in this case raised money for an unregistered commodity pool, commingled, and then lost or misappropriated a substantial portion of the funds. Key points:

- CME and CFTC case
- Unregistered commodity pool
- Solicited among fellow church members
- CME disciplinary action
- Published a book on day trading in the midst of his problems
- Trivette died before CFTC case was finished
- Wife reached consent agreement with CFTC, sanctions waived

Case Summary

Donald Trivette had been raised on a farm in North Carolina, studied agricultural economics, and graduated in May 1972 with a B.S. degree. Ten years later, he worked for a brokerage firm in the same state. In 1993, he moved to Chicago, where he traded futures and options for his own account at the Chicago Mercantile Exchange (CME) and was registered with the CFTC.

In 1995, Trivette persuaded members of his church to invest in a commodity pool he would set up. In total, about seven of his fellow parishioners along with other acquaintances invested more than $100,000.

Trivette commingled the investors' money with his own and some of this was misappropriated to meet personal needs. His S&P 500 trading lost money in each year from 1996 to 1999; however, investors were provided with false reports that indicated otherwise.

On October 12, 1998, Trivette was subject of a Chicago Mercantile Exchange Business Conduct Committee action, stemming from a prior investigation in which he was found to be in violation of CME Rule 432.I, "making verbal or written material misstatements to the Board, a committee, or Exchange employees." He was suspended from the exchange for two years.

When investors sought to redeem their funds in 1999, Trivette was unable to comply placing some of the blame on the CME, saying it had seized the funds. Ironically, as late as November 1998, in the middle of his legal problems Trivette published a small book entitled *A Professional Look at S&P Day Trading*.

The CFTC initiated a civil action on April 6, 1999, and on September 28, Trivette was arrested, though he died unexpectedly on December 6, 2001, before the legal process had been completed. The CFTC reached a consent agreement with the now deceased Trivette's wife, Meredith, who was the administrator of his estate. She agreed that the commission was justified in its actions against her late husband. The commission agreed to dismiss its complaint and to not seek restitution against the estate, given its reported minimal assets.

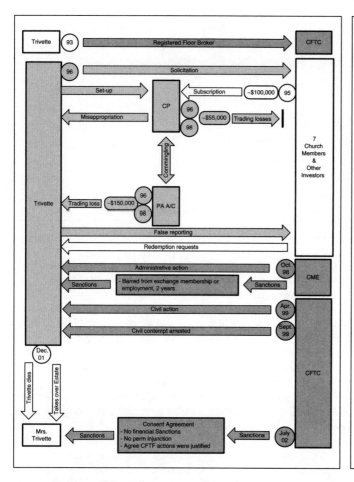

Fraud Facts
- Alleged Acts Date: 1995
- Enforcement Date: April 6, 1999
- Main Defendants **(hedge fund–related): Donald Trivette**
- Most Serious Charge: Misappropriation, Fraud
- Damages $actual **($2005): >$100,000 ($128,000)**
- No. of Investors: 7
- Highest Court: Civil
- Most Severe Sentence: Sanctions waived

Sanctions:

- Donald Trivette: CME membership and employment suspended two years
- Donald Trivette: (deceased before completion of court action)
- Meredith Trivette (wife): agreed to consent judgment, sanctions waived

Cases:

- *CME v. Trivette* (985629BC, administrative)
- *CFTC v. Trivette* (99cv00054, civil, W. Dist. N.C.)

The main defendant in this case was the subject of prior enforcement actions. He reoffended by operating several unregistered commodity pools. The violations included misrepresentation, disclosure, fraud, and misappropriation. Key points:

- CFTC case
- Unregistered CPOs
- Prior enforcement action by the SEC
- Unusual loan arrangements with investors
- Insignificant amount of real investment
- Employed Ponzi tactics
- A number of family members involved
- Settled in a series of consent agreements including substantial restitution

Case Summary

In the mid- to late 1980s, Joseph McGivney managed a rapidly growing mini-financial conglomerate that included a brokerage, insurance agency, commodities trader, trust company, some print shops, and Wealth Unlimited, a unit offering investment seminars to the general public. The group's parent company (JPM Industries) went public in July 1985 and within one year its share price had risen from $2 to $7, at which point its market capitalization was $236 million, with a price-earnings-ratio (PER) of about 300×.

However, at around the same time McGivney also found himself to be the subject of SEC enforcement action centering on his issuance of $11 million of promissory notes to some 500 investors and a failure to disclose that the collateral supporting the transaction was never put in place. The SEC also maintained that McGivney and his financial companies had to be registered as investment advisers to offer his seminars. In a consent agreement, McGivney agreed to a permanent injunction against selling promissory notes. As a consequence, the NASD later refused to approve McGivney's application for continued membership. A related action, CFTC Docket #87–3-SD, revoked the registrations of the same McGivney entities because of the NASD action.

On April 12, 1999, the CFTC filed an eight-count civil complaint against McGivney and associate Edwin Koziol, and six related corporate entities, including commodity pools and CPOs (99cv2357, N. Dist. Ill.). Also named as relief defendants were McGivney's ex-wife and current girlfriend for receiving ill-gotten gains. The complaint alleged that commencing as early as January 1993 McGivney et al. had operated as unregistered CPOs; solicited investors; made misrepresentations; accepted some $958,000 in the form of "loan agreements" from around 105 of investors; commingled the funds of the different commodity pools; failed to make certain disclosures while acting as CTAs; and misappropriated a substantial portion of the funds being managed.

In July 2000, the defendants and CFTC reached a series of consent agreements to settle the case. These agreements called for McGivney and Koziol to jointly and severally be liable for restitution of $755,085, plus prejudgment interest of $115,950. In addition, McGivney, Koziol and JPM, Inc. were also jointly and severally liable for a further restitution of $49,000 plus $3,693 prejudgment interest to a subgroup of 49 investors who participated in a separate "Rebate Pool." As relief defendants, McGivney's ex-wife Marita and girlfriend Leslie Wnukowski, herself an AP of her own CTA, were ordered to disgorge a total of $268,920. The combined restitution of all the defendants amounted to some $1.2 million including prejudgment interest. McGivney, Koziol, and Wnukowski were also barred from the industry and permanently injuncted against future violations. Wnukowski later appealed revocation of her registration, but her appeal was denied.

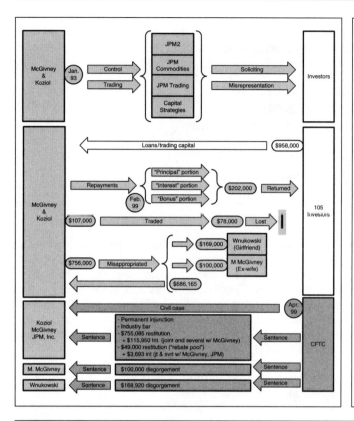

Fraud Facts

- Alleged Acts Date: January 1993
- Enforcement Date: April 12, 1999
- Main Defendants (**hedge fund–related**): **Koziol, J. McGivney**, M. McGivney Wnukowski (**Capital Strategies, JPM, Inc., JPM2, Inc. JPM Commodities, Inc., JPM Investments, Inc.**, JPM Traders, Inc.
- Most Serious Charge: Misappropriation, fraud
- Damages $actual (**$2005**): >$755,000 (**$880,000**)
- No. of Investors: 105
- Highest Court: Civil
- Most Severe Sentence: $1.2 million restitution and disgorgement, registrations revoked

Sanctions:

- Edwin, A. Koziol, Jr.: $871,000 restitution (w/McGiveny), permanent injunction
- Edwin, A. Koziol, Jr.: $53,000 restitution, Perf. Rebate pool (w/McGivney and JPM)
- Joseph, P. McGivney: $871,000 restitution (w/McGiveny), industry bar
- Joseph, P. McGivney: $53,000 restitution, Perf. Rebate pool (w/Koziol and JPM)
- JPM, Inc.: $53,000 restitution, Perf. Rebate pool (w/Koziol and McGivney)
- Marita McGivney: $100,000 disgorgement (deferred for 3 years)
- Leslie Wnukowski: $170,000 restitution, registration revoked

Cases:

- *SEC v. McGivney*
- *CFTC v. McGivney* (99cv2357, civil, N. Dist. Ill.)

The defendant formed two unregistered commodity pools and recruited acquaintances as investors in what became a Ponzi scheme. Key points:

- CFTC case
- Ex-broker with undisclosed NASD sanctions
- Two unregistered commodity pools
- Affinity aspect involving local church parishioners
- Defendant was a Sunday school teacher
- Very little money ever invested
- Most of money misappropriated

Case Summary

On February 2, 1994, the Dow Jones index hit a post-1987 high. Around this time, Donald James had reportedly terminated his employment as a broker in Asheville, North Carolina, and with his wife moved to the Atlanta area. Apparently, the NASD had some questions about this termination and James seemingly refused to, or was unable to, provide sufficient answers. There is a record of the NASD levying a fine of $20,000 on James in February 1997 for failing to provide this information and barring him from associating with any NASD member.

After moving to Dunwoody, Georgia, just north of Atlanta, James, then still in his mid-30s, became active in his local church, including teaching a Sunday school class. Over the next four years, James solicited fellow church members to invest in two unregistered commodity pools—Franklin Thomas & Company and Franklin Thomas Investments, LP, convincing about 25 church members and others to invest around $5 million during this time.

To bolster his marketing pitch, James misrepresented his trading experience saying he never lost money and that he was trading commodity futures and promised returns of as much as 18 percent per month on the investments. According to one parishioner friend at the time, James claimed that "God helped him make his trades" and that he would not make a trade unless he prayed about it."

Another said that "God had given (James) a formula to trade options." The reality was that before 1997 only about 4 percent ($200,000) of the investor money was ever invested, and 60 percent of this ($120,000) was lost in trading. And, after 1997, no investments were made. Whatever money was not being expended in maintaining the Ponzi scheme that the fund had become was consumed for personal expenses, including a $1.9 million home on seven acres of land in Alpharetta, where he moved in 1997.

The scheme began to unwind in late 1998, when investors sought to redeem some or all of their, by then, fictitious wealth from the pools and only received excuses and bounced checks in return. On April 9, 1999, several of these investors confronted James at his home. There he admitted to having lost all the money and to have stopped trading a year earlier due to a "mental block." On April 15, the CFTC filed a civil complaint followed over the next few days with orders for expedited discovery, a restraining order, and appointment of a receiver. A criminal case was filed on December 28. James was arrested a month later and, in March 2000, was sentenced to 51 months in prison, three years of supervised release, $100 special assessment and $3.33 million restitution. On July 10, 1999, Jameses' home and contents were sold in an auction.

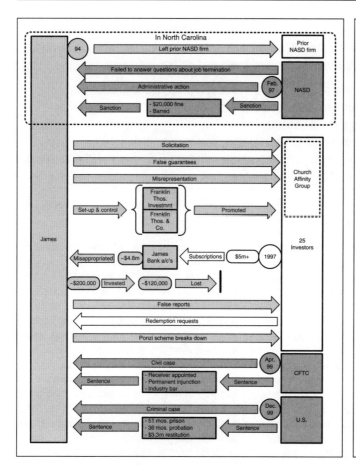

Fraud Facts

- Alleged Acts Date: 1995
- Enforcement Date: April 6, 1999
- Main Defendants **(hedge fund–related): James (Franklin Thomas & Co., Franklin Investments)**, Donald James, Inc.
- Most Serious Charge: Misappropriation, fraud
- Damages $actual **($2005): >$5 million ($5.8 million)**
- No. of Investors: 25
- Highest Court: Criminal
- Most Severe Sentence: 51 months' prison, 3 years' probation, $3.55 million restitution, industry ban

Sanctions:

- Donald E. James: 51 months' prison, 3 years' probation, $3.33 million restitution, industry bar

Cases:

- *NASD v. James* (Administrative Proceeding, Feb. 1997)
- *CFTC v. James* (99cv00967, civil, N. Dist. Ga.)
- *U.S. v. James* (99cr00712, criminal, N. Dist. Ga.)

Two overlapping cases: one a civil action in which a commodity pool operator deceived a group of related investors, the other, a criminal action in which an individual related to the other investors by marriage, defrauded them and others. Key points:

- CFTC civil case (Tennessee) plus a U.S. Attorney's Office criminal case (Alabama)
- Two-tier fraud where one deceptive entity invested in another
- In part operated as a Ponzi scheme
- Main victims and one perpetrator related by family ties
- New Jersey defendant, who was registered with the CFTC, was not charged with misappropriation or other criminal charges

Case Summary

Edwin Jay Sheldon, a resident of Little Falls, New Jersey, was the owner, principal, and Associated Person of commodity pool operator Applied Capital Management, LLC, which managed a commodity pool, Fair Haven Futures Fund. In late 1997, Sheldon hosted a meeting in New York with Kenneth and Mary Duke, a wealthy couple from Tennessee, and another couple from Birmingham, Alabama, Charles Powell and Wanda Powell, who was also Kenneth Duke's sister. At this meeting, Sheldon made numerous misrepresentations about the fund and his experience. For example, that apart from one minor instance, he had never made a monthly loss in seven years of commodity trading and that investors could not lose more than 10 to 12 percent, as that was the maximum amount invested. He also stated that he required investor approval to invest more than 15 percent in the futures markets.

Powell was an unregistered securities agent based in Birmingham and principal of the unregistered Alpha Group, the vehicle used by his brother-in-law, Kenneth Duke, and others to invest in the Fair Haven Futures Fund. During 1998, the Dukes, along with other members of the Alpha Group, invested about $334,000 into Fair Haven out of a total, of nearly $1 million the Alpha had previously raised from some 20 investors. Throughout 1998 while the Fairhaven Fund was

steadily losing money, Sheldon continued to write reports to the investors stating otherwise. Efforts to maintain the look of normalcy included calculating an NAV that hid the trading losses by netting them off against the receivable of supposed management fees due from Powell's Alpha Group, as well as Ponzi-style recycling of fictitious profits or redemptions to Alpha Group investors amounting to $47,831 during 1998. However, by December of that year the losses drove Sheldon to shut down the fund. At that time its net assets were virtually nil.

On January 15, 1999, Powell was indicted by a grand jury in Shelby County Alabama on fraud and securities charges related to the loss of almost $1 million by more than 20 of the investors in his Alpha Group. In April 1999 the CFTC filed a civil complaint against Sheldon, Applied Capital Mgmt., and Charles Powell. Sheldon and Applied Capital agreed to a Consent Order with the CFTC, which included a permanent injunction and joint and several payment of restitution of $334,000 over a five-year period. Sheldon was also barred from the commodity futures industry. A default judgment and permanent injunction was entered against Powell.

In the separate Shelby County criminal action, Powell was sentenced to 46 months in prison, supervised release of three years, and ordered to pay restitution of $317,500 to one couple and one individual.

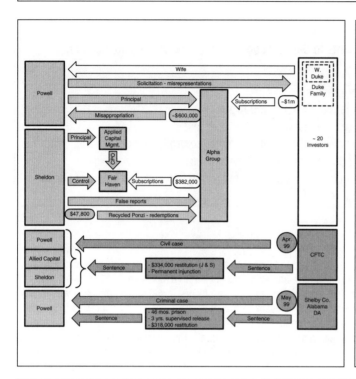

Fraud Facts

- Alleged Acts Date: Late 1997
- Enforcement Date: April 28, 1999
- Main Defendants **(hedge fund–related):** Powell, **Sheldon, Applied Capital Mgmt., Fair Haven Futures Fund**
- Most Serious Charge: Fraud
- Damages $actual **($2005): $652,000 ($770,000)**
- No. of Investors: Approximately 20
- Highest Court: Criminal
- Most Severe Sentence: 46 months' prison, $652,000 restitution, industry bar

Sanctions:

- Charles E. Powell: 46 months' prison, 3 years' probation, $317,500 restitution
- Edwin J. Sheldon: $334,000 restitution (joint and several), industry bar, permanent injunction
- Applied Capital Management, LLC: $334,000 restitution (joint and several)

Cases:

- *CFTC v. Sheldon* (99cv00138, civil, E. Dist. Tenn.)
- *U.S. v. Powell* (99cr00183, criminal, N. Dist. Ala.)

Two defendants utilized offshore and onshore companies and promotions as well as inappropriate bank accounts to defraud commodity pool investors. Key points:

- CFTC case
- Made use of BVI companies
- Ran soliciting seminars in Cancun and Aruba
- About 5 percent of money invested and all of it lost
- Investor money was directed to bank accounts controlled by defendants, where it was commingled and used for personal expenses
- Seemingly no effort made to prolong deception with Ponzi-like recycling of capital
- Oddly, no known criminal case was ever pursued

Case Summary

In the fall of 1997, David Loyd and Richard Tichy of Fort Lauderdale, Florida, put into motion an elaborate scheme of offshore and onshore companies to defraud more than 100 investors who thought they were investing nearly $3 million in commodity futures. Prior to this, the two perpetrators were both Associated Persons of a CTA–introducing broker, First Resource & Capital Management, where Loyd had been registered and Tichy was not.

The scheme involved Europacific Equity and Capital Management, a Florida-based commodity pool, and two British Virgin Islands (BVI) entities, International Investment Group, Ltd., and Tortola Corporation Company, Ltd., the former acting as the manager of Europacific and the latter a promotional vehicle.

The coconspirators issued promotional literature and ran investment seminars in Aruba and Cancun that made numerous misrepresentations about their investment business, describing, among other things, Tichy's trading experience and track record. Investors were told that Tichy had developed computer programs to trade commodities, including one strategy that utilized "a very sophisticated and complex program composed of ten noncorrelated S&P 500 index trading computer models."

It was further claimed that Tichy had invested his own money in these strategies and that his performance was proof that they worked, having produced a return of 72 percent in the first two months of 1998. They predicted the oddly precise minimum return for the year of 134.21 percent.

The money raised in the promotion was mostly or entirely directed to a Tichy-controlled, U.S.-based Charles Schwab trading account in the name of Europacific. The investor money in this account was commingled and misappropriated to pay personal expenses. Of around $2.3 million deposited only about $134,000 (approximately 6 percent) ended up at one of the two trading accounts, Linnco Futures Group, in Chicago. All of this money was lost and the accounts were closed in December 1998. These losses were not disclosed to the investors, who received false reports detailing double-digit gains per month. By August 1968, these reports claimed that returns had exceeded 50 percent year to date (YTD) and 60 to 70 percent was projected for the year.

By the start of October 1998, investors tried without success to redeem their shares. This failure likely led to the subsequent involvement of the CFTC. A civil complaint followed in May 1999. Loyd settled the case in a consent agreement that stipulated $2.9 million in joint and several restitution plus interest. Tichy's lack of cooperation resulted in a default judgment on him and the three corporate defendants, which added a civil penalty of $7.9 million, including triple damages. No criminal charges were filed against Tichy despite his actions and subsequent lack of cooperation.

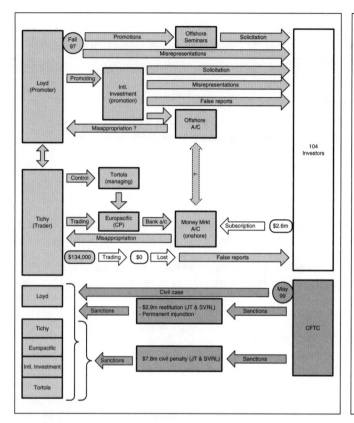

Fraud Facts

- Alleged Acts Date: November 1997
- Enforcement Date: May 5, 1999
- Main Defendants **(hedge fund–related): Loyd, Tichy, Europacific Equity, Intl. Investment, Tortola Corp.**
- Most Serious Charge: Fraud, misappropriation
- Damages $actual **($2005): $2.6 million ($3.0 million)**
- No. of Investors: 104
- Highest Court: Civil
- Most Severe Sentence: $7.8 million civil penalty, $2.8 million restitution, permanent injunction

Sanctions:

- Civil fine (joint and several)
- David Michael Loyd, Richard Tichy, Europacific Equity and Capital Mgmt., Int'l Investment Group, Tortola Company Ltd.
- $2.9 million restitution (joint and several), permanent injunction (all)
- Richard Tichy, Europacific Equity and Capital Mgmt., Int'l Investment Group, Tortola Company Ltd.
- $7.8 million civil fine (joint and several)

Cases:

- *CFTC v. Europacific* (99cv06560, civil, S. Dist. Fl.)

The defendant was the chief financial officer of an investment adviser/pool operator who defrauded his employer by allocating losing personal account (PA) trades to the funds the firm managed. Key points:

- No regulatory or civil actions, only criminal
- Hedge funds and adviser were the victims of fraud
- Defendant acted as a rogue trader, but was a CFO not a trader
- In a regulated entity, the CFO's PA trading should have been subject to compliance

Case Summary

Bruce Berkowitz was the CFO of Gotham Capital, a hedge fund investment adviser. While employed there, he became actively involved in trading S&P index options for his own account. To what extent this personal account trading was reported to his employer is not known; however, it appears that this trading lost Berkowitz millions of dollars.

Berkowitz sought to recoup his losses by defrauding Gotham Capital. He did this by continuing to trade S&P index options, even though he was now allocating his losing trades to Gotham's three hedge funds, while keeping the winning trades in his personal account. By the time these trades were discovered in June 1999, Berkowitz had redirected $4 to $5 million of losses to Gotham funds. Berkowitz was arrested on June 22, the same day a criminal complaint was filed with the U.S. District Court for the Southern District of New York.

After initially pleading "not guilty," by mid-August, Berkowitz changed his plea to "guilty." Berkowitz was sentenced to 37 months in prison followed by 36 months of supervised release and ordered to pay restitution equivalent to 20 percent of his gross monthly income from the time he commenced supervised release.

One unusual aspect of this case is the apparent lack of any regulatory or civil action. This may be due to the fact that Berkowitz or Gotham Capital was not registered with any regulator. Incidentally, Gotham Capital was founded in 1985 by Joel Greenblatt, the author of several popular books on value investing.

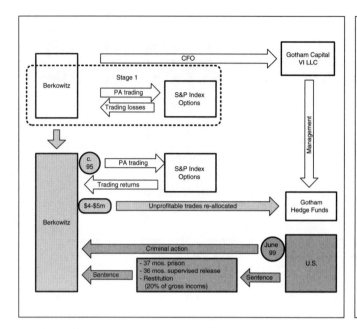

Fraud Facts

- Alleged Acts Date: 1995
- Enforcement Date:
  June 23, 1999
- Main Defendants **(hedge fund–related): Bruce Berkowitz, Gotham Capital Mgmt.**
- Most Serious Charge:
  Securities fraud
- Damages $actual **($2005): $4.5 million ($5.27 million)**
- No. of Investors: NA
- Highest Court: Criminal
- Most Severe Sentence:
  37 months' prison,
  3 years' probation,
  20 percent gross income

Sanctions:

- Bruce Berkowitz: 37 months' prison, 3 years' probation, restitution: 20 percent of gross income

Cases:

- *U.S. v. Berkowitz* (1:99cr00736, criminal, S. Dist. N.Y.)

Believing he qualified for exemption, the defendant in this case operated an unregistered commodity pool and accepted money from a small number of investors. When he had lost substantially all of that money, he sought to disguise the fact with false reports, admitting the truth to his investors when the deception was no longer sustainable. Key points:

- CFTC case
- Unregistered commodity pool
- Defendant Godres believed pool was exempt from registration
- All investor money lost through trading
- Godres sought to replace losses by trading with his own money
- Covered up losses by sending false reports to investors
- CFTC ordered restitution

Case Summary

Ross Godres, a native of Lafayette, Colorado, had been involved in the bullion business, where he came into contact with precious metals investors and saw the possibility of trading as a principal on their behalf. On May 3, 1993, Godres established the Navco Precious Metals Fund, and, on May 18, he submitted to the CFTC copies of documents he had given to prospective investors in his new fund. In submitting these documents, he also asserted that the fund would be exempt from having to register with the CFTC as a commodity pool operator because it had less than $200,000 capital and less than 15 investors. (The Commission's response, if any, is not known.)

After setting up a trading account with a futures commission merchant, Godres started to trade sometime after June 30, 1993. Over the course of that year, he received investment capital from five individuals totaling $60,750. However, Godres went on to lose all but $530 within one year and closed the trading account. Instead of disclosing the loss, he took measures to conceal it, including sending investors fictional performance reports. From September 1993, as his losses were mounting, Godres sought to make up the deficits by trading his own capital, but by June 1994, this effort had failed. From that time until June 1996, the deception campaign continued until it could no longer and Godres wrote to the investors, telling them the truth.

Three years were to pass before the CFTC took action, bringing an administrative proceeding against Godres, having already accepted an offer of settlement from him. He was ordered to cease and desist from his violative conduct, pay restitution plus interest, and be barred from registering with the CFTC.

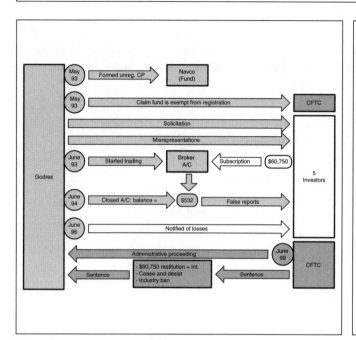

Fraud Facts

- Alleged Acts Date: June 1993
- Enforcement Date: June 28, 1999
- Main Defendants **(hedge fund–related): Godres, Navco Precious Metals Fund**
- Most Serious Charge: Fraud, misappropriation
- Damages $actual **($2005): $60,000 ($80,000)**
- No. of Investors: 5
- Highest Court: Administrative
- Most Severe Sentence: $60,750 restitution, industry bar

Sanctions:

- Ross R. Godres: $60,750 restitution plus interest, cease-and-desist order, industry ban

Cases:

- *In the Matter of Godres* (CFTC Docket #99–13, Admin. Proc.)

In this case, a registered commodity trading and commodity pool adviser lost all or most of the investment capital in his two commodity pools and caused violations by acting to deceive his investors about these losses over a period of several years. Key points:

- CFTC case
- Registered CTA/CPO
- Solicitation to an affinity group
- Loss of substantially all of investor money
- Failure to disclose losses
- Use of false reports to maintain deception
- Misappropriation of approximately 10 percent of money invested
- Civil case resulting in consent order to pay restitution and Industry bar

Case Summary

In January, February, and March 1989, Morris Benun, at that time a resident of Brooklyn, New York, applied for membership and registration with the National Futures Association (NFA) and the CFTC as a CTA, CPO, and introducing broker. A few months later the memberships and registrations were effective. In October 1990, around the time the CFTC alleged that his violative conduct began, Benun withdrew his registration as an introducing broker. The violations cited by the CFTC concerned two commodity pools that the defendant ran: Benun Fund and Aspen Capital Management. Around $5.2 million was raised from 27 individuals for these funds. Eighteen of these investors were from Brooklyn, 17 from one ZIP code, suggestive of an affinity group. Three of members of this group were rabbis, at least one, also named Benun, was possibly a relative, and several others appear to be related members of two or more of the other victim families.

It was not alleged Benun caused any violations in creating his funds or in soliciting for investors. There

were also no serious misrepresentations alleged in the marketing of the funds. Benun's violations involved his actions to disguise substantial losses with false reports. This deception went on for as long as six years, although it is not clear when the losses became substantial—and whether these investors pressured him to redeem some or all of their fictitious profits and whether Ponzi-like tactics were used to prolong the fraud. There was also one charge filed against Benun of converting $49,531 of client money for his own use.

While Benun had withdrawn as a CPO, CTA, and member of NFA on May 31, 1996, there is no evidence of any legal or regulatory action against him until the CFTC filed a civil complaint in July 1999. The action resulted in a consent agreement in which Benun was ordered to pay restitution of $1,046,516, a sum that included disgorgement of the $49,531 misappropriated. He was also barred from the industry and permanently enjoined from further violations.

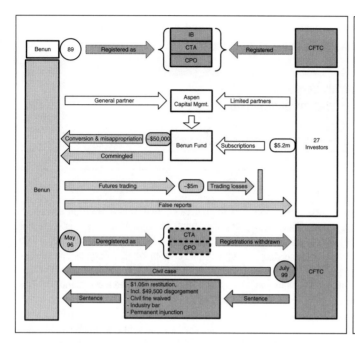

Fraud Facts
- Alleged Acts Date: 1990
- Enforcement Date: July 2, 1991
- Main Defendants **(hedge fund–related): Benun (Aspen Capital Mgmt. Fund, Benun Futures Fund)**
- Most Serious Charge: Fraud, false reports
- Damages $actual **($2005): $5.2 million ($6.1 million)**
- No. of Investors: 27
- Highest Court: Civil
- Most Severe Sentence: $1.05 million restitution, industry bar

Sanctions:
- Morris J. Benun: $1.047 million restitution, including $49,531 disgorgement, civil fine waived, industry bar, permanent injunction

Cases:
- *CFTC v. Benun* (99cv04822, civil, S. Dist. N.Y.)

Two individuals solicited investors for an unregistered commodity pool, lost some in trading, and misappropriated the balance. Key points:

- CFTC case
- Unregistered commodity pool and operators
- Most of investor cash was misappropriated
- Deception lasted three years
- Evidence of prior legal troubles that should have deterred investors

Case Summary

This is a thinly documented case. The two defendants, Richard Belz and Andrew Cafferky, both residents of Tennessee and neither registered with the CFTC, solicited on behalf of an unregistered commodity pool, Safetrak Group, Ltd. Beginning in 1994 and extending through to 1997, the pair raised around $596,000, $459,000 of which was misappropriated and more than $137,000 of losses were incurred in trading.

From the available documents, it is unclear whether the trading losses led, lagged, or were contemporaneous with the misappropriations. More clear is the fact that things were starting to unravel by 1997. There is an NFA Notice (I-97–07) of March 27, 1997, that asked anyone that had an account with or had transacted business with Belz, Cafferky, Blue Chip, or Safetrak, to contact the NFA Compliance Department immediately.

In April 1998, there was a record of a property transfer from Richard Belz and his wife for $159,000. There was also a private civil action filed against Blue Chip Information Corp. in July 1998— a compromise was reached in that case. Then on July 19, 1999, the CFTC filed a civil complaint. This action was resolved on September 3, 1999, with a consent agreement in which the defendants were joint and severally liable to disgorge $596,000 plus interest, with payments to be made over a five-year period. They also received permanent injunctions and were barred from the industry.

As a footnote, both Cafferky and Belz had filed bankruptcy petitions in November 1987 and February 1989, respectively, and Richard Belz and a company named Capital Investments were named as defendants in a private securities–commodities action in the Eastern District of Tennessee in May 1995, the latter a date overlapping with the events of this case.

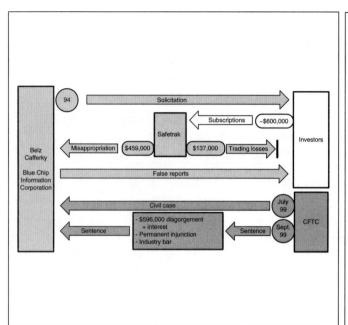

Fraud Facts
- Alleged Acts Date: 1994
- Enforcement Date: July 19, 1999
- Main Defendants **(hedge fund–related): Belz, Cafferky (Blue Chip Info. Corp., Safetrak Group)**
- Most Serious Charge: Commodity fraud, misappropriation
- Damages $actual **($2005): $600,000 ($760,000)**
- No. of Investors: NA
- Highest Court: Civil
- Most Severe Sentence: $60,750 restitution, industry bar

Sanctions:

- Richard G. Belz: $596,581 disgorgement (joint and several), industry bar, permanent injunction
- Andrew E. Cafferky: $596,581 disgorgement (joint and several), industry bar, permanent injunction
- Blue Chip Information Corporation: $596,581 disgorgement (joint and several), industry bar, permanent injunction

Cases:

CFTC v. Belz (99cv00378, civil, E. Dist. Tenn.)

The defendant, a broker with prior financial difficulties who was a registered floor broker with a seat on a commodity exchange, created a commodity pool partnership with one limited partner and then defrauded that partner of over $1 million. Key points:

- CFTC case
- Registered floor broker with seat on Kansas City Board of Trade
- Prior financial and legal problems, including defaulting on a promissory note
- Defrauded commodity pool with just one limited partner
- Administrative and criminal actions, no civil action

Case Summary

In 1993 the defendant, Max Walters, a CFTC-registered floor broker and member of the Kansas City Board of Trade, formed Chaparral Investments, LP, and acted as its general partner. At that time, he solicited a friend, Leland Brewer, to be an investor. In doing so, Walters made a number of misrepresentations as well as omissions, including the fact that he had a computer-based trading system that had produced an annual return of 600 percent. He also claimed that his trading was conservative and that it would not include overnight trading of futures and options.

Beginning in August 1993, Brewer became a limited partner of Chaparral and, between then and August 1996, invested a total of $1.15 million in addition to a personal loan extended to Walters for $.5 million. During this period, Walter provided Brewer with false reports of Chaparral's performance, including a false IRS form 1099 showing purported partnership profits for 1994. By September 1996, Brewer believed he had accrued cumulative trading profits of $945,000, when, in fact, the partnership had losses totaling $811,000.

In October 1996, Walters returned $8,994 to Brewer and admitted that Chaparral had lost the majority of its assets. The CFTC subsequently filed a complaint that same month and in January 2000 criminal charges were also filed. In its investigations, the CFTC found that Walters had misappropriated $872,129 from Chaparral, though this was offset by $53,000 that had been transferred from his own account to Chaparral's. Walters was subsequently sentenced to 27 months in prison in the criminal case and ordered to pay a civil penalty of $2.4 million on top of restitution of more than $1.64 million.

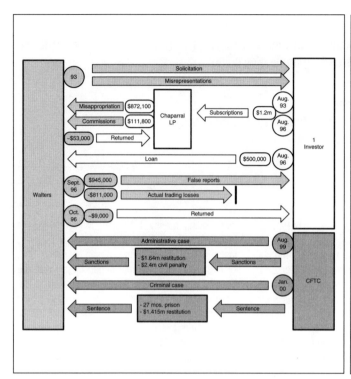

Fraud Facts
- Alleged Acts Date: August 1993
- Enforcement Date: August 10, 1999
- Main Defendants **(hedge fund–related): Walters, Chaparral Investments**
- Most Serious Charge: Commodity fraud, misappropriation
- Hedge Fund Role: Defrauded by general partner
- Damages $actual **($2005): $1.64 million ($2.0 million)**
- No. of Investors: 1
- Highest Court: Criminal
- Most Severe Sentence: 27 months' prison, $2.4 million civil fine, $1.6 million restitution

Sanctions:
- Max E. Walters: 27 months' prison, 3 years' supervised release, cease-and-desist order, industry bar, $1.64 million restitution, $2.61 million civil penalty

Cases:
- *CFTC v. Walters* (99–15, administrative)
- *U.S. v. Walters* (00cr00026, criminal, W. Dist. Mo.)

The main defendant solicited money for a then unregistered commodity pool, commingled and directly received money, and then lost much of it trading while reporting to the investors that profits were being made. Key points:

- CFTC case
- Unregistered commodity pool
- CTA and CPO registered before case was brought
- Civil and criminal cases filed
- Class action against brokers/intermediaries

Case Summary

In September 1997, Peter John Berzins of Houston, Texas, applied to the NFA for registration as a principal, branch manager, and associate member in connection with an entity called the Infinity Group, Inc., which was itself applying for NFA membership and status (presumably with the CFTC) as a CTA and CPO in September 1997 and was granted status in these applications in November 1997. There appears to have been another individual who was an Associated Person of Infinity, but this person remained unnamed in the cases and likely was not involved in the violations.

The Infinity Group's address was listed as Beaver Dam, Virginia, a rural hinterland of Richmond. In a civil complaint filed in August 1999, the CFTC charged that Berzins had commenced his violative conduct from at least 1996 by soliciting for an unregistered commodity pool—probably the Infinity Fund, which had not applied for registration until September 1997.

Berzins was also charged with misrepresenting his past performance in marketing his fund. These solicitations succeeded in attracting around $1 million from as many as 25 or more investors. According to the CFTC charges, over the next several years, through March 1998, reports to the investors continued to maintain that their investments were earning double-digit returns when, in fact, they

were losing money. Finally, in March 1998, the investors were informed that all of their money was lost in difficult trading conditions in February 1998.

Regulatory enforcement action began with the Texas State Securities Board. They referred the case to the CFTC, which brought the civil action mentioned above. In February 2000, several of the investors (referred to as the "Bisselle Group") brought a Maryland civil action that evolved into a subsequent class action and, in June 2001, Berzins was indicted on 14 counts in a Maryland criminal case. With Berzins also subject to criminal prosecution, the class action focused on other defendants that could be shown to bear some financial liability, including a number of the financial intermediaries that had been involved in the trades, but in the end this number was reduced to three: Newhall Discount Futures & Options, Matthew Bowyer, one of Newhall's employees, and First American Discount Corp.

Ultimately, a settlement was reached that included provision of an investor compensation pool of $200,000. In the CFTC case, Berzins was ordered to pay restitution of $1.4 million and in the criminal case, sentenced to 24 months in prison. The NFA also took action against Berzins and Infinity in withdrawing their various professional registrations.

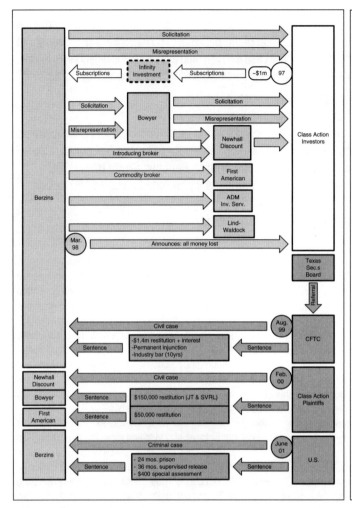

Fraud Facts

- Alleged Acts Date: 1996
- Enforcement Date: August 24, 1999
- Main Defendants (**hedge fund–related**): Berzins, **Infinity Investments**
- Most Serious Charge: Commodity fraud, misappropriation
- Damages $actual (**$2005**): over $1 million (**$1.25 million**)
- No. of Investors: (qualified as class action in Maryland)
- Highest Court: Criminal
- Most Severe Sentence: 24 months' prison, $1.4 million restitution

Sanctions:

- Peter John Berzins: 24 months' prison, 36 months' supervised release, $1,424,456 restitution, permanent injunction, industry bar (reviewable after 10 years)
- Matthew Raymond Bowyer: 150,000 restitution (joint and several with Newhall)
- Newhall Discount Futures: $150,000 restitution (joint and several with Bowyer)
- First American Discount Corp.: $50,000 restitution

Cases:

- *CFTC v. Berzins* (99cv00592, USDC ED Va.)
- *Bisselle v. Berins* (00cv00339, USDC Md.)
- *U.S. v. Berzins* (01cr00353, USDC Md.)

In this case, the defendant issued fraudulent notes to a large number of foreign corporate investors and then lost a substantial portion of the principal in reckless trading. He sought to conceal it by issuing false NAV reports. The case also involved the sale of the defendant's futures brokerage, which was a subsidiary of a company being sold to a large bank. Key points:

- SEC, CFTC, private, and U.S. criminal cases
- Largest securities fraud up to that time
- Principal defendant Armstrong spent seven years in jail for contempt for noncooperation
- Defendant's brokerage, Republic was directly implicated as a criminal conspirator
- Fraud unraveled a $10 billion acquisition offer to Republic Group from HSBC
- Armstrong lost $550 million in trading and misappropriated around $180 million
- Armstrong was imprisoned for 60 months
- Republic was to pay $556 million in restitution

Case Summary

The main case against Martin Armstrong and his group of "Princeton" companies concerned the issuance of $3 billion of "Princeton Notes" to some 139 Japanese institutional investors during the years 1992–1999.

The notes generally purported to pay these institutions an annual coupon rate of 4 percent with the principal to be invested in U.S. government securities. The most serious violations in this case were the result of increasingly desperate actions taken by Armstrong to cover mounting trading losses. Other violations were caused by misrepresentations in the initial marketing of the notes.

Matters were made more complex due to Armstrong's co-opting and manipulating Japanese broker-dealer entities Cresvale International and Republic Securities, which took on a dimension of its own by the later stages of the fraud when UK-based HSBC Holdings sought to acquire Republic Bank from Edmund Safra in a $10.3 billion deal. The fraud undermined the value of Republic, which caused the deal to unravel.

Japanese financial regulators began investigating Cresvale International's Tokyo branch around May 1999 after an official questioned why a Department Head had signed a routine letter to a client. On September 9, Japanese regulators ordered suspension of business at Cresvale and by the end of the month the SEC had filed civil charges against Armstrong and his companies. Other case filings followed including CFTC administrative and civil, a private RICO prosecution brought by the Japanese victims of the Notes, and criminal cases against both Armstrong and Republic.

The complaints filed indicated that substantial misrepresentation was employed in the marketing of the notes, including Armstrong's historic performance and qualifications. The misrepresentation continued in the management of the invested note principal, which was supposed to be invested in U.S. government securities. Investors had also been told that each investor's assets would be kept in a segregated account. Once it proved difficult to manage margin requirements across the different accounts, the management was simplified by commingling investor funds.

Making matters worse for Armstrong, his undisclosed efforts to add value through trading led to significant net losses by early 1995, and these mounted until he was as much as $500 million in the red during 1999. These losses drove Armstrong to implement a Ponzi scheme. To maintain this deception, he enlisted complicit assistance from his broker-dealers, Cresvale International, which he controlled, and Republic Securities New York, where he had co-opted the services of the president of the Futures Department. Among the most egregious acts of these aiders and abettors, was Republic's issuance of as many as 400 falsified NAV letters to the note investors.

Well before sentencing Armstrong had been jailed for what turned out to be seven years for contempt because he would not cooperate with the SEC in trying to locate assets. He was later sentenced to 60 months in prison as well. In its own criminal case, Republic was ordered to pay $606 million restitution and $5 million in fines, and its registration was revoked. Three of the individual aiders and abettors were ordered to pay a total of nearly $11.5 million restitution and several million in fines.

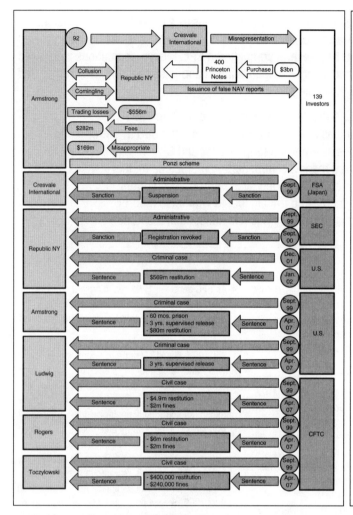

Fraud Facts

- Alleged Acts Date: June 1992
- Enforcement Date: September 1999
- Main Defendants (**hedge fund–related**): **Armstrong**, Ludwig, Rogers, Toczlowski, Cresvale Intl., Princeton Econ., Princeton Global, Republic Securities N.Y., HSBC, **Princeton Global SPVs,**
- Most Serious Charge: Criminal conspiracy, Wire fraud, misappropriation, commingling
- Damages $actual (**$2005**): plus $700 million (**$814 million**)
- No. of Investors: 139
- Highest Court: Criminal
- Most Severe Sentence: 60 months' prison, $606 million restitution

Sanctions:

- Martin Arthur Armstrong: $60 months' prison, 3 years' supervised release, $80 million restitution
- Harold L. Ludwig: 36 months' probation, $4.9 million restitution, $2 million fines
- William H. Rogers: 60 months' probation, $6 million restitution, $2 million fines
- Maria Toczlowski: 36 months' probation, $400,000 restitution, $240,000 fines
- Cresvale Intl Ltd. Tokyo Branch: business suspension
- Republic New York Securities Corp.: $569 million restitution, registration revoked

Cases:

- *SEC v. Armstrong* (99cv09667, civil, S. Dist. N.Y.)
- *CFTC v. Princeton* (99cv09669, civil, S. Dist. N.Y.)
- *U.S. v. Armstrong* (99cr00997, criminal, S. Dist. N.Y.)
- *Yakult v. Republic* (00cv01512, civil, S. Dist. N.Y.)
- *U.S. v. Republic* (01cr01180, criminal, S. Dist. N.Y.)
- *U.S. v. Ludwig* (04cr00742, criminal, S. Dist. N.Y.)

With a substantial history of prior enforcement actions as a broker-dealer, the defendant relocated to another state to pursue a commodity newsletter business, which evolved into an unregistered CPO and several unregistered CPs. Misrepresentations were used to raise money and commingling, misappropriation and false reporting were employed in managing the money. Key points:

- Long history of prior securities violations dating back to 1974
- Earlier SEC violations as a broker-dealer and company CEO in Detroit
- Later CFTC violations as a newsletter publisher and CPO in Kauai, Hawaii
- Was a widely followed market commentator on precious metals
- Used newsletters to solicit, included false performance figures
- Sought to cover up increasing trading losses with false reports
- Ultimately received a prison sentence and substantial restitution

Case Summary

David T. Marantette III is a member of old Detroit family (its downtown has a Marantette Street). In 1963, he graduated from Georgetown University with an economics degree and joined Marantette & Co., his family's Detroit-based stockbroking company. In 1972, this firm was acquired by another Detroit broker, Wm C. Roney & Co., where Marantette became a branch manager. In 1974, he began publishing the *Goldstock Letter* on precious metals. From about this time, Marantette's professional work record closely paralleled his regulatory enforcement record, which began in April of that same year, when he received a four-week suspension as a broker-dealer from the SEC (Administrative Proceeding 3–4391).

Between 1976 and 1992, there were five additional enforcement actions brought against Marantette and his associated financial companies, including:

- An SEC administrative action for misrepresentations in a newsletter in 1980 ("Dear Dow Letter")
- Defendant in a private RICO prosecution in 1987 related to a takeover he engineered (this was dismissed)
- Charged with violating securities law in 1991 for questionable loans and stock transfers

- An SEC action in 1992 resulting in a consent order for engaging in a fraudulent scheme, resulting in a permanent ban from the securities industry

By 1994, David Marantette was living in Kauai, Hawaii, and engaged in publishing newsletters. The following year, he established Troubadour, Inc., an unregistered commodity operator and several unregistered commodity pools, including Troubadour I, Troubadour II (in 1996), and Cycles in Gold (in 1998) and raised over $2 million from more than 100 investors around the United States. Evidence later showed that from 1998, Marantette published false, overinflated performance reports for his funds. In August 1999, newspapers reported that Troubadour's gold futures fund had collapsed, and on September 22, the CFTC filed a civil commodities fraud suit followed by a criminal fraud suit in February 2002. The latter resulted in a prison sentence of 28 months, with three years of supervised release, and restitution of $336,000. In the civil case, Marantette's charges included operating an unregistered commodity pool, misrepresentation, issuing false reports, commingling and misappropriation. He was ordered to pay restitution of $2.25 million, including prejudgment interest and a contingent civil fine of up to $700,000.

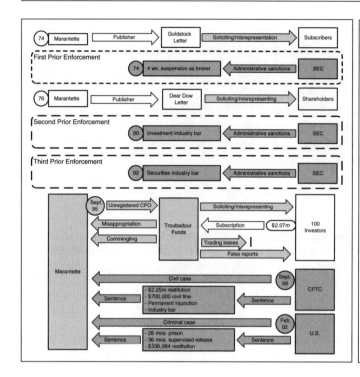

Fraud Facts

- Alleged Acts Date: 1995
- Enforcement Date: September 1999
- Main Defendants (**hedge fund–related**): **Marantette (Troubadour, Inc., Troubadour I & II, Cycles of Gold)**
- Most Serious Charge: Commodity Fraud, wire fraud, misappropriation, commingling
- Damages $actual (**$2005**): plus $1.8 million (**$2.1 million**)
- No. of Investors: 100
- Highest Court: Criminal
- Most Severe Sentence: 28 months' prison, $2.25 million restitution

Sanctions:

- David T. Marantette, III: 28 months' prison, 36 months' supervised release, $336,000 restitution, $2.25 million restitution, $700,000 civil fine, permanent injunction, bar against future registration (CFTC)

- Troubadour, Inc.: Restitution as above (joint and several), permanent injunction

Cases:

- *In the Matter of Marantette* (SEC 3–4391, admin.)
- *In the Matter of Marantette* (SEC 3–5809, admin.)
- *In the Matter of Marantette* (SEC 3–7842, admin.)
- *SEC v. Marantette* (91cv74500, civil, E. Dist. Mich.)
- *CFTC v. Marantette* (99cv00653, civil, Dist. Hi.
- *U.S. v. Marantette* (02cr00043, criminal, Dist. Hi.

In this case, a hedge fund blow-up became a crime when one of its principals defrauded it with a scam investment in an alleged attempt to save it. Key points:

- SEC case
- Hedge fund blew up months after launch
- Desperate and inappropriate measures taken to recoup losses
- Misguided rescue effort was a scam involving a Lithuanian bank
- One of the adviser's principals was a Russian national with mob connections
- Situation was not disclosed to the investors

Case Summary

In late 1996, a newly formed San Francisco investment adviser, Morgan Fuller Capital Management, LLC, solicited investors for the Paradigm Capital Fund and succeeded in raising an initial $825,000 from seven investors.

Paradigm commenced trading in January 1997, pursuing the portfolio manager Charles Seavey's short-bias strategy in the belief the U.S. market and technology shares in particular were overvalued and due for a decline. The strategy proved to be disastrously wrong, and by February 18 the fund's NAV had dropped to $305,325, a loss of more than half its value. (Two examples of the fund's short positions were cited: Henderson Technology, which subsequently rose by 50 percent, and put options on the S&P100, which rose by 10 percent, causing massive losses.)

In a misconceived effort to recoup the lost value, one of the firm's directors, Alexander Lushtak, a Russian national, recommended investing two-thirds of Paradigm's remaining assets ($240,000) in Bankas Hermis shares. Hermis was a Lithuanian bank with which Morgan Fuller had an ongoing investment banking relationship. Lushtak proposed the purchase of a 15,000-share block owned by his girlfriend, Tanya Khabay, which could be sold for a substantial profit as Khabay would settle for immediate liquidity. In reality, Khabay had already sold most of her shares and therefore could not deliver them, and, furthermore, Lushtak had misappropriated the money to pay for the shares.

The SEC charged that once the other Morgan Fuller principals and the trader Seavey became aware of the fraud they allowed two letters, dated April 4 and July 29, 1997, to be sent to Paradigm's investors, which misled them or misrepresented the true state of affairs. In this way, those charged had aided and abetted the fraud.

Lushtak, affiliated with other securities frauds and similar perpetrators who preyed upon the Russian community, soon faced federal criminal charges and was convicted of money laundering and sentenced to 71 months' prison and $3 million restitution. The SEC brought administrative proceedings against the Morgan Fuller principals, including Lushtak, and also against Seavey, the trader, in October 1999, and all received moderate fines, suspensions, censures, and cease-and-desist orders.

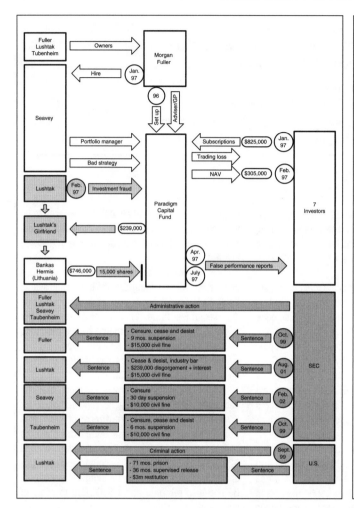

Fraud Facts

- Alleged Acts Date: February 1997
- Enforcement Date: June 23, 1999
- Main Defendants **(hedge fund–related): James Fuller, Alexander Lushtak, Charles Seavey, Gordon Taubenheim, Morgan Fuller Cap. Mgmt., Paradigm Capital Fund**
- Most Serious Charge: Money laundering
- Damages $actual **($2005): $240,000 ($300,000)**
- No. of Investors: 7
- Highest Court: Criminal (Lushtak only)
- Most Severe Sentence: 71 months' prison, $3 million restitution (Lushtak criminal), $234,000 disgorgement, $35,000 fines

Sanctions:

- James Fuller: $15,000 civil money penalty, cease-and-desist order, 9 month suspension
- Alexander Lushtak: 71 months' prison, 3 years' probation, $3,009,486 restitution SEC) $239,000 disgorgement, cease-and-desist order, industry bar
- Charles Seavey: $10,000 civil penalty, censure, cease-and-desist order, 30-day suspension.
- Gordon Taubenheim: $10,000 civil penalty, censure, cease-and-desist order, 6-month suspension

Cases:

- U.S. v. Lushtak (99cr363, criminal, N Dist Ca.)
- *SEC v.* Taubenheim (98cv01348, civil, N. Dist. Ca.)
- *SEC v. Fuller* (Admin. Proc. 3–10073, administrative)
- *SEC v. Seavey* (Admin. Proc. 3–10336, administrative)
- *SEC v. Taubenheim* (Admin. Proc. 3–10074, administrative)

A stockbroker created a fictitious hedge fund and enticed his family and friends to invest in it. Misappropriations and trading losses wiped out much of the NAV and further deception led to criminal charges. Key points:

- State of Pennsylvania case
- Fictitious hedge fund created by a stockbroker
- Marketed largely to family and friends, but also to clients
- Criminally charged and tried by Pennsylvania state courts

Case Summary

In 1985, William Pangrass joined Thomas McKinnon Securities, Inc., a stockbroking firm in Allentown, Pennsylvania, and the following year landed a stockbroking position with the Allentown office of Merrill Lynch.

From available reports, it appears that three years after joining Merrill Lynch, Pangrass started promoting an unregistered and possibly wholly fictitious hedge fund, the "Pangrass Family Hedge Fund," to family, friends, and clients of Merrill Lynch. Seed capital of $150,000 was contributed by his parents, Betty and William Sr., and over time this was followed by additional sums from his sister and brother-in-law and from a second cousin. All told, there were about 22 subscribers who invested up to $1.1 million, including at least one Merrill Lynch client.

In 1992, with his hedge fund still operating, Pangrass was terminated from his job and a report was filed with the Pennsylvania regulator. The words "low production" were used to describe the reason for his termination. It is not known if his hedge fund activities provoked an internal investigation by Merrill as well as by the Pennsylvania Securities Commission. Pangrass's registration was also withdrawn at that time.

Though still unregistered, and still nominally managing his hedge fund, Pangrass subsequently joined the Vanguard Marketing Corp., believed to be the company that marketed the Vanguard mutual funds in 1996. Pangrass again became registered in March 1998.

On November 8, 1999, criminal charges were filed against Pangrass by the Pennsylvania Securities Commission for theft by deception and securities fraud. This resulted from further investor complaints, exacerbated by the mounting losses of Pangrass's fund and the appearance of wrongdoing—including, possibly, evidence turned up from the earlier investigation.

In his defense, Pangrass claimed that he had used the majority of the fund's money for investments and had incurred most of his losses from these investments. State investigators concluded that Pangrass had diverted around $293,000 to his personal account, some of this allegedly to pay for his two daughters' education. He had also returned about $100,000 to some of his investors.

On April 8, 2000, Pangrass pled guilty to 12 counts of theft by deception and one count of securities fraud and was sentenced the following August to up to six years in state prison and ordered to repay $1.2 million to his investors.

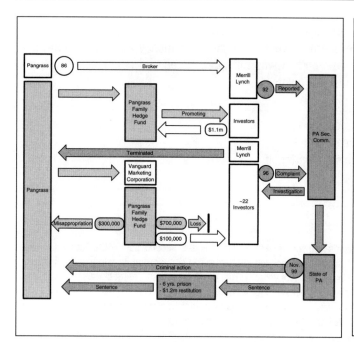

Fraud Facts

- Alleged Acts Date: 1991
- Enforcement Date: November 8, 1999
- Main Defendants **(hedge fund–related): William Pangrass, Jr., Pangrass Family Hedge Fund**
- Most Serious Charge: securities fraud
- Damages $actual **($2005): $1.2 million ($1.5 million)**
- No. of Investors: Approximately 22
- Highest Court: State Superior Court
- Most Severe Sentence: 6 years' prison, $1.2 million restitution

Sanctions:

- William Pangrass Jr.: 2 to 6 years' prison, $1.2 million restitution

Cases:

- *Commonwealth of Pennsylvania v. Pangrass* (CP-48-CR-3237–1999, criminal, Northampton Co., Pa.)

The defendant, a former broker, created two unregistered commodity pools and utilized misrepresentations to solicit from investors. Some of this money was subsequently lost in trading, while a larger proportion was misappropriated and commingled with the defendant's personal funds. Key points:

- CFTC case
- Unregistered commodity pools
- Administrative proceeding only
- Commingling and misappropriation
- Ponzi tactics

Case Summary

In April 1985, George Velissaris registered with the National Futures Association as an Associated Person of Paine Webber, Inc. Three and a half years later, in January 1989, his status as an AP was withdrawn as was his NFA associate membership. The circumstances suggest Velissaris left Paine Weber and the commodities industry at that time.

In April 1996, the CFTC claimed that Velissaris had created ACG Partners I, the first of two unregistered commodity pools. Between that date and July 1998, he solicited investment capital for these pools, making misrepresentations about them in doing so. Around $323,000 was raised for the first pool. Of this sum, $61,000 (19 percent) was lost in trading and $99,000 (31 percent) was misappropriated. In a Ponzi-like recycling of money, some of the cash raised in the second pool (ACG Partners II) was used to pay some of the investors in the first pool. The CFTC later also charged that Velissaris had commingled $82,000 of the investor's money with his own after transferring the sum to his personal checking account.

On December 16, 1999, the CFTC announced that it had initiated administrative proceedings against Velissaris and that it had simultaneously accepted an offer of settlement from him—indicating that they had been negotiating for some time previously. Without an admission of guilt, Velissaris consented to the publishing of the CFTC's charges against him and to abide by CFTC sanctions including, a cease-and-desist order, a permanent injunction against future violations, and $103,663 restitution plus interest.

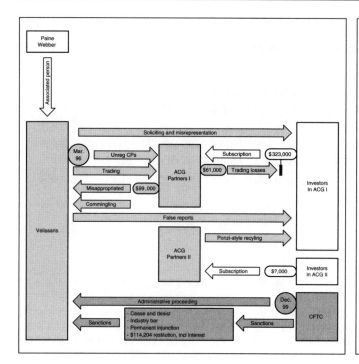

Fraud Facts

- Alleged Acts Date: March 1996
- Enforcement Date: December 16, 1999
- Main Defendants **(hedge fund–related): Velissaris (ACG Partners I LP, ACG Partners II LP)**
- Most Serious Charge: Misappropriation
- Damages $actual **($2005): $114,200 ($133,000)**
- No. of Investors: NA
- Highest Court: Administrative
- Most Severe Sentence: $114,200 restitution, industry bar

Sanctions:

- George W. Velissaris: $114,204 restitution, industry bar, permanent injunction

Cases:

- *CFTC v. Velissaris* (00–02, CFTC administrative)

The defendant in this case pursued an incorrect directional strategy that lost the majority of the fund's value. He then covered up the losses using forged statements. Key points:

- Largest hedge fund loss due to fraud to that date
- Fund and fund adviser created by a 28-year-old who was sole shareholder and the only active officer
- Losing directional strategy covered up with falsified reports for 39 months
- Class actions successful in reaching settlements for $64 million
- Berger jumped bail and became a fugitive before sentencing in a criminal case in which he pled guilty
- FBI Most Wanted list

Case Summary

In 1996, Michael Berger, a 28-year-old Austrian emigre, set up the Manhattan Fund. Berger managed the Investment Adviser (Manhattan Capital Management) with six employees and served as the president, company secretary, and sole shareholder. The fund with no employees had three directors, but, apart from Berger, they had no contact with the business and there were no board meetings. During its short life, the fund attracted some $592.8 million in capital from more than 200 investors. Of this sum, $143.1 million was redeemed by investors and roughly $393.1 million (around two-thirds of its NAV) was lost in trading.

Berger, like many other managers at the time, believed that the U.S. technology stocks were overvalued and heavily sold-short shares in this sector, quickly resulting in the large losses. At that point, Berger chose to hide the losses by creating fictitious trading reports. These false reports were sent to the fund administrator, Fund Administration Services (FAS) of Bermuda, while the broker-dealer, Financial Asset Management, Inc., of Columbus, Ohio, were convinced to send monthly statements to him rather than to the administrators. This deception continued for the next 39 months. Berger also told FAS to ignore parallel (and accurate) valuations it received from Bear Stearns Securities, saying that the Bear Stearns numbers did not reflect the entire portfolio. FAS then unknowingly prepared what were false NAVs and distributed these to the investors.

By the start of 2000, Berger was no longer able to hide the mounting losses and, before the end of January, the fund's accountants refused to sign off on the past three years accounts. This forced Berger to admit to the administrator that there were substantial problems and misrepresentations. Soon after, a similar message was sent to the investors. Lawsuits followed: an SEC civil suit, a criminal suit, and private suits including class actions, which also targeted the fund's brokers, administrator, and auditor. The auditor and administrator, both Bermuda entities, eventually settled the litigation at a reported cost of $32 million each. Cases against the large U.S. parent companies of these entities, Deloitte & Touche and Ernst & Young, were dismissed along with that against Bear Stearns Securities.

In its civil case, the SEC obtained a judgment against Berger for more than $20 million. In the criminal court, Berger sought to withdraw his guilty plea to pursue an insanity defense involving a jury trial, which would have caused much embarrassment to Bear Stearns, which Berger sought to implicate. These maneuvers failed and on the day he was to be sentenced, Berger became a fugitive. In 2007, he was rearrested in Austria and is, at this writing, awaiting extradition.

In addition to the $143 million redeemed prior to the collapse (approximately 24 percent of capital invested), $36.5 million (approximately 6.2 percent) was distributed when the fund was frozen, $64 million (approximately 11 percent) was paid in settlements, and $20 million (approximately 3 percent) is still due from Berger.

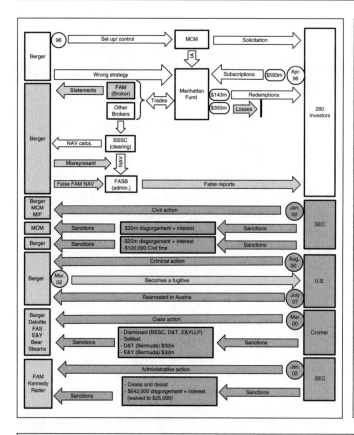

Fraud Facts

- Alleged Acts Date: 1996
- Enforcement Date: January 18, 2000
- Main Defendants (**hedge fund-related**): **Michael Berger, Manhattan Cap. Mgmt. Inc., Manhattan Fund Ltd**. Financial Asset Mgmt. Fund Administration Services, Deloitte & Touche, Bear Stearns
- Most Serious Charge: Misrepresentation, absconding
- Damages $actual (**$2005**): Approximately $400 million (**$490 million**)
- No. of Investors: 280
- Highest Court: Criminal
- Most Severe Sentence: Likely prison sentence, $20 million restitution, $64 million settlements

Sanctions:

- Michael Berger: $20,007,233.68 disgorgement plus interest plus $100,000 civil penalty (not paid, fugitive)
- Manhattan Cap Mgmt. Inc: $20,007,233.68 disgorgement plus interest plus $100,000 civil penalty (not paid, fugitive)
- Debra Kennedy: Cease-and-desist order
- James Rader: Cease-and-desist order
- Financial Asset Mgmt.: $641,877 disgorgement plus interest waived to $25,000
- Deloitte & Touche (Bermuda): $32 million settlement
- Ernst & Young (Bermuda): $32 million settlement

Cases:

- *SEC v. Berger* (00cv00333, civil, S. Dist. N.Y.)
- *U.S. v. Berger* (00cr877, criminal, S. Dist. N.Y.)
- *Cromer v. Berger* (00cv2284, civil class action, S. Dist. N.Y.)
- *Argos v. Berger*
- *In the matter of FAM* (SEC Admin. Proc. 3–10670)

The defendant, with a prior record of petty crime, created an unregistered, unaudited hedge fund group. Having raised a substantial amount of money using misrepresentation, he operated it as a Ponzi scheme and misappropriated and lost a majority of the capital over the next several years. Key points:

- SEC and CFTC case
- Mobley had been implicated in petty financial crimes in Toledo, Ohio, before he set up his Florida-based hedge fund group
- Funds were unregistered and unaudited
- Defendant became a financial pundit, claimed to use a computer black box and wrote an introduction to *Trade Your Way to Financial Freedom* by Van K. Tharp
- Family members employed in all key managerial positions

Case Summary

In a February 14, 2000, article entitled "King of Naples," *Barron's* broke the story of a substantial hedge fund fraud being perpetrated by David Mobley, Snr. and his Maricopa Fund organization against more than 350 investors centered in Naples, Florida. Up to that point, Mobley appeared to be a successful fund manager who claimed that his then $450 million fund group produced an average return of 51 percent per year, performance, which entitled him to a salary of $1 million and bonus of $2 million a year. Mobley portrayed himself as a computer genius who had developed a model called "Predator."

Barron's revealed what investors did not know—that Mobley had an undisclosed criminal past in Toledo, Ohio, before coming to Naples and that most of the activities of the Maricopa Funds organization were a complete fraud in support of Mobley's misappropriation of investor assets. The article triggered a call for wholesale redemptions that could not be met and drove Mobley to confess to the authorities, who, after investigation, responded with civil and criminal suits. He was indicted by a federal grand jury on 20 counts of fraud, tax evasion, and money laundering, ultimately pleading guilty to seven of these counts and was sentenced

to the maximum 17.5 years in prison and ordered to pay $76 million in restitution.

Mobley's fraud was perpetrated without detection for over seven years due to: the use of unregistered staff and funds, extensive employment of family members as company officers and staff, and the lack of an outside auditor. There were also telltale signs that, in aggregate, could have raised concerns such as: mention of a black-box computer model, claims of consistent unrealistically high performance, lavish charitable donations, and an outwardly luxurious life style.

At about the time he was prosecuted for the Maricopa fraud, Mobley was also tried and later convicted for his part in a major real estate scandal known as "Stadium Naples," for which he received a further two concurrent five-year terms, along with a number of other individuals including senior Collier County officials. Three and a half years were taken off of Mobley's sentence for his cooperation in this case.

As of the last receiver's report in the class-action suit (filed November 30, 2006), $39,735,132 had been paid to 274 Maricopa claimants and around $1.7 million remains of the total $41.4 million for distribution.

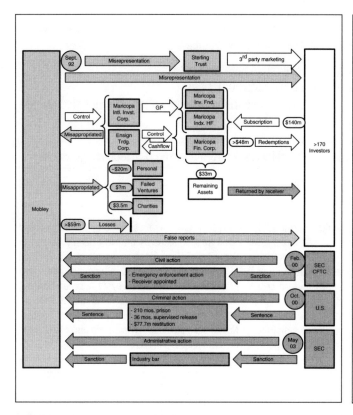

Fraud Facts

- Alleged Acts Date: September 1992
- Enforcement Date: February 22, 2000
- Main Defendants **(hedge fund–related): David Mobley Sr., Maricopa Investment Fund Ltd., Maricopa Index Hedge Fund, Ensign Trading Corp., Maricopa Financial Corp.**
- Most Serious Charge: Money laundering (interstate commerce)
- Damages $actual **($2005): $59 million ($82 million)**
- No. of Investors: >170
- Highest Court: Criminal
- Most Severe Sentence: 210 months' prison, 3 years' probation, $76 million restitution

Sanctions:

- David Mobley Sr.: 210 months' prison, 3 years' probation, $76,230,452.92 restitution
- David Mobley Sr.: Permanent injunction, industry bar, receiver appointed

Cases:

- *SEC v. Mobely* (00cv01316, civil, S. Dist. N.Y.)
- *CFTC v. Mobley* (00cv-1317, civil S. Dist. N.Y.)
- *U.S. v. Mobley* (00cr00071, criminal, M. Dist. Fl.)
- *Doroski v. Mobley* (00cv0587, civil-class act, S. Dist. Ca.)

The defendant was the general partner of two hedge funds, both of which he defrauded for eight years by creating a Ponzi scheme. Key points:

- Largest hedge fund fraud in New Jersey to that date
- Major criminal case, managed by state authorities
- Defendant Natale had serious prior securities violations that were not disclosed to investors
- Fraud was continued over an eight-year period
- One of a group of frauds triggered by losses from shorting U.S. technology stocks

Case Summary

In 1992, John Natale set up Cambridge Partners, LP, and over the following eight years used this and a second fund, Cambridge Partners II, LP, to defraud about 180 investors out of some $40 million.

At the outset, Natale used false performance reports to attract some 60 limited partners who subscribed a minimum of $50,000 for the first fund. He also failed to report prior securities violations to investor prospects. According to reports, Natale lost $20,000 early on, betting against rising technology stocks in the United States and like others before him, he chose to deceive rather than admit the loss and commenced what became a long trail of false reports. The fraud only came to light eight years later, in 2000, when one investor sought to redeem what had turned into a fictitious $12 million investment, at a time when there was only $3 million remaining in the entire fund. Having run out of alternatives, Natale turned himself in to the New Jersey Attorney General's Office.

A civil case was prosecuted by the State based upon investigations by the New Jersey Bureau of Securities Enforcement on behalf of the Division of Consumer Affairs, and a criminal case was prosecuted by the State Deputy Attorney General, who represented the Financial Crimes & Antitrust Bureau within the Division of Criminal Justice. Natale did a plea deal. By pleading guilty to fraud in the criminal case in March 2000, he received a 10-year prison sentence for which he would be eligible for parole after serving four years. He was also ordered to pay $51 million in restitution and was permanently barred from the securities industry.

The investigation and trials turned up the evidence of Natale's prior history of disciplinary problems including suspension from the CBOE and a $15,000 fine in 1986 for making unauthorized trades while employed with Dillon Read, and being barred from the American Stock Exchange and fined $50,000 in 1996 for submitting trade records with altered dates and times.

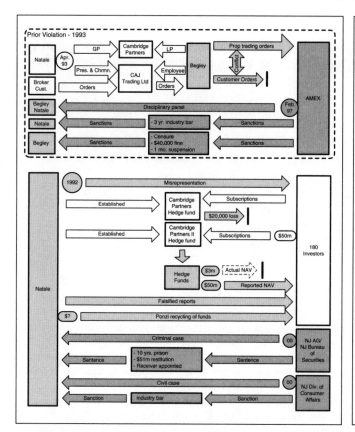

Fraud Facts

- Alleged Acts Date: April 1992
- Enforcement Date: March 3, 2000
- Main Defendants **(hedge fund–related): John Natale, Cambridge Partners, Cambridge Partners II, CAJ Trading**
- Most Serious Charge: Securities fraud, misrepresentation
- Damages $actual **($2005): $40 million ($55 million)**
- No. of Investors: 180
- Highest Court: State Court, Superior Court
- Most Severe Sentence: Criminal, 10 years' prison, $51 million restitution

---

Sanctions:

- John Natale: 120 months' prison, $51 million restitution, industry bar
- Cambridge Funds: Court-appointed receiver

Cases:

- *N.J. v. Natale* (N.J.DA, criminal, Superior Court, Newark, N.J.)
- *N.J. v. Natale* (Div. Cnsmr. Affrs., civil, Superior Court, Newark, N.J.)

In this case, the defendant did business as an unregistered commodity pool operator and made misrepresentations in attracting investors. He subsequently commingled and misappropriated the funds that he raised. Around half of the money was lost in trading. Key points:

- CFTC case
- Chulik solicited funds for and operated an unregistered commodity pool
- Funds commingled and used for personal trading
- More than $500,000 of commingled funds were subsequently lost in futures trading
- Additional commingled monies were misappropriated for personal use
- Investors were deceived by omission and misrepresentation
- Civil and criminal cases were filed

Case Summary

Mark Chulik registered as a commodity trading adviser with the CFTC on March 20, 1990. About one year later, in March 1991, without having registered as a commodity pool operator, Chulik began soliciting investors for Westgate Partners, a de facto commodity pool. These efforts, which crossed state lines, resulted in investment subscriptions from at least 14 investors. A total of about $1,160,000 had been raised and deposited in Westgate's account at Wells Fargo Bank.

For reasons that are not entirely clear, in December 1994, Chulik commingled and transferred a substantial portion of the investor assets at Wells Fargo Bank to his own personal trading account in Chicago. These combined funds were used to trade futures contracts, trades that subsequently lost more than $500,000. Some of the commingled funds were also misappropriated for Chulik's personal use.

In addition to nondisclosure of commingling and other required investor information, Chulik also resorted to the distribution of falsified performance reports to further disguise the true state of affairs from his investors.

The CFTC filed a civil complaint in the Central District of California against Chulik and his operating entities on March 9, 1999. On October 17, 2000, criminal charges were also filed in California (*USA v. Chulik*). As a result of these actions, Chulik was found guilty of four counts of felony fraud and sentenced to 15 months' prison and 36 months' supervised release. He was also liable for restitution of $1,273,567.55.

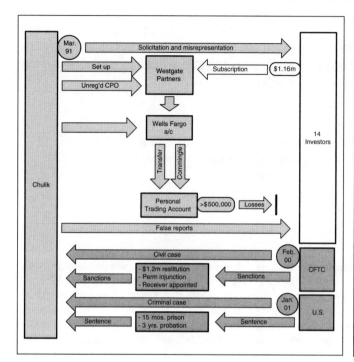

Fraud Facts

- Alleged Acts Date: March 1991
- Enforcement Date: March 9, 1999
- Main Defendants **(hedge fund–related): Mark E. Chulik, Westgate Partners, MEC Mgmt., MEC Cap. Mgmt.**
- Most Serious Charge: Mail fraud
- Damages $actual **($2005): $1.136 million ($1.6 million)**
- No. of Investors: 14
- Highest Court: Criminal
- Most Severe Sentence: Criminal, 15 months' prison, 3 years' probation, $1,175,555 restitution

Sanctions:

- Mark Chulik: 15 months' prison, 3 years' probation, $1.2 million restitution

Cases:

- *CFTC v. Chulik* (99cv02412, civil, C. Dist. Ca.)
- *U.S. v. Chulik* (00cr01044, criminal, C. Dist. Ca.)

The defendant created a group of unregistered and largely bogus funds and marketed them to a number of individuals living in one rural locale. By commingling and moving funds through several accounts, the defendant was able to misappropriate much of the money and lost some of it trading. Key points:

- CFTC case
- Set up four unregistered commodity pools
- Rural Wisconsin resident solicited a group of friends in rural Alabama
- Misrepresented fund history and performance
- Transferred money to personal accounts
- Commingled personal trading and investor trading

Case Summary

In 1996, Michael Konkel created four business entities that he promoted as commodity pools and for which he solicited investment capital from retail investors. None of these entities were registered as commodity pools with the CFTC nor was Konkel registered as a CPO. His violative conduct also included making false claims regarding the history and performance of these entities.

Konkel was also registered with the CFTC as an Associated Person for two registered CPOs—i.e, introducing brokers—Commodity Programs, Inc., from October 1996 to February 1999, and World Capital Brokerage Services, Inc., from January 1999 to December 1999. He was also registered as the branch manager of these entities.

Konkel's solicitation efforts, especially those among a group of individuals residing in Henry County, Alabama, succeeded in raising at least $1.3 million for his "funds" The evidence shows that around $950,000 of this money was withdrawn from the funds accounts and transferred to Konkel's personal account, and from there some $270,000 was deposited in Konkel's personal commodities trading account at Iowa Grain, a registered futures commission merchant, and some $200,000 deposited in two personal securities trading accounts with Bear Stearns. Ultimately, about $200,000 of the Iowa Grain account money was lost in trading.

In May 2000, the CFTC filed a civil complaint charging him with four counts of fraud and operating as an unregistered commodity pool operator, commingling, and failure to report to pool participants. A consent agreement was reached in May 2001, which ordered Konkel to pay $790,882.01 restitution, including interest, and a $440,000 civil fine. He was also subject to a permanent injunction against future violations. As of August 2001, the receiver recorded that the Konkel investors had received a total of $195,749.

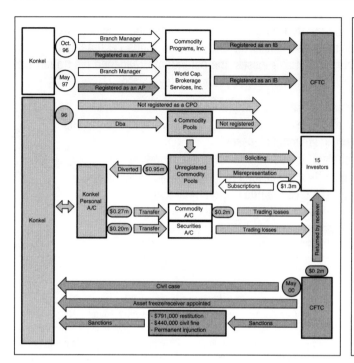

Fraud Facts

- Alleged Acts Date: 1996
- Enforcement Date: May 1, 2000
- Main Defendants **(hedge fund–related): Michael Konkel, Ad Astra, Inc., Ice Cap. Mgmt, Inscape Funds, Venture Fund**
- Most Serious Charge: Mail fraud
- Damages $actual **($2005): $870,000 ($1.1 million)**
- No. of Investors: Approximately 15
- Highest Court: Civil
- Most Severe Sentence: $791,000 restitution, $440,000 civil fine, permanent injunction

Sanctions:

- Michael Konkel: $790,900 restitution, $440,000 fine, permanent injunction

Cases:

- *CFTC v. Konkel* (00cv00547-MHT, civil, M. Dist. Ala.)

The defendant in this case created an unregistered hedge fund based on numerous misrepresentations after incurring losses on the personal funds he managed. When the hedge fund began suffering major losses, the defendant broadened his fraudulent activities, including a Ponzi scheme, to maintain assets. Key points:

- The defendant lost money in a prior fund he managed
- A new fund was marketed to investors using multiple misrepresentations
- Investor money incurred substantial losses
- Deception was maintained to secure additional subscriptions
- Some investors relayed their suspicions to the FBI, which investigated
- Higgins was imprisoned for 18 months in a criminal action
- Receiver brought in, but unclear how much money was recovered
- Defendant Higgins's sentence did not include restitution or fines

Case Summary

In the mid- to late 1990s, Michael Higgins lived in the San Francisco area managing the Ballybunion Fund, an unregistered hedge fund investment adviser funded with his own capital. In December 1998, after suffering substantial trading losses, Higgins began soliciting prospective outside investors. In doing so, Higgins made numerous material misrepresentations regarding the history and performance of the fund in order to make it more appealing. The deception was successful and, by May 1999, the fund had $6 million in assets and ultimately grew to $7.6 million.

While subscriptions increased, the Ballybunion Fund incurred significant losses that in May 1999 amounting to roughly $2.4 million of the $6 million that had been subscribed to that date (–40 percent). Higgins falsified his performance reports to hide the burgeoning losses and to keep new investor's cash coming in. Deceptive measures included forging broker and auditor's reports. False performance data were also distributed to a third-party data vendor.

When two investors later sought $2.7 million of redemptions from the fund, Higgins progressed to a Ponzi scheme, using new investor subscriptions to pay older investor redemptions. At some point, some of the investors became suspicious enough to contact the FBI, which investigated and then referred the case for criminal trial.

Higgins was arrested on May 9, 2000, and a civil complaint was filed by the SEC the following day with a criminal complaint filed a month later. On July 6, he pleaded guilty to one count of securities fraud as part of a plea agreement and was sentenced to 18 months' imprisonment and 36 months' supervised release. In the civil action, a permanent injunction order was issued against Higgins. The civil court also appointed a receiver in October 2000, which completed its work by the end of January 2002 after making several distributions to the investors.

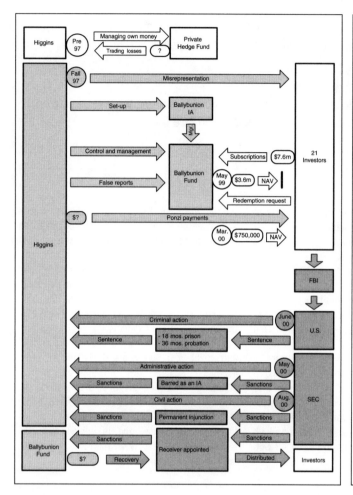

Fraud Facts

- Alleged Acts Date: 1997
- Enforcement Date: May 10, 2000
- Main Defendants **(hedge fund–related): Michael Higgins, Ballybunion Capital Associates, Ballybunion Capital Partners**
- Most Serious Charge: Securities fraud
- Damages $actual **($2005): $7.6 million ($8.6 million)**
- No. of Investors: Approximately 21
- Highest Court: Criminal
- Most Severe Sentence: 18 months' prison

Sanctions:

- Michael Higgins: 18 months' prison, 3 years' probation, permanent injunction

Cases:

- *U.S. v. Higgins* (00cr307, criminal, N Dist. Ca.)
- *SEC v. Higgins* (00cv001657, civil, N Dist. Ca.)
- *In the Matter of Michael Higgins* (Admin. Proc. 3–10492)

In this case, the defendant failed to register as a commodity trading adviser or to disclose this fact to his investors, believing he was exempt. Key points:

- CFTC case
- Administrative proceeding only
- Engaged in commodities trading and solicitation of investors while unregistered
- Improperly claimed exemption from registration as a CTA
- Fined $10,000

Case Summary

Stanley Harley was active in investment advice in the 1990s following an earlier career as an aeronautical engineer and aviator, including a stint at the Navy's "Top Gun" school. After receiving an MBA in 1989, he set up Harley Capital Management in 1991, where he managed accounts that traded securities and. later, commodities futures. He was also an occasional commentator in *Barron's* and other financial periodicals and maintained a Web site and a market newsletter.

While setting up his investment adviser, he registered with the state of California. According to the CFTC complaint, Harley had at some point also registered with the SEC. However, he withdrew his SEC registration effective October 20, 1997, due to changes in the law regarding registration with the state and minimum assets to qualify for SEC registration.

From November 1998, Harley started to manage a number of accounts that traded commodities futures. In July 1999, he filed a notice of exemption with the CFTC in an effort to avoid registration as a CTA. The basis for the exemption was his alleged registration with the SEC; however, at that time, Harley was no longer registered with the SEC. Despite this fact, Harley held himself out as a CTA, thereby misrepresenting himself to his investors.

On May 31, 2000, having already reached an agreement with Harley, the CFTC filed an order instituting administrative proceedings. Without admitting or denying the CFTC's allegations, he acknowledged its jurisdiction and agreed to be served with the order, which included provisions to cease and desist and to comply with the Commodities Act and was ordered to pay a civil penalty of $10,000.

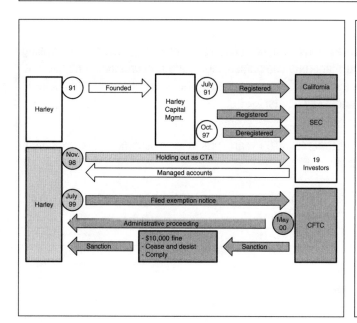

Fraud Facts

- Alleged Acts Date: November 1998
- Enforcement Date: May 31, 2000
- Main Defendants **(hedge fund–related): Stanley Harley, Harley Capital Mgmt.**
- Most Serious Charge: Unregistered CTA
- Damages $actual **($2005)**: $10,000 **($11,300)**
- No. of Investors: 19
- Highest Court: Administrative
- Most Severe Sentence: $10,000 civil fine

Sanctions:

- Stanley Harley: $10,000 civil fine, cease-and-desist order, compliance order

Cases:

- *In the matter of Harley* (CFTC 00–20)

This case involved an extensive criminal conspiracy in which elements of organized crime were able to infiltrate the investment industry and create an enterprise comprising over 100 individuals and numerous companies, legitimate and criminal. A hedge fund and its manager were one of several channels used by the criminal enterprise to defraud several union pension funds. Key points:

- Among the largest criminal cases
- >100 arrests and indictments, >100 years' prison term sentences, approximately $90 million restitution
- RICO subject
- Hedge fund was a small part of the total criminal enterprise, but played a similar role to most of the other perpetrators

Case Summary

On June 14, 2000, the U.S. Department of Justice issued a press release announcing: "the largest number of defendants ever arrested at one time on securities fraud related charges, and one of the largest number ever arrested in a criminal case of any kind." At its core is a series of RICO racketeering prosecutions against members of the Bonanno and Colombo Mafia families and DMN Capital Investments, a criminal enterprise masquerading as an investment bank. From that core, the network extended out into four main areas of exploitation: (1) manipulation of publicly traded securities; (2) union pension fund kickback schemes; (3) private placement and Internet ventures; and (4) brokers.

Over 120 individuals were arrested related to 19 companies and 16 private placements, 10 individuals associated with organized crime, a former NYPD detective, 57 stockbrokers, 21 broker-dealer/financial adviser firms, 30 company officers, an attorney, and two accountants. All told, the losses were estimated at $50 million, partly due to the rapid action of law enforcement in winding the scheme up before it got bigger.

Among the many separate strands of felonious activity was one hedge fund and manager, TradeVentureFund and its principal, Glenn Laken. His activities were mainly within the subgroup of schemes targeting union pension funds. In outline, the schemes involved the co-opting of corrupt union officials by Mafia operatives, the directing of their pension funds assets via selected investment managers, who would kickback a portion of these assets to the Mafia interests. The primary channel for defrauding the unions was via two nonhedge fund investment advisers, who largely directed the investments into a corrupt real estate investment trust (REIT). The hedge fund scheme was an alternative channel in which Laken invested in risky strategies and paid kickbacks from inflated commissions.

Laken was arrested on June 14, 2000. In the subsequent criminal case, Laken, who initially pled not guilty, changed his plea after arranging a deal with the prosecution to plead guilty to one count of conspiracy to defraud the United States (securities fraud). He was sentenced to 63 months in prison, two years of supervised release, and fined $100,000.

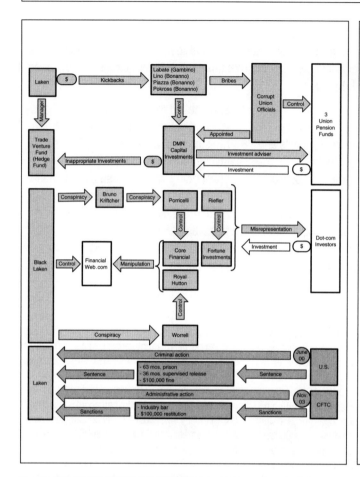

Fraud Facts

- Alleged Acts Date: 1995
- Enforcement Date: May 31, 2000 (Laken: 14 June 2000)
- Main Defendants **(hedge fund–related):** (over 100 nonhedge fund defendants) **Glenn Laken, TradeVentureFund**
- Most Serious Charge: Racketeering, criminal conspiracy, murder (alleged), securities fraud conspiracy
- Damages $actual **($2005):** Approximately $90 million **($100 million) (est. hedge fund portion $6.6 million)**
- No. of Investors: Implicitly all pension fund holders
- Highest Court: Criminal
- Most Severe Sentence: 121 months' prison/$22 million restitution

Sanctions:

- Cary Cimino: 121 months' prison, 3 years' supervised release,
- James Labate: 87 months' prison, 3 years' supervised release, $22.2 million restitution
- Robert Lino: 83 months' prison, 3 years' supervised release, $15.9 million restitution
- Mitchell Cushing: 70 months' prison, 3 years' supervised release
- Roger Detrano: 70 months' prison, 3 years' supervised release
- Frank Persico: 65 months' prison, 3 years' supervised release
- Glenn Laken: 63 months' prison, 2 years' supervised release, $6.6 million restitution, $100,000 fine

Cases:

- *Lino* (00cr00632, criminal, S. Dist. N.Y.)
- *U.S. v. Laken* (00cr00651, criminal, S. Dist. N.Y.)
- *U.S. v. Cushing* (00cr01098, criminal, S. Dist. N.Y.)
- *U.S. v. Dacunto* (00cr00620, criminal, S. Dist. N.Y.)

The main defendant created a number of unregistered commodity investment entities and used numerous misrepresentations, an unconventional loan, and offers of guaranteed downside protection to lure investors. When minimum losses were exceeded, investors pressed for enforcement. Key points:

- CFTC case
- Administrative case
- Three unregistered commodity pools and six managed trading accounts
- False claims of a proprietary computer trading system
- Represented historical hypothetical trades as real trades, including a return of 969 percent for 1997
- Did not disclose historic trading losses

- Scheme aided and abetted by colleague (second defendant Park), who was registered as an Introducing Broker
- Investors thought they were subscribing via an unusual bank loan funding and maximum loss guarantee agreement (see diagram), but none of this was honored
- Commingled investor funds
- Lost majority of asset value in trading

Case Summary

The two defendants, Seungho Kim and John Ki Park, were friends and former partners in a prior business venture. Park had been an Associated Person of an introducing broker, Lind-Waldock Financial Partners, Inc., while Kim had never been registered in any capacity.

In October 1997, Park assisted Kim in setting up an unregistered commodity pool operator, Houston System Trading (HST), followed by three unregistered commodity pools, namely Austin, Match, and JKP. HST operated out of Kim's offices (i.e., JKP) and Kim introduced HST to a futures commission merchant, where HST set up a trading account.

In marketing the venture to prospective investors, numerous misrepresentations were made, including a claim to be using a proprietary computer trading program developed by Kim's brother. The program was, in fact, an off-the-shelf program that identified buy and sell points. Historic performance claims, like a gain of 969 percent in 1997, were also misrepresented as real when they turned out to be a paper-traded backtest. Kim's actual trading, using the computer system on his own and in conjunction with his brother, incurred losses of more than $67,000. Investors were also told that losses would be guaranteed not to exceed 20 percent. Park provided ongoing assistance to Kim in the management of the funds to the extent that some investors believed he was directly involved with them rather than being employed by an entirely separate company.

Kim also sought to fund investor subscriptions via a bank loan of $10,000 for each account. In return,

investors were to pay HST $600 per month per unit, for a period of 18 months, generating $10,000 of principal and $800 of profit for HST. Kim had a goal of attracting 20 investors and $200,000 for each of his three commodity pools. Only about $52,000 was ever raised. Added to this, Kim had about $111,000 of his own money invested. He never obtained any bank loans as represented. In reality, the HST commodity pools lost 53 percent of their asset value.

When investors became concerned at not receiving monthly performance reports as promised, they discovered that the funds had lost more than the guaranteed 20 percent. At that point, some of these investors sought to remove their money; but Kim instead promised to honor the 20 percent guarantee—and failed to do so.

On June 30, 2000, the CFTC initiated administrative proceedings and simultaneously accepted an offer of settlement from the defendants Kim, Park, and HST. In the settlement, the defendants neither admitted nor denied the CFTC's findings but agreed to the CFTC publishing its findings and imposing sanctions. Kim was ordered to pay $86,498 restitution plus $14,000 prejudgment interest on a 10-year payment plan, together with a contingent civil fine of $50,000. He was effectively barred from the industry. Park was ordered to pay restitution of $35,000 with interest of $6,200 and a contingent civil fine of $35,000, also with a 10-year payment plan. He was not barred from the industry but suspended for six months.

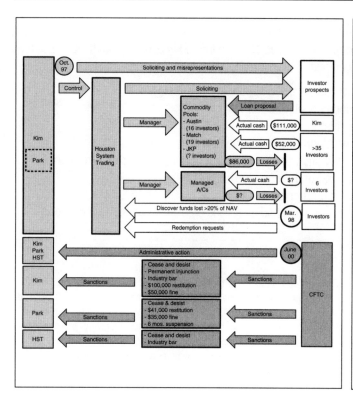

Fraud Facts

- Alleged Acts Date: October 1997
- Enforcement Date: June 30, 2000
- Main Defendants **(hedge fund–related): Kim, Park (Houston Systems, Austin, JKP, Match)**
- Most Serious Charge: Commodity fraud
- Damages $actual **($2005): $52,000 (approximately $60,000)**
- No. of Investors: 41
- Highest Court: CFTC administrative proceeding
- Most Severe Sentence: $121,500 restitution, $85,000 contingent fines, industry bar

Sanctions:

- Seungho Kim: $100,498 restitution plus interest, $50,000 civil fine, industry bar
- Houston System Trading: Restitution and fine, joint and several (with Kim), cease-and-desist order, industry bar
- John Ki Park: $41,200 restitution plus interest, $35,000 civil fine, 6-month suspension

Cases:

- *CFTC v. Kim* (00–24, CFTC administrative proceeding)

The defendant in this case solicited funds from investors for trading futures and options. Most of the money was directed to unregistered commodity pools, where it was misused or misappropriated. Key points:

- Successful private action awarded significant damages
- Unregistered commodity pool operator
- Fund had no trading history
- LP Agreement had no biography of the manager
- Approximately $0.5 million, that is, 50 percent of the capital, came from one individual living in Hong Kong
- Most of the assets misappropriated
- Perpetrator later claimed to have had a nervous breakdown and a bipolar disorder

Case Summary

Robert Dormagen resided in Ravenswood, West Virginia, a small town on the Ohio River in a region considered part of Appalachia. From there he operated numerous investment scams over a period of years. His basic MO was to pose as a trader of futures and options and, later, as an exempt unregistered commodity pool operator. Individuals were solicited to purchase units in one or another of his limited partnership "funds": Capital Asset Management & Research or Capitol Group III. He and his wife were the executives of Delta Financial Corp., the general partner of these "funds."

Dormagen collected nearly $1 million of investment capital from around 20 individuals, including $500,000 from a UK national (Mumford) living in Hong Kong. (How this person came to know a small trader in West Virginia and subsequently invest such a large sum in "funds" that, in themselves, did not comprise more than $1 million, remains a mystery.)

Most of the invested capital was cycled through one or more bank accounts where it was generally commingled and misappropriated to meet personal expenses. A small proportion of the money was used for trading that mostly lost money. False reports were produced by Dormagen, giving "investors" the impression that the trading was profitable. Some of the capital was recycled to the investors in a Ponzi-like fashion.

On May 18, 1999, Mumford filed a civil complaint against Dormagen, Delta Financial Corp., and Delta Trading Co., charging breach of contract and seeking damages of $427,000. Mumford had already received $73,000 after requesting his account be closed. In his case, Mumford pointed out that his agreement with Delta included a provision that the account would be closed automatically if it declined by 25 percent. The court granted Mumford a judgment in his favor for $427,000.

On July 3, 2000, the CFTC filed a civil complaint against Dormagen. This was, in effect, superseded by a grand jury indictment and the filing of criminal charges on March 22, 2001. A plea bargain by Dormagen resulted in a 54-month prison sentence and restitution of $852,626.

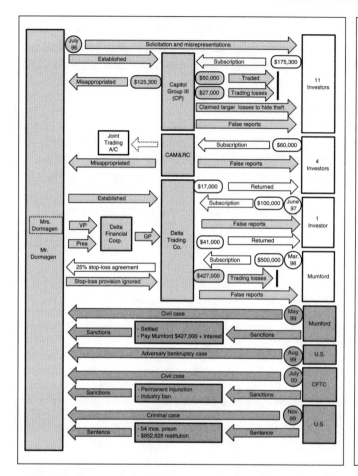

Fraud Facts

- Alleged Acts Date: March 1996
- Enforcement Date: July 2000
- Main Defendants **(hedge fund–related): Dormagen, Commodity Group III, Delta Financial Corp., Delta Trading Co.**
- Most Serious Charge: Securities fraud
- Damages $actual **($2005): $850,000 ($1,030,000)**
- No. of Investors: Approximately 20
- Highest Court: Criminal
- Most Severe Sentence: 48 months' prison, $850,000 restitution

Sanctions:

- Robert L. Dormagen: 54 months' prison, $850,000 restitution, industry bar

Cases:

- *Mumford v. Dormagen* (99cv00413, civil, S. Dist. W.V.)
- *U.S. v. Dormagen* (01cr00093, criminal, S. Dist. W.V.)
- *CFTC v. Dormagen* (00cv00567, civil, S. Dist. W.V.)

The hedge fund manager in this case was accused in an investor class action of securities fraud and manipulation after acquiring an outsized position in a small company. The suit was settled, although there were subsequent actions over the implementation of its terms. Key points:

- No regulatory or law enforcement action taken
- Investor class action
- Acquisition of single 55 percent position being 25 percent of a small company
- Settlement reached but disagreement over effective date of NAV for redemption
- Investment target NetSol International held global rights to assign Internet domain names
- NetSol was listed in the United States but had its headquarters in Pakistan

Case Summary

Jonathan Iseson had 20 years of investment experience prior to setting up the fund Blue Water in 1999. Most of his experience, which included Keefe, Bruyette & Woods, and Montgomery Securities, was concentrated in the areas of trading convertibles, arbitrage, and market-making in OTC and listed equities. Blue Water attracted about $70 million in subscriptions from approximately 60 clients, a high proportion of whom were institutional investors.

In June 1999, the first year of operations for Blue Water, Iseson started buying shares of NetSol International, a listed subsidiary of Network Solutions, a company headquartered in Pakistan and the United Kingdom. In 1993, this small company won an exclusive contract to develop a domain names registration service for the Internet, which included .com, .net, and .org domains. In 1995, the company got the right to charge a fee for registering names.

Between June 1999 and June 2000, Blue Water acquired a 25 percent stake in NetSol for around $43 million. At that time the position represented around 55 percent of Blue Waters NAV. During this same period, NetSol shares rocketed from $4 to a high of $80 in February 2000. However, the price started to collapse when Blue Water stopped buying and by the start of June 2000 it was below $100.

This, a number of Blue Water's investors maintained, was in violation of the fund's prospectus.

In a $100 million suit (later a class action) filed at the end of June 2000, these investors accused Blue Water of securities fraud and manipulation, which netted Blue Water managers a $12 million performance fee.

During the suit, as the share price dropped below $10, Iseson created a NetSol shareholder's group, comprised almost entirely of Blue Water fund interests, and initiated a proxy fight in an effort to wrest control of the company, including a physical occupation of the company offices and getting a court to appoint a receiver. This was later reversed by another court, even though NetSol was badly damaged by the actions. In the Blue Water shareholder suit, an agreement had been reached on December 14, 2000. The settlement was encompassed in a court-approved "stipulation" that called for a standstill period, a redemption plan covering all shareholders, no admission of guilt, and a partial meeting of legal costs by Blue Water. In separate civil cases with two of its investor groups, Common Sense Partners and Phoenician Trading, the Blue Water funds received an adverse judgment for $1.29 million plus interest and in a further judgment Jonathan Iseson was assessed $365,238.97 for the balance of what became an uncollected judgment in the Phoenician action. Iseson was ordered to pay this money from fees he received from Blue Water that were subsequently deemed to be illegal transfers.

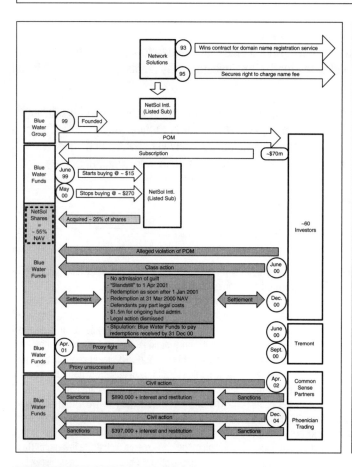

Fraud Facts

- Alleged Acts Date: 1998
- Enforcement Date: June 26, 2000
- Main Defendants **(hedge fund–related): Gillies, Iseson, Rovell, Shogren, Blue Water Funds, JDI Mgmt., Tuna Capital**
- Most Serious Charge: Securities fraud
- Damages $actual **($2005)**: Approximately $160 million **(approximately $180 million)**
- No. of Investors: Approximately 70
- Highest Court: Civil (private)
- Most Severe Sentence: None (cases dismissed)

Sanctions:

- Blue Water Fund(s): "Tremont Stipulation," pay redemptions prior to 12.31.00
- Blue Water Fund(s): $396,541.51 plus interest damages to Phoenician Trading
- Blue Water Fund(s) $890,000 plus interest to Common Sense Partners

Cases:

- *Tremont v. Blue Water* (00cv3768, civil, S. Dist. N.Y.)
- *Lewis v. Blue Water* (00cv4215, civil, S. Dist. N.Y.)
- *Phoenician v. Blue Water* (013659, civil, S. Dist. N.Y.)

The main defendant, who controlled a broker–issuer and one or more foreign hedge funds was alleged to have colluded, bribed, and manipulated foreign state privatization assets and thereby defrauded the fund's U.S. investors. Key points:

- Not an SEC or CFTC case
- U.S. case centered on bribery of foreign government officials (Republic of Azerbaijan)
- First hedge fund case to involve the Foreign Corrupt Practices Act
- Defendant sought to gain control of state oil company via privatization vouchers
- U.S. hedge fund main victim of fraud but also complicit in knowing of bribery
- Most defendants foreign entities
- Assets involved were foreign assets

Case Summary

Viktor Kozeny was nicknamed "the Pirate of Prague," in the early 1990s after his high-profile actions in manipulating the Czech privatization program. By mid-1997, while avoiding prosecution by Czech authorities, Kozeny involved himself in the privatization voucher market in the former Soviet Republic of Azerbaijan. The most sought-after prize in this program was Socar, the state oil company. In a short space of time: Kozeny set up Minaret, a large brokerage operation in the Azeri capital of Baku, and purchased nearly 27 percent of the total issue of privatization vouchers through Minaret and Oily Rock, another offshore company he controlled.

When the Azeri State Privatization Committee (SPC) declared that foreign nationals were also required to purchase four "options" per voucher, Kozeny purchased around twice as many as needed—he reportedly had between 1.4 million and 1.9 million vouchers and so needed 7.6 million options, but he purchased more than 15.7 million. The options were initially issued at the equivalent of $0.50 and in quick succession were increased to $1.00 then $25.00 by government decree.

In an effort to both assemble a controlling stake in Socar and to make a quick windfall profit on his options—which he had purchased at an average price of around $0.40—Kozeny sought to bring in several large foreign investment partners. The centerpiece of this strategy was an extravagant celebrity party hosted at his Peak House mansion in Aspen, Colorado, in December 1997. These efforts brought in two additional investor pools in May 1998. The larger of these was centered on Omega Investors, a New York hedge fund group that, after due diligence, invested around $127 million in vouchers and options

and Marlwood, a subsidiary of AIG, which purchased some $15 million of these assets.

By December 1999, everything had changed. Omega and Marlwood were pursuing Kozeny as well as his assets and associates in civil and criminal court actions in London, the Bahamas, Colorado, and New York. The main charges against these parties included conspiracy to defraud, money laundering, racketeering, and manipulation.

The charges were largely derived from Kozeny's actions in allegedly marking up the option prices sold on to the investors (from around $0.40 to $25), in violation of the agreements with these investors. This transaction would have netted Kozeny an undisclosed profit of roughly $24.60 on some 2.68 million options, or around $66 million on the Omega portion and an additional $8 million on the Marlwood options.

Kozeny was also charged with moving tens of millions of dollars to companies unrelated to the vouchers and options, some of which were involved with his personal possessions, of which his Aspen house was a chief beneficiary ($9.7 million). The legal actions in Colorado were intended to place a lien on that asset.

In subsequent prosecutions, the U.S. Justice Department brought criminal charges against Kozeny and several of his associates, most of whom reached plea agreements. Kozeny became a fugitive and was ultimately arrested in the Bahamas and extradited to the United States. The U.S. charges centered on the bribes paid to Azeri officials in violation of the Federal Corrupt Practices Act and the Travel Act.

Sentences are being held in abeyance awaiting the outcome of other cases in the United Kingdom. Omega, though the main victim of Kozeny's dealings, nevertheless had to do a deal with the Justice Department and pay a civil fine of $500,000 to avoid prosecution.

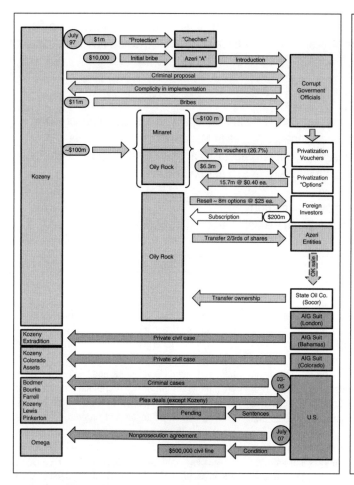

Fraud Facts

- Alleged Acts Date: August 1997
- Enforcement Date: July 19, 2000
- Main Defendants **(hedge fund–related): Kozeny, Oily Rock, Omega Advisors, Pharos Fin., Blueport Intl.**
- Most Serious Charge: Foreign Corrupt Practices Act
- Damages $actual **($2005)**: Approximately $140 million **(approximately $163 million)**
- No. of Investors: Not known
- Highest Court: Criminal
- Most Severe Sentence: Pending

Sanctions:

- Hans Bodmer: Pending
- Frederic Bourke, Jr.: Pending
- Thomas Farrell: Pending
- Clayton Lewis: Pending
- Viktor Kozeny: Pending
- David Pinkerton: Pending
- Omega Advisors, Inc.: $500,000 civil fine

Cases:

- *Daventree v. Azerbaijan* (1:02cv06356, civil, S. Dist. N.Y.)
- *U.S. v. Farrell* (1:03cr00290, criminal, S. Dist. N.Y.)
- *U.S. v. Lewis* (1:03cr00930, criminal, S. Dist. N.Y.)
- *U.S. v. Bodmer* (1:03cr00947, criminal, S. Dist. N.Y.)
- *U.S. v. Kozeny* (1:05cr00518, criminal, S. Dist. N.Y.)
- *Omega v. Lewis* (1:06cv00834, civil, S. Dist. N.Y.)
- *U.S. & Omega* (nonprosecution agreement, S. Dist. N.Y.)

In this case, the defendant operated two unregistered commodity pools as a Ponzi scheme over a number of years and then became a fugitive when law enforcement investigated. Key points:

- CFTC case
- Unregistered commodity pools
- Over 500 investors lured into Ponzi scheme that operated over a number of years
- Scheme was run from defendant's offices in Marion, Indiana
- Over $20 million subscribed, but only about $3 million invested and $1.6 million remaining; i.e., approximately $10 to $15 million missing
- 7.5 percent funds recovered
- Main defendant a fugitive since 2000
- Criminal sentence is pending defendant Ferguson's arrest

Case Summary

Between November 1981 and August 1988, Phillip Ferguson of Summitville, Indiana, the central character in this case, was an Associated Person of two futures commission merchants and an introducing broker. By 1997, Ferguson was doing business variously as Ferguson Financial, B&F Trading, and, First Investor's Group, the latter two of which were unregistered commodity pools and unincorporated in any state. Ferguson was the unregistered commodity pool operator of these two entities. Through his own efforts and with the assistance of other individuals (Eltzroth, Johnson, Miller, and Wilson) acting as IBs, he raised more than $20 million, much of it retirement assets, from more than 500 individuals.

Toward the middle of 2000, suspicious activity was noticed during an audit. That, in turn, kicked off investigations by state and federal enforcement authorities. The investigations found that most of the money was never invested but recycled in a Ponzi scheme—and by June 2000, Ferguson became a fugitive. Several legal actions followed the investigations. Most of the plaintiff's claims were aggregated in a civil case, *CFTC v. Ferguson.*

The CFTC charged Ferguson with failure to register (as a commodity pool operator), providing false statements to investors, and failure to produce documents (to the CFTC). A criminal case followed once Ferguson fled justice. In his absence, he was given a default sentence and ordered, jointly and severally with his companies, to pay $12.8 million restitution and $10.8 million civil penalties. Prosecutors had more success with Ferguson's accomplices, who did not flee and who each entered into consent agreements with the commission requiring additional restitution and fines.

A receiver had been appointed by the court and some 546 claims were made, almost all from investors. In a distribution agreement, the investors and creditors were returned some $1.77 million, around 7.5 percent of their original investments.

In 2004, another criminal action indicted Ferguson, who was still at large with eight counts of mail fraud, tax evasion, and money laundering.

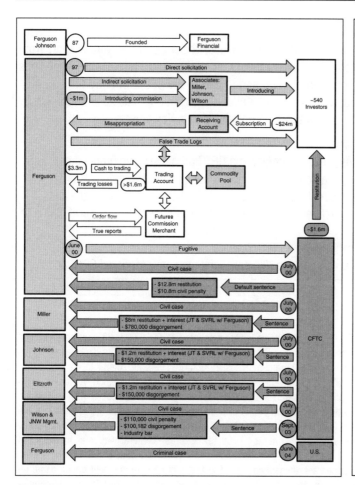

Fraud Facts

- Alleged Acts Date: 1997
- Enforcement Date: July 28, 2000
- Main Defendants **(hedge fund–related):** Eltzroth, **Ferguson,** Miller, Wilson, **B&F Trading, Ferguson Financial, First Investors Gp**
- Most Serious Charge: Securities fraud, mail fraud, tax evasion, money laundering
- Damages $actual **($2005): $24.5 million (approximately $27.7 million)**
- No. of Investors: Approximately 540
- Highest Court: Criminal
- Most Severe Sentence: $12.8 million restitution, $10.8 million civil fine (criminal penalties pending, defendant at large)

Sanctions:

- Phillip L. Ferguson: $12.8 million restitution, $10.8 million civil penalty (remains a fugitive)
- Geoffrey Eltzroth: $75,000 restitution, $25,000 civil penalty
- David Johnson: $1.2 million restitution (joint and several with Ferguson), $150,000 disgorgement, $150,000 civil penalty
- Thomas Miller: $8 million restitution (joint and several with Ferguson), $780,000 civil penalty
- James N. Wilson: $100,182 disgorgement, $110,000 civil penalty, permanent injunction
- JNW Mgmt.: $100,182 disgorgement, $110,000 civil penalty, permanent injunction

Cases:

- *CFTC v. Ferguson* (1:00cv0300, civil, N. Dist. In.)
- *U.S. v. Ferguson* (2:04cr00041, criminal, N. Dist. In.)

The defendant, a registered commodity pool operator and commodity trading adviser fraudulently operated three commodity pools over a period of ten years. Apart from disguising sums lost trading through misrepresentation and Ponzi tactics, violations included commingling, misappropriation and in one of the pools, offering to guarantee profits as returns on personal loans. The defendant also sought to avoid enforcement by moving investor funds to unregistered commodity pools. Key points:

- Originally an NFA case
- Continuing violations became subject of a CFTC administrative proceeding
- One investment fund was comprised of personal loans to the defendant
- Defendant used a personal bank loan to purchase CDs to replace fund assets and also to serve as collateral on the loan, but did not disclose collateral status to investors
- Managed to keep scheme going for 10 years
- Defendant's failure to comply with NFA sanctions may have triggered CFTC action

Case Summary

In 1986, William Billings of Bartlesville, Oklahoma, created a commodity pool, Bilcom, and a peculiar collective debt funding vehicle, the "20 percent Fund." The latter entity was available to individuals who wished to invest with Billings via personal loans in return for a compounding 20 percent per annum return. The 20 percent loan capital was to be primarily used by Billings to invest in futures markets.

Some $1.1 million was raised for these two entities. Violations appeared from the earliest stages, including commingling of investor capital with Billing's own personal capital.

In December 1988, Billings registered Billfund Inc., with the NFA as a CPO and CTA and himself as their AP. In 1992, Billings created another commodity pool, Billfund, LP, and offered his investors the opportunity to transfer their investments to the new fund. By this time, however, it appears that though some investors withdrew their money, most of the investor money had been lost in trading and misappropriation.

The new Billfund LP pool turned out to be an effort to raise new money in a Ponzi-like scheme, both to have capital to meet redemptions and to disguise the prior losses. The new money in the Billfund

LP amounted to $555,000. Billings, however, still needed more cash to close the gap created by his losses and, in 1994, he sought to do this with a $300,000 bank loan. This money was used to purchase a certificate of deposit (CD) in Billfund LP's name, which served both as collateral on the loan and as a (now encumbered) Billfund asset. The CD used as collateral was later increased to three with a combined value of $425,000.

The first signs of enforcement action came on April 7, 1998, when the NFA issued a member responsibility action barring Billfund from trading and acting in any capacity requiring registration and ordered it to close down its accounts and transfer the assets to a proper party. The NFA issued a complaint to Billfund in December 1998, based on his alleged conversion of fund assets, implying that he did not transfer assets to a proper person as directed in April 1998. The NFA status of Billings and Billfund was withdrawn at the same time.

On July 17, 2000, the CFTC filed administrative proceedings against Billings and Billfund, Inc., resulting in a civil fine of $400,000, to be paid over a 10-year period as well as cease-and-desist and permanent injunction orders and an industry bar.

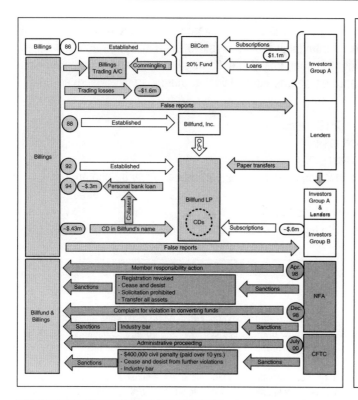

Fraud Facts

- Alleged Acts Date: 1999
- Enforcement Date: June 26, 2000
- Main Defendants **(hedge fund–related): Billings, Billfund**
- Most Serious Charge: Commodity fraud, fraud
- Damages $actual **($2005): $409,000 (approximately $490,000)**
- No. of Investors: 40
- Highest Court: CFTC administrative proceeding
- Most Severe Sentence: $400,000 civil fine, registration revoked, industry bar

Sanctions:

- William, G. Billings: $400,000 civil fine, Associated Person status withdrawn, cease-and-desist order, permanent injunction, industry bar
- Billfund, Inc.: cease-and-desist order, permanent injunction, industry bar, registration revoked

Cases:

- *NFA/Billfund* (Member Action 98ARA00001)
- *NFA/Billfund* (Member Action 98BCC00020)
- *In the matter of Billings* (CFTC Admin. Proc. 00–25)

The main defendants in this case used an unregistered commodity pool operator and misrepresentation to solicit from individual and Fund-of-fund investors, some of whom were complicit or negligent. Defendants also used fraud to open and maintain trading accounts with FCMs and misappropriated investor money from trading accounts. Key points:

- Several interrelated CFTC cases
- Ponzi scheme based in Utah
- Unregistered CPOs and CPs
- One group of cases involved sales of notes purporting to pay 32 percent per annum
- Main defendant taught ethics at college
- Criminal trial ended with a jury dismissing more serious charges against several of the defendants

Case Summary

BIRMA/Brockbank comprises a set of interrelated cases based in and around Salt Lake City, Utah, during the years 1999–2002. At its core, it involved two groups of unregistered commodity pools and commodity pool operators. One of these groups comprised two individuals—Stephen Brockbank and Carol Love—and BIRMA, the unregistered CP they founded. The other was made up of three individuals—Allen Andersen, John Garrett, and Robert Heninger and two CPs they created, Gahma Corp. and Vision Capital. The two groups were related by money Gahma allocated to BIRMA, to be managed by Brockbank. Two other individuals also provided funds to Brockbank/BIRMA, one (Purser) was a prominent local attorney who acted as a third-party solicitor for BIRMA, the other (Jones) was a multimanager fund.

The CFTC pursued two cases against Andersen, Garrett, and Heninger; one concerning the Gahma pool, which invested in BIRMA, and the other, the Vision pool, which invested in Platinum Holdings, an offshore fund registered in Nevis. Both pools were similar in purporting to offer investors notes that paid 32 percent per annum, compounding over 10-years. In both cases, the only assets available to generate the 32 percent returns were the investments in other manager pools (e.g., BIRMA or Platinum). The CFTC also alleged negligent due diligence, misrepresentation, commingling, misappropriation,

and failures to disclose, charges that were more or less common to all of the defendants in all of the cases referenced here.

In an unusual twist, the state of Utah also filed criminal charges against Andersen, Garrett, and Heninger, to which Garrett and Heninger pled guilty to reduced charges. The state pursued criminal charges against Andersen, the most junior of all the defendants, and in a subsequent four-day jury trial; Andersen was acquitted of all charges. This led to a dropping of all charges against Garrett and Heninger. This, in a way, cast a shadow over all the defendants in the other cases, although the civil actions had a lower threshold of guilt to satisfy. The Vision defendants were also successful in claiming that the CFTC did not have jurisdiction over Vision since it did not actually trade in commodities.

The CFTC was generally more successful in pursuing its civil actions against Brockbank, Love, BIRMA, and Gahma (as well as Jones and Purser), where cash was more directly invested in securities and commodities (rather than notes) and where BIRMA, being a U.S. company, had a more accessible record of transactions in evidence. The CFTC obtained consent orders from the accused and imposed substantial sanctions, including restitution of around $2 million, disgorgement of about $400,000, and civil fines of roughly $1 million.

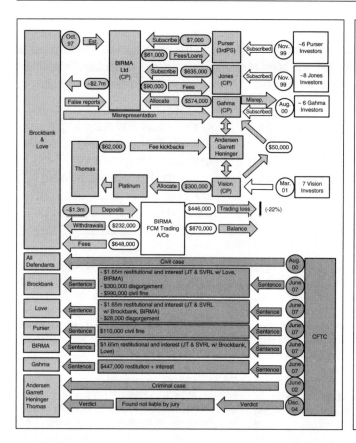

Fraud Facts

- Alleged Acts Date:
  October 1999
- Enforcement Date:
  August 8, 2000
- Main Defendants
  (hedge fund–related):
  Andersen, Brockbank,
  Garrett, Heninger,
  Love, Purser, Thomas,
  BIRMA, Gahma, Vision,
  Platinum Hldgs.
- Most Serious Charge:
  Commodity fraud
- Damages $actual
  ($2005): $1.6 million
  ($1.9 million)
- No. of Investors: 27
- Highest Court: Civil
- Most Severe Sentence:
  $2.1 million restitution
  plus interest, $328,000
  disgorgement, $1.1
  million fines, permanent
  injunctions

Sanctions:

- Allen Andersen: Jury found not liable
- Stephen W. Brockbank: $1.65 million restitution plus interest (joint and several with Love & BIRMA), $300,000 disgorgement, $990,000 civil fine, permanent injunction.
- John Garrett: Jury found not liable
- Robert Heninger: Jury found not liable
- Carol J. Love: $1.24 million restitution (joint and several with Brockbank & BIRMA), $28,000 disgorgement, permanent injunction
- Donald J. Purser: $110,000 civil fine, permanent injunction
- Birma Limited: $1.24 million restitution (joint and several with Brockbank & BIRMA), permanent injunction
- Gahma Corporation: $364,700 restitution plus interest, permanent injunction

Cases:

- *CFTC v. Brockbank* (2:00cv00622, civil, Dist. Utah)
- *CFTC v. Gahma* (1:02cv00101, civil, Dist. Utah)
- *CFTC v. Vision Cap.*(2:04cv00804, civil Dist. Utah)

As the administrator of the soft-dollar program of his employer, a hedge fund investment adviser, the defendant allowed violations in the use of soft dollars. The defendant was also responsible for filing disclosures with the SEC and failed to disclose some uses of soft dollars. Defendant's employer, was found to have caused violations in its supervision of the defendant. Key points:

- SEC case
- Part of an industry-wide sweep by the SEC
- Administrative proceeding only
- Improper use of soft dollars and lack of supervision

- Nonresearch-related business travel, personal travel, and marketing fees
- Failure to disclose use of commissions to investors
- Censure and fine imposed, including the hiring of a compliance consultant and employment of a compliance director

Case Summary

The abolition of fixed commissions in 1975 inadvertently created a legal conflict for funds: obligated to seek the lowest commission while still paying higher commissions for now unbundled research services. To eliminate this conflict, the SEC amended the Securities Exchange Act with Section 28(e) to include a "safe harbor" for funds to pay additional sums for research without facing charges. However, this exemption also gave rise to a substantial "soft dollar" industry and widespread abuse of its boundaries.

In February 1995, the SEC again reviewed controls on the use of soft dollars and, in particular, the use of wider disclosure to investors. These measures were put into practice in September 1995, and, according to the *Wall Street Journal*, "In January, the SEC began a wide-ranging examination of 100 brokerage firms . . . mutual funds and other investment advisers." The first of these cases was filed on October 2, 1995. From that date through to April 13, 2000, actions were filed against at least 12 investment advisers: Tandem, Oakwood, Parnassus, Renaissance, Fundamental, Sweeney Capital, Shawmut, Fleet, Republic New York, Schuylkill, Marvin & Palmer, and East West).

In February 1997, the clients of one of the then largest hedge funds, Dawson-Samberg, with about $3 billion under management, were notified that it was under investigation for soft dollar practices for the period 1995–1996. Dawson-Samberg announced that it would reimburse its investors $1.5 million plus interest for losses due to its nonconforming actions. As reported, the reimbursement was the result of an internal review by Dawson-Samberg, which found that it had received $940,000 in soft dollars in 1995–1996 and had paid $75 million in commissions.

On August 3, 2000, the SEC published an order instituting administrative proceedings against Dawson-Samberg—whose name had since changed to Dawson-Giammalva Capital Management—and its treasurer, Judith Mack. (The SEC had, at the same time, accepted on offer of settlement from Dawson and Mack.) The SEC had found that the soft-dollar violations had commenced from August 1994 and continued until November 1996, and that they comprised $174,000 of soft dollars that were improperly used to pay nonresearch-related business travel expenses, $35,700 used to pay personal (nonbusiness) travel expenses, and $270,000 used to pay marketing referral fees—that is, a total of $479,799 in violations, plus an unstated amount of "other undisclosed expenses."

At the time of the violations Judith Mack, as treasurer of Dawson-Samberg, had responsibility for administering the firm's soft-dollar program as well as the annual Form ADV soft-dollar disclosures. Mack had delegated the reviewing of soft-dollar expense claims to her assistant, but was still held liable. Dawson-Samberg was also held to be guilty of improper supervision of Mack.

Much of the problem had been traced to distribution of American Express credit business cards to staff in August 1994. Dawson-Samberg had arranged for the card's invoices to be paid by soft-dollar vendors, but this procedure required that Mack (or other Dawson-Samberg staff) review the charges and separate out the inappropriate charges prior to the soft-dollar vendors and brokers settling the invoice. When Mack delegated this responsibility to her assistant, this review and separation did not happen, and as a result, the brokers paid the full amounts.

The SEC settlement called for Dawson-Giammalva and Mack to be censured, cease and desist from further violations, and for Dawson-Giammalva to pay a civil fine of $100,000 and Mack to pay $20,000. Dawson-Giammalva was also required to hire a compliance consultant to carry out a review and to hire a director of compliance.

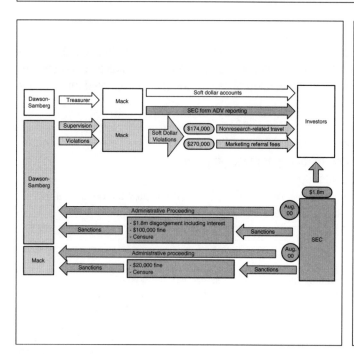

Fraud Facts
- Alleged Acts Date: August 1994
- Enforcement Date: August 3, 2000
- Main Defendants **(hedge fund–related): Mack, Dawson-Samberg**
- Most Serious Charge: Soft dollar violations
- Damages $actual **($2005): $1.4 million ($1.9 million)**
- No. of Investors: NA
- Highest Court: Administrative
- Most Severe Sentence: $1.8 million returned to investors, including interest, $120,000 fines, censure

Sanctions:

- Judith, A.Mack: $20,000 fine, censure
- Dawson-Giammalva Capital Mgmt.: $1.8 million disgorgement including interest, $100,000 fine, censure

Cases:

- *SEC v. Dawson-Giammalva* (3–10261, administrative)

An unregistered commodity pool operator had created four unregistered commodity pools and, with other defendants, employed substantial misrepresentation and fraud in soliciting from individuals. The defendants then continued the fraud as a Ponzi scheme. The central defendant lost about 50 percent of assets and misappropriated much of the remainder. Key points:

- CFTC case
- Unregistered CPO and four unregistered CPs
- Most assets either lost in trading or misappropriated
- Utilized Ponzi-type fund recycling
- CFTC intervened in central defendant's Chapter 7 bankruptcy action to retain direct access to defendant's assets

Case Summary

In early 1989, Leonard Nauman of Minnesota formed a company, Pension America International (PAI), which, according to reports, was intended to be a brokerage firm. It is not clear whether it ever functioned as such; nor does it appear that Nauman or PAI were registered with any securities or commodities regulator.

In 1992, Edward Kirris was hired as vice president of PAI. Kirris had been registered with the National Futures Association as an Associated Person of Morgan Stanley Dean Witter since 1985. Shortly after joining PAI, Kirris had solicited investors for the first of what eventually were four unregistered commodity pools operated by PAI: Commodity Timing, LLC, Future Profit Making, LLC, Selective Futures Mgmt., LLC, and Specialized Commodity Timing, LLC. It is likely that Nauman wanted to avoid registering with the CFTC by creating these four small pools, each of which would be exempt, rather than one large one, which would not. Nauman wrote to pool investors making that claim, even though, as was proved later, it was an erroneous claim. Kirris, in soliciting for investors, added to the misrepresentations regarding past performance, Nauman's experience and the risks of the commodity pool investments. In total, about $634,000 were raised from some 36 investors.

Nauman took responsibility for the trading of these accounts, even though his trading generally incurred losses that were often substantial. From an early stage, Nauman also made large-scale withdrawals from the accounts, which were variously redirected: to his own personal trading accounts, redirected to another nonfinancial company he owned (Kidz FirstInternational), used

to pay his personal expenses, or used to arrange loans from the same funds. A small proportion of the funds were recycled back to investors as per a Ponzi scheme. Overall, approximately half of the assets were lost in trading and half were misappropriated. False reports were issued to investors to conceal the losses for as long as possible.

Possible signs of strain started coming to light in 1999, perhaps due to the fact that money could no longer be recycled to a sufficient degree. In March, the future profits making (FPM) trading accounts were empty. In November, Nauman reorganized the management of the funds, hiring another executive, William Relf, and moving the operations of the four commodity pools to the principal's residential addresses.

When investors in the SCT and CTS pools requested the return of their money, Relf and Kirris offered false promises of future returns in order to deter the calls for redemption. For reasons not stated, Nauman fired Kirris in January 2000, and the CFTC filed a civil complaint in September 2000.

Perhaps seeking to avoid enforcement action, Nauman filed for Chapter 7 voluntary bankruptcy in December 2000. The CFTC intervened in the bankruptcy proceedings to "except a debt from discharge" so that the assets would be available for the investors. The substance of the civil case was settled in a series of consent orders agreed with each of the defendants in turn. Nauman, along with the commodity pool defendants, were jointly and severally ordered to pay $556,452 in restitution together with $68,800 interest, together with a civil fine of $242,431, to be paid once restitution was fulfilled. The other defendants received lesser sanctions.

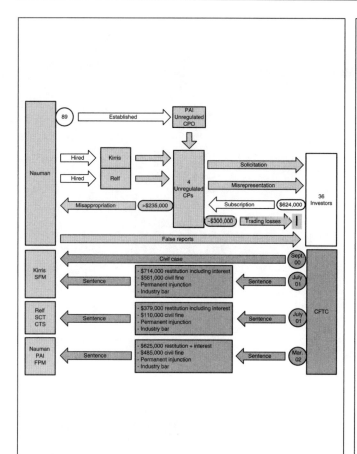

Fraud Facts

- Alleged Acts Date: April 1997
- Enforcement Date: September 6, 2000
- Main Defendants **(hedge fund–related): Kirris, Nauman, Relf, Commodity Timing Specialist, Futures Profit Making, Pension America, Selective Futures Mgmt., Specialized Commodity Timing**
- Most Serious Charge: Fraud
- Damages $actual **($2005)**: Approximately $600,000 **(approximately $700,000)**
- No. of Investors: 36
- Highest Court: Civil
- Most Severe Sentence: $556,500 restitution, $561,500 civil fine, permanent injunction, industry bar

Sanctions:

- Nauman, Leonard, G.: $556,452 restitution (joint and several), $484,862 civil fine, permanent injunction
- Pension America Inc.: $556,452 restitution (joint and several), $484,862 civil fine, permanent injunction
- Leonard, G. Nauman: $68,800 restitution (joint and several)
- Pension America Inc.: $68,800 restitution (joint and several)
- Futures Profit Making LLC: $68,800 restitution (joint and several)
- Edward, S. Kirris III: $448,079 additional restitution, $561,452 civil fine
- Edward, S. Kirris III: $265,706 restitution (joint and several), permanent injunction
- Selective Futures Management: $265,706 restitution (joint and several), permanent injunction
- William, J. Relf: $110,000 civil fine, permanent injunction
- William, J. Relf: $266,675 restitution
- Specialized Commodity Timing: $266,675 restitution
- William, J. Relf: $112,375 restitution
- Commodity Timing Specialist, LLC: $112,375 restitution

Cases:

- *CFTC v. 1Pension America* (00cv02071, civil, USDC Minn.)
- *Nauman 11, Chap. 7* (00–45285, bankruptcy, USDC Minn.)

CHAPTER 5

Summary: Case Group Characteristics

The case studies in this book provide the reader with a chronological, comparative survey of the first 100 known occurrences of hedge fund fraud in U.S. jurisdictions. This body of information will allow, for the first time:

- The establishment of "hedge fund fraud" with its own unique population and characteristics, as a defined subsector of securities fraud.
- A complete chronological narrative history of the specific crime from its first case in August 1968 up to the 100th adjudicated case in September 2000.
- A standardized format with facts and figures making it possible to contrast and compare one case with another or one aspect across many cases.
- A minimally sufficient statistical set of cases from which important baseline measurements can be directly obtained, such as frequency of fraud.
- A database from which statistical inferences about aggregate characteristics can be made, including more solid foundations for profiling and predictive modeling.

In order to develop the applications identified in the last two areas, "baseline measurements" and "statistical inferences" for modeling, the data in the individual cases must be aggregated and then resorted amongst a set of new data-fields that are indicative of characteristics at the group and subgroup levels within the total set of 100 cases.

The conclusions are arranged in two broad groups; one for the factors that run through the entire data set and serve to exemplify hedge fund fraud as a distinct group, the second divides the 100 case set into four subgroups that distinguish some of the basic differences between cases.

Taken together, these "cross-sectional" views of the data create a more accurate and objective description of the crime that serves to both dispel certain myths and misconceptions as well as providing the foundation for a more comprehensive response to the crime.

COUNT

The first question to address with the aggregate data is, how many hedge fund frauds have there been? Prior to the publication of this book, practitioners could not answer this question. Even an order of magnitude approximation would have been difficult to estimate. The SEC has come close to an answer, though it generally does not distinguish hedge funds from other securities fraud cases. An accurate count also requires a combination of SEC cases with CFTC cases involving commodity trade advisers (CTAs), commodity pools (CPs), and commodity pool operators (CPOs) in addition to other cases in which these two federal agencies were not involved.

One combined census of hedge fund fraud cases that was prepared by the SEC and CFTC is shown in Figure 5.1. It covers enforcement actions by both agencies for the period 1999 to 2003. It shows 81 actions over this four-year time span (a rate of 3 percent of all actions). This conveys no sense of the number of cases during anything like the length of time that hedge funds have been operating. It also does not include cases brought by a range of parties, which could variously include: state security boards, state and federal Attorney's General, private prosecutions, and class actions.

While limited to 100 cases, the book covers a 32-year time period beginning with the first known case in 1968. And, indirectly also covers the earlier 19 years (or 51 years in total) from the date the first hedge fund appeared in 1948 until 1968, during which time there were no known fraud cases. This claim is mitigated by the fact that there were hardly any hedge funds operating until the late 1960s and because most of the frauds, numerically, have occurred since the late 1990s or 2000s. However, balancing against this limitation there is also the fact that any case that is less than 3–5 years old has a good chance of still being open or subject to appeal.

Certainly, the figure of 100 cases to 2001 is a reasonably meaningful value given the time span of these cases relative to the total history of hedge funds and

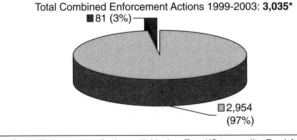

Total Combined Enforcement Actions 1999-2003: **3,035***
■ 81 (3%)

□ 2,954 (97%)

☐ All Other Enforcement Actions ■ Hedge Fund/Commodity Pool Actions

* SEC enforcement actions during 1999-2003 totaled 2,789. CFTC enforcement actions during the same period totaled 246.

FIGURE 5.1 SEC and CFTC Hedge Fund/Commodity Pool Enforcement Actions
Source: "Testimony of Patrick J. McCarty, General Counsel of the Commodity Futures Trading Commission before the U.S. Senate Committee on Banking, Housing and Urban Affairs," July 15, 2004, page 4. (There is a footnote under the chart referring to the source of the SEC data being: "Implications of the Growth of Hedge Funds" Staff Report to the United State Securities and Exchange Commission, September 2003, page 73.)

it allows for the passage of enough time for any appeals to have played out. It also provides a rough-and-ready order of magnitude of "hundreds" for the total number of cases.

What more can be said about the total number of fraud cases, a number that increases week-by-week, if not day-by-day? While no attempt has been made to validate the total number of cases that currently exist beyond the first 100, from files kept on the more recent cases an estimate of around 300 cases in total might not be too far off the mark.

FREQUENCY

More than the count, the frequency is the defining measure of risk. It is the frequency per unit of time that is the probability that a fraud will or will not occur, that fraud is a function of time. Frequency as a statistic is also further decomposable in several other dimensions that describe its stability and trend and whether there are any other factors, like time, that exhibit a pattern of relationship to the frequency.

The date of the first filing of criminal, civil, or administrative charges has been used throughout this book as the effective date for a given case. A graph of the dates of the first 100 cases is shown in Figure 5.2.

The raw frequency rate for the entire period works out to be around 32 cases per year (100 cases/380 months). However, visual inspection of the bar graph of frequency suggests that there was little or no trend in the rate of fraud until at least the 1990s. In the 30-year time span from 1972 to 1992, there were only 11 cases in total, or about 0.4 cases per year. Most of these years had no new cases filed, and only one year (1988) had more than one case appearing in the year.

The early years from 1968 to 1972 correspond with one of the most serious periods of economic and financial crises since World War II. There were as many as

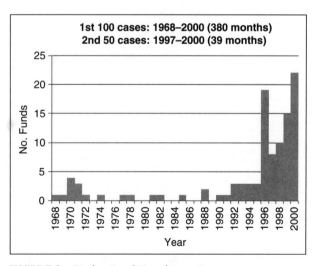

FIGURE 5.2 Hedge Fund Frauds per Year

10 known cases in just those four years, an implied rate of 2.5 per year. However, the total duration of this behavior was too short, singular, and isolated in time to extrapolate much meaning from it.

Given these observations, it might be fair to assume that prior to 1992, hedge fund fraud was a rarity—or that it was simply not a subject worthy of study. It rated a footnote in a paper on hedge fund risks, little more. But from 1992, that all changed with signs that the number of fraud cases was increasing to levels not seen in the preceding 30 years, and seemingly growing in number over time, (a trend that has continued to the present).

The 80 cases that were recorded between 1992 and 2000 represent an average rate of nearly nine cases per year, although the rate of new cases was far from constant in these years, increasing at a rate of about 35 percent per annum. By all measures, the year 1996 was exceptional. There were 19 new cases recorded in that year, up from just three cases per year in each of the previous four years, and substantially higher than any of the following three years. The year 1996 represents a surge probably fueled by a regulatory campaign to stem perceived market excesses and punish some of its prime movers.

A different perspective on the rate of frauds can be gained from a comparison of the number of frauds per year divided by the number of hedge funds existing in a given year, as shown in Figure 5.3.

This graph shows the frequency of frauds per year declining rapidly in the earlier years, reflecting the rising number of funds, followed by a long period in which the rate stabilized with slight fluctuations in a narrow range of between roughly a quarter and three-quarters of a percent per year. The figure of less than 1 percent per annum can be contrasted with Figure 5.1. It shows hedge fund and related commodity fund frauds to comprise around 3 percent of enforcement actions for the four-year period 1999 to 2003. The less than 1 percent figure does reflect to some degree the probability or risk of being invested in a hedge fund that becomes embroiled in fraud charges. In its most simple terms, it implies that an investor with a hypothetical portfolio of 100 hedge funds might be likely to experience one fraud per year. A more realistic hedge fund, or fund-of-funds

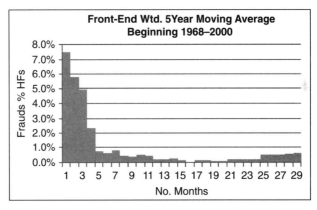

FIGURE 5.3 Number of Hedge Fund Frauds/Number of Hedge Funds

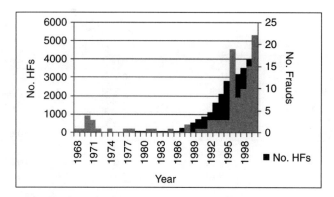

FIGURE 5.4 Number of Hedge Fund Frauds/Number of Hedge Funds

portfolio of 20 funds, could be expected to encounter a fraud around once in five years. Of course, this statistic does not suggest whether the frauds are randomly distributed across funds of all types or more heavily concentrated in certain types of funds. Nor does it factor in the amount of money lost or the number of investors victimized in each case.

Figure 5.4 illustrates the relationship between the number of funds and the number of frauds and seems to suggest that the latter is a function of the former.

DISTRIBUTION OF CASES BY ENFORCEMENT AGENCY AND CASE LOCALE

Although the SEC is the dominant enforcement agency with responsibility for hedge fund fraud, the majority (56 percent) of the first 100 cases, which include commodity trading advisers and commodity pool operators, have been pursued by the CFTC. By contrast, the SEC led on 43 percent of the cases and 10 percent were handled by both (i.e., a total of 89 percent were headed up by one or the other or both of these agencies). That left 10 percent that were instigated by another enforcement agency—several of which, such as the stock markets, commodity exchanges, and NASD are under the supervision of the SEC (as is the CFTC itself), and those not supervised by the SEC, such as state attorneys general and state securities bureau.

While it is tempting to draw contrasts between the SEC and CFTC cases, it can be a mistake to make too much of their differences due to substantial overlaps in funds that are both hedge funds and commodity pools (a May 2003 SEC roundtable panel claimed that 55 percent of the top 100 hedge funds were run by CPOs). However, the effect of there being two large regulators is to cause some noise in the interpretation of fraud in the hedge fund sector, especially in the need to be registered. The CFTC cases also exhibit a geographical anomaly in the number of fraud cases occurring in Illinois, the location of the main futures and options exchanges and historically the geographic center of America's commodity economy.

	Actual/	Percent Distribution			
	Predicted	Cases	HF+CPO	HF	CPO
D.C.	15.5	2.0%	0.4%	0.7%	0.3%
West Virginia	15.5	1.0%	0.0%	0.0%	0.9%
Alabama	15.5	3.0%	0.1%	0.1%	0.2%
Michigan	12.4	4.0%	0.2%	0.1%	0.3%
Oklahoma	10.4	2.0%	0.1%	0.0%	0.2%
Kansas	7.8	1.0%	0.2%	0.2%	0.1%
Wyoming	7.8	1.0%	0.1%	0.0%	0.5%
Utah	5.2	2.0%	0.2%	0.0%	3.6%
Georgia	2.8	2.0%	1.0%	1.4%	0.7%
Indiana	2.8	2.0%	0.4%	0.1%	0.7%
Colorado	2.6	4.0%	1.2%	0.8%	1.5%
Wisconsin	2.2	1.0%	0.4%	0.3%	0.1%
Minnesota	1.8	2.0%	1.1%	1.0%	1.1%
Florida	1.7	7.0%	3.0%	1.9%	4.1%

FIGURE 5.5   States with Greater than Expected Number of Cases

One of the possible conclusions drawn from the aggregation of cases is a counterintuitive geographic bias in the location of fraud cases (apart from the CFTC–Illinois bias already mentioned). Although the largest number of fraud cases does occur where most hedge funds are located, the number of cases in the major centers is consistently below the proportion of hedge funds located in that center. For example, the state of Connecticut accommodated nearly 7.5 percent of hedge funds and CPOs (223) in around 2000 and yet was only responsible for one of the 100 fraud cases. That suggests that the state was about 13 times underrepresented in fraud cases (assuming that the number of cases would be roughly in line with the number of funds). Similarly, New York had about 41 percent of the funds and only some 25 percent of the fraud cases, an underrepresentation of cases to funds of about 1.6 times. The table in Figure 5.5 lists the states where fraud is underrepresented, relative to the number of funds located there.

At the opposite end of the spectrum, Alabama, with only four hedge funds plus CPOs, 0.14 percent of the total, had four of the 100 cases, an overrepresentation of nearly 29 times its pro rata. While Figure 5.6 presents states roughly in line on a pro rata basis, those states with an underrepresentation of cases are shown in Figure 5.7.

One inference to make from these geographical observations is that there is less relative risk in the financial centers than in remote locations. Another inference is that states with a small resident population of hedge funds and CPOs are more likely to suffer a higher rate of fraud.

LOSSES

While all of the 100 cases represent incidences of suspected fraud in hedge funds or commodity pools, not all of the cases have hedge fund investors as fraud victims. Of the cases presented, 69 (69 percent) do have hedge fund investor/victims where both

	Actual/	Percent Distribution			
	Predicted	Cases	HF+CPO	HF	CPO
North Carolina	0.5	1.0%	1.3%	0.6%	2.0%
Tennessee	0.6	1.0%	1.0%	0.4%	0.3%
Iowa	0.7	1.0%	0.7%	0.1%	1.4%
Massachusetts	0.8	2.0%	4.0%	5.6%	2.6%
New York	0.8	25.0%	40.5%	52.3%	29.6%
Illinois	0.9	11.0%	9.0%	4.8%	12.8%
Texas	1.1	4.0%	3.3%	3.1%	1.6%
Washington	1.1	1.0%	0.8%	0.8%	1.7%
California	1.2	9.0%	10.8%	14.2%	7.7%
Maryland	1.2	1.0%	0.6%	0.3%	0.8%
Missouri	1.4	1.0%	0.5%	0.3%	0.7%
Pennsylvania	1.5	2.0%	1.0%	0.6%	1.4%

FIGURE 5.6 States Roughly in Line with Expected Number of Cases

	Actual/	Percent Distribution			
	Predicted	Cases	HF+CPO	HF	CPO
Alaska	0.0	0.0%	0.2%	0.1%	0.3%
Arizona	0.0	0.0%	0.6%	0.6%	0.6%
Arkansas	0.0	0.0%	0.1%	0.0%	0.1%
Delaware	0.0	0.0%	0.2%	0.1%	0.1%
Hawaii	0.0	0.0%	0.2%	0.3%	0.2%
Idaho	0.0	0.0%	0.1%	0.1%	0.1%
Kentucky	0.0	0.0%	0.2%	0.2%	0.2%
Louisiana	0.0	0.0%	0.2%	0.1%	0.3%
Maine	0.0	0.0%	0.0%	0.0%	0.0%
Mississippi	0.0	0.0%	0.0%	0.0%	0.1%
Montana	0.0	0.0%	0.0%	0.0%	0.1%
Nebraska	0.0	0.0%	0.2%	0.1%	0.3%
Nevada	0.0	0.0%	0.5%	0.1%	0.9%
New Hampshire	0.0	0.0%	0.1%	0.0%	0.3%
New Mexico	0.0	0.0%	0.3%	0.3%	0.3%
North Dakota	0.0	0.0%	0.1%	0.0%	0.2%
Oregon	0.0	1.0%	0.0%	0.1%	0.0%
Rhode Island	0.0	0.0%	0.1%	0.1%	0.1%
South Carolina	0.0	0.0%	0.3%	0.0%	0.1%
South Dakota	0.0	0.0%	0.1%	0.0%	0.6%
Vermont	0.0	0.0%	0.0%	0.0%	0.4%
Virginia	0.0	0.0%	0.9%	0.1%	0.1%
Connecticut	0.1	1.0%	7.5%	7.1%	7.8%
New Jersey	0.3	3.0%	5.3%	0.8%	9.5%

FIGURE 5.7 States with Less than Expected Number of Cases

the number of investor entities (individuals and corporations) and the amount lost due to fraud are known or able to be reasonably estimated.

Of the 31 cases without hedge fund investor/victims, 13 (42 percent of this group), were cases where the nature of the violations do not directly correspond to specific victims, crimes such as insider trading, short-selling, soft-dollar broking, and

Table 5.1 Summary Statistics for Cases with Known Hedge Fund Investor–Victims

Total Number of Cases	69 Cases
Total number of known investor–victim entities (including estimates)	10,425 investors
Total sum of known money lost in fraud in 2005 dollars	$2.9 billion
Average number of investor/entities per case	151 investors
Average loss to fraud per case in 2005 dollars	$42.7 million
Average loss per investor per case in 2005 dollars	$282,586

issuing violations. A further 10 cases had hedge fund investor–victims but available information was not sufficient to determine or reasonably estimate the number. In the last group of eight, the available information was insufficient to determine the type of investors involved.

Table 5.1 shows summary statistics for the 69 cases where there were known hedge fund investor–victims.

Figure 5.8 suggests that there is little or no correlation between the number of investors and the amount of money lost to fraud.

Figure 5.9 displays the same data but in a chronological order. The general pattern of noncorrelation of victims and money appears to persist, but there is also a greater awareness of a sensitivity to outliers, particularly in one of the victim data points and in three of the money data points. (These were less glaring in the previous graph because it was plotted on a logarithmic scale). The case in point was that of Hubshman (Case 2). This self-proclaimed hedge fund of the late 1960s—a time when there were probably not more than 100 hedge funds in existence—was reportedly a fund that was registered with the SEC and one that had a modest minimum cash threshold for investors and had over 3,000 investors.

Given the small sample size of the cases (100 cases) and the smaller subset of cases with known values for victims and losses (69), there is a great disinclination to

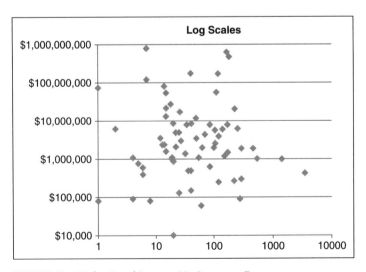

FIGURE 5.8 Hedge Fund Losses: No Investors/Losses

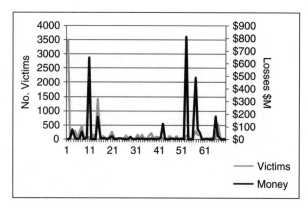

FIGURE 5.9 Victims and Losses: Chronological Order

throw out any data. However, taking the least destructive path by eliminating just one victim number brings these two data-series closer together. To see this better, the remaining numbers have been transformed in two ways: They have been restated as natural log values and the money values have been transposed by the standard error so their scale effectively starts at zero as does the number of victims. The final transformed values are shown in Figure 5.10.

The regression R-square for the above series is 0.31 with a significant T-stat above 4.0. This shows a moderate underlying relationship between the number of victims and the amount of money lost. This is a common-sense proposition, along the same lines as the earlier observation—that the number of frauds corresponds roughly with the number of hedge funds. These conclusions do not have to be true a priori. However, it is reasonable that they are, and it suggests fraud has a dimensional property in the hedge fund universe much the same way that jails tend to be in towns of a certain size.

Replotting the initial x–y graph with the elimination of the single outlier in the victim data series, restating the remaining data in natural log scales, and rebasing the losses data by subtracting the minimum value from all values (normalizing) produces Figure 5.11. In this portrayal, a trendline has been overlaid and the trend

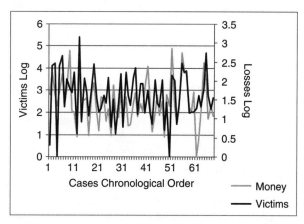

FIGURE 5.10 Victims and Losses: Chronological Order (log scales and adjusted range)

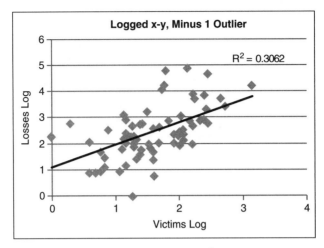

FIGURE 5.11   Victims vs. Losses Logged x–y

can be clearly seen. Several outliers easily observable in the chronological graph remain among the losses data.

VIOLATIONS

Hedge fund fraud violations—the laws, regulations, and rules contravened—are drawn from two primary sources reflecting the two main fund regulators, the Securities and Exchange Commission Acts and the Commodity Exchange Act. Beyond these, other violations are derived from the U.S. criminal code (Title 18 of the U.S. Code), the laws and regulations of individual states and state regulators, the rules of individual stock and futures exchanges, and professional associations (including NASD, NFA, and bar associations).

There is a considerable degree of parallelism as well as divergence between these codes reflecting the overlapping jurisdictions of federal and state governments, as well as between one state and another, and the lack of a seamless fit in the regulation of commodity pools and hedge funds, registered and not registered. The resulting duplication and inconsistency shows up in the first 100 cases in the following principal ways:

- Many commodity pools and hedge funds are virtually indistinguishable in their structure and management.
- Most hedge funds make use of futures and options, which are themselves under the jurisdiction of the CFTC.
- ETFs are increasingly taking on the attributes of futures and options, but are under the jurisdiction of the SEC.
- While it is a violation for a commodity pool to be unregistered, it is not currently a violation for a hedge fund to be unregistered as long as it is exempt.
- The SEC and the CFTC may both be plaintiffs in a case or either one.
- Individual states may bring their own cases whether the CFTC or SEC have brought a case or not.

Rank	No.	Code	Section	Subject
1	45	Commodity Act	4b(a)(i)	Fraudulent contracts for sale of commodities
2	43	Commodity Act	4b(a)(ii)	False reports or statements
3	38	Commodity Act	4o(1)	Use of mail to defraud or cheat
4	33	Securities & Exchange Act 1934	10(b)	Fraudulent contracts for sale of securities
5	31	Securities & Exchange Act 1934	R10b-5	Fraudulent means, statements, practices
6	27	Commodity Act	4m(1)	Use of mail by registered CTA/CPO & exceptions
7	24	Commodity Act	R 4.20(c)	Commingling property of commodity pool
8	22	Securities Act 1933	17(a)	Use of mail to defraud or cheat
9	21	United States Code	18:1341	Frauds and swindles (criminal)
10	19	Commodity Act	4b(a)(iii)	Willful deception in execution of orders

FIGURE 5.12   Ten Most Frequently Cited Violations (all enforcement agencies/codes)
Note: Measured by number of cases in which section is cited.

There are some 851 individuals and corporate defendants in the first 100 cases. Each of these defendants could be the subject of multiple counts of violation and violation of multiple provisions of the acts, regulations, and so on. In total, there were 2,634 separate violations (a specific section of a code cited as a charge against a defendant) cited—averaging just over three per defendant and nearly 27 per case. (Most of these violations refer to different sections of the same few acts rather than different acts).

These figures were adjusted to reflect the distribution of sections of the legal codes across the cases—counting each case as a 1 if a section of a code has been cited in that case (ignoring how many times it may have been cited in a particular case) and a 0 if it was not cited at all (in relation to any defendant in any action grouped with that case).

The Code column in Figure 5.12 reflects the split between CFTC cases (Commodity Act) and SEC cases (Securities & Exchange Act and Securities Act), as well as the split between administrative and civil cases on the one hand (all of the aforementioned codes) and criminal cases (United States Code) on the other.

Restating the same top ten rankings for the CFTC and SEC codes separately yields Figures 5.13 and 5.14, respectively.

CASE GROUPING

While there is no necessity or intrinsic basis for creating case-type groups for the hedge fund fraud cases—in fact, even the category "hedge fund fraud" does not yet exist as a distinct crime category—there are a number of benefits in attempting

Rank	No.	Code	Section	
1	45	Commodity Act	4b(a)(i)	Fraudulent contracts for sale of commodities
2	43	Commodity Act	4b(a)(ii)	False reports or statements
3	38	Commodity Act	4o(1)	Use of mail to defraud or cheat
4	27	Commodity Act	4m(1)	Use of mail by registered CTA/CPO & exceptions
5	24	Commodity Act	R 4.20(c)	Commingling property of commodity pool
6	19	Commodity Act	4b(a)(iii)	Willful deception in execution of orders
7	18	Commodity Act	R 4.21	Delivery of required disclosure document
8	17	Commodity Act	4o(1)(B)	Engaging in any fraudulent transaction
9	16	Commodity Act	R 4.22	Providing monthly account statements
10	14	Commodity Act	4n(4)	CPO providing monthly account statements

FIGURE 5.13   Ten Most Frequently Cited Violations (CFTC)
Note: Measured by number of cases in which section is cited.

Rank	No.	Code	Section	
1	33	Securities & Exchange Act 1934	10(b)	Fraudulent contracts for sale of securities
2	31	Securities & Exchange Act 1934	R10b-5	Fraudulent means, statements, practices
3	22	Securities Act 1933	17(a)	Use of mail to defraud or cheat
4	15	Investment Advisers Act 1940	206(2)	Use of fraudulent means (by Investment Advisers)
5	14	Investment Advisers Act 1940	206(1)	Fraudulent transactions (by Investment Advisers)
6	8	Investment Advisers Act 1940	204	Reports by investment advisers
7	6	Investment Advisers Act 1940	206(4)	Fraudulent practices (by Investment Advisers)
8	6	Securities Act 1933	5(a)	Sale or delivery of unregistered securities
9	6	Securities Act 1933	5(c)	Use of mails for unregistered securities
10	4	Securities & Exchange Act 1934	15(c)(1)	Fraudulent means by brokers or dealers

FIGURE 5.14   Ten Most Frequently Cited Violations (SEC)
Note: Measured by number of cases in which section is cited.

to do so. The most powerful reason for doing so is the possibility of a schema that juxtaposes cases on a like-for-like basis. Doing so could yield insight into the causes of fraud, information that could greatly assist in the prediction of such crimes. A more modest potential benefit of putting cases into groups is simply to aid in the explanation of the case material.

As the previous paragraph implied, many ways of defining groups exist depending upon the objective sought. Some of the criteria considered for creating fraud case groups include:

- Time period (when the crimes were committed)
- Amount of money lost to fraud
- Type of perpetrator
- Hedge fund role in fraud
- Type of enforcement action taken
- Type of sentence or sanctions meted out
- Sequence of events in the crime
- Criminal MO
- Sections of the legal code from which perpetrators can be charged

The greatest limitation for selecting criteria is the lack of consistent data across all of the cases. Another shortcoming of many of the grouping criteria is the lack of any obvious predictive value in the results.

The basic selection of the book's content has, in effect, created a first group—hedge funds that have experienced fraud up to mid-2000. This initial group has 100 members in its class. Further divisions within the first group are essentially based upon finding criteria that move similar cases closer together and dissimilar cases further apart. Furthermore, the total set of groups, so defined, should include all cases and no case should qualify for more than one group.

The categories were ultimately defined by empirical inspection of the case data aimed at identifying descriptive factors that quantified the degree of similarity or dissimilarity between cases. Over time the search for factors changed from the consideration of many to the choice of the minimum number required to associate or disassociate any two cases.

In retrospect, while all fraud cases have been found to have elements of deception and theft, it was the nature of the theft that helped most to categorize the majority of securities fraud cases examined here. The case data suggested that the most elemental associative factors were whether misappropriation and/or trading losses were notable features of the case. This observation generated three initial case groups, cases in which there were:

1. Substantial trading losses but little or no known misappropriation
2. Substantial misappropriation with little or no known trading losses
3. Both trading losses and misappropriation

These three presumptive groups contained 76 percent of all of the 100 cases, and comprised 24 percent, 24 percent, and 28 percent, of the total, respectively. The remaining 24 percent of cases comprised a fourth catchall group.

SCHEMATIC ORGANIZATION OF CASE GROUPS

Figure 5.15 shows the logical organization of the four fraud case groupings in the form of Euler's circles. The main features of this ordering are:

- Two subgroups: {M,L,ML},{O}
- Four subsubgroups: {M},{L},{ML},{O}
- Three related groups: {M},{L},{ML}
- One catchall group: {O}

Loss-Driven Frauds (Groups 1 and 2)

Among the 100 cases surveyed in this book, the most common factor indicative of causation is the presence of financial investment loss, generally substantial loss. In more than half of all cases (52 percent) the commission of fraud was preceded by the appearance of such losses, although this appearance was partly or entirely hidden

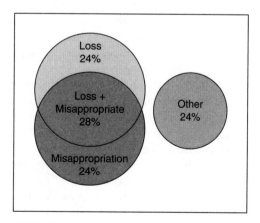

FIGURE 5.15 Overlapping Circles Diagram; "Loss, Misappropriation, Other"

from the investors). The losses in each case varied from deficits that accumulated over months or even years, to sudden dramatic losses in which the fund was essentially wiped out within one month.

The presence and preponderance of these cases indicate that for a narrow majority of the hedge fund cases, the frauds were not premeditated. Theft was not the initial business plan. Loss-driven frauds are represented at all levels of monetary scale and for all types of enforcement action. They also appear to be randomly distributed with respect to hedge funds and commodity pools.

Two of the case groups derive from these loss-driven frauds. One, comprising 28 percent of all cases and just over half of the cases in this group, are frauds in which the investment loss was followed by misappropriation of remaining or other investor money. The other group, comprising 24 percent of all cases and just under half of the cases of this type, are cases where misappropriation did not appear to be part of the crime, but some form of false reporting was. In other words, the perpetrator lost money trading and lied to the investors to cover up the loss, but was not known to have also stolen some or all of any of the remaining money.

Forty-two percent of the two loss-driven groups (22 percent of all cases) involved Ponzi schemes to aid the deception. Significantly, half of the loss–misappropriation group employed Ponzi schemes as opposed to just one-third of the loss-only—that is, nonmisappropriation—group. This may support the inference that the Ponzi tactic is more important as a component of theft rather than an aid to cover-up.

The biggest case in this large group was the late 1998, $814 million (in 2005 constant dollars) fraud of the Princeton Economics Group and its mercurial manager Martin Armstrong (Case 79). This case was in the loss-only group.

Misappropriation (Group 3)

The group containing cases of loss–misappropriation comprises 28 percent of all cases. In addition to the instances of misappropriation in this group, there is a further 24 percent of cases that comprise the third major group in which there was misappropriation but without any major or known prior trading losses. The cases in this latter group are most clearly examples of premeditated crimes, crimes with no pretext, entities that sought criminal gains from the outset. The most criminal of these are a subgroup of four cases that represent instances of racketeering—operations of organized crime, though at least one of these (Case 14, Princeton-Newport) was dismissed and shown to be without substance. In total, misappropriation is present to a significant degree in 52 percent of cases.

Superficial observation of the data of this group suggests two possible biases— one being that all of these cases appear to have occurred in the earlier half of the time period for all the cases, and two, being a lower average and maximum value for money lost to fraud (as compared to the group one subgroup representing cases of loss without misappropriation). The latter observation, if valid, may imply that the intentional thefts actually have lower total losses than the unintentional ones. What may at first seem to be a bizarre conclusion may make sense if one considers that criminals that set out to steal money using money management as a front are generally not in a position to raise as much money from investors as bona fide managers. The largest fraud, measured by amount lost to fraud in this group, was the $13.4 million in 1998 and documented in Case 62, Chateauforte/Busch.

Group 4

The fourth group has been designed as a catchall for all of the remaining case types. In aggregate, it contains 24 percent of cases comprised of five subgroups as follows:

- Misuse of funds (7%)
- Disclosure (6%)
- Insider trading (5%)
- Manipulation (4%)
- Solicitation violations (2%)

This group bears one subtle property in common: Their losses tend to be indirect to the investors. Some approach the degree of victimless crimes. To this extent, the violations also tend to be more technical, with enforcement brought by regulators.

Misuse of Funds

Seven percent of the cases fall into this group. The group includes all instances where the fund manager sought to obtain a personal financial advantage from the funds under management. The misuse fell short of theft in that the investor's funds were not removed; but in some cases they may have lost some value as a result of the misuse, such as where best execution was not sought. These cases tend to involve smaller sums of fraudulent losses and lesser levels of enforcement action and all involve people and institutions that are registered as brokers, if not also as fund managers. The maximum fraudulent loss here is $8.7 million (Case 19, Stotler).

Disclosure

While lack of disclosure is almost the definition of fraud itself, and is intrinsic to almost every case, the crimes placed in this group, just 6 percent of the cases, are those in which lack of disclosure is the core of the crime and other, generally more serious aspects, such as misappropriation, or even lesser offenses such as the issuing of false reports, may not be present. The offenses in these cases tend to be more technical in nature. However, despite the technical nature of these crimes, the group includes one of the largest financial penalties, $405 million that resulted in Case 65, BOA/D.E. Shaw. This seeming anomaly was due to the fact that the disclosure related to the valuation of a substantial merger.

The disclosure cases are also often ones where the final charges are to some extent a default, as, for example, when investor–victims either failed to make a strong fraud case against a fund manager or where the fund was depleted of assets and disclosure became the best grounds to go after the deeper pockets of accountants or other parties related to the main defendants.

Insider Trading

Insider trading is represented by five cases, one of which, Case 9, Nemeroff, was not only dismissed, but was judged to be "malicious prosecution" where the plaintiffs were fined for legal costs. The largest case in this group was Case 13, Boesky, in which fines of $94 million were levied.

Market Manipulation

There are four cases in this group, two of which are straightforward manipulation, one of which is a short-selling violation and the other relates to the sale of restricted stock. The largest case is that of Case 17, Salomon, which incurred $300 million of sanctions.

Solicitation Offenses

There are only two cases in this group (Case 64 PRIME/Zadeh, Case 90 HARLEY), which represents probably the most minor violations of all cases, both of which involve improper approaches to prospective hedge fund investors.

SUMMARY

Reflecting on a much more serious fight, Winston Churchill famously characterized the present as being "the end of the beginning" rather than the "beginning of the end," so it is here in the search for understanding of the problem of hedge fund fraud. In the five or more years that I have turned this subject over, it had always appeared that the present-day approach of due diligence was a brave start in tackling this problem, but never more than a start.

For me the ambitions of due diligence always seemed so self-limiting that they could do little to shed light on the problems it tried hard to address. From the outset, it seemed compromised by the conflicting goal of covering certain hind parts with legal armor. Yet, after so many decades of soldiering on with this cumbersome inquisition-styled methodology, little was still known about this crime, except that it was growing rapidly and the prospect to alter its progress seems remote.

By 2009, we had reached a point where hedge fund fraud had attained the unimaginable level of loss of $50 billion with the life savings of thousands of ordinary investors consumed without much redress. At this same moment in time, almost all of the regulatory machinery of the state has been nearly crushed by overwhelming economic circumstances to the extent that lawmakers are collectively going back to square one in a massive rethink about how we do business and go about our affairs.

At the start of this study, I had already tackled the majority of the question of "Why hedge funds fail?" and devised efficient means for evaluating the potential for such failures, even though fraud was a nagging final issue to wrestle with and there was the hope that it could be dispensed with quickly. The only conviction in initially tackling this issue was the cost and inefficiency of existing methods. Sometime later the problem cast itself in a more basic light, which was the implication of applying legal logic to what was more properly understood as a scientific inquiry. A good starting point for the application of science was the assembly of a sufficient body of comparative data. That was the immediate and most basic goal of this work. The assembly of this basic data is to serve as a foundation for subsequent analysis. That remains the central achievement of writing this book—the "end of the beginning."

Beyond the laying of this foundation, some sketches have been made of what a superstructure might look like. How we might proceed to direct the light that better information offers and toward that end, some rudimentary analysis has been done to see what can stand up. And, what can be seen is something of the extent and nature of this type of fraud. While it is the purpose of a casebook to leave much of the further concluding to those who use it, there is just one further philosophic vantage point that has been opened up here—that is the view that scientific inquiry can illuminate things in such a way that we can suffer fewer faults and more efficiently utilize our resources. Further than that, there is the need to accept that failure is intrinsic to life and fraud is part of failure. With better knowledge and tools, we should be capable of significantly reducing the occurrence of fraud, but even a sharp reduction will not banish this crime; therefore, we must also find better ways to live with what remains.